Emerging Areas of Human Rights in the 21st Century

This book includes a set of studies and reflections that have emerged since the adoption of the Universal Declaration of Human Rights in 1948. Encompassing a number of rights, such as the right to environmental protection, the right to humanitarian aid and the right to democratic governance, this collection focuses on issues and areas that were not originally mentioned or foreseen in the Declaration but that have since developed into salient topics.

These developing rights are considered in the light of contemporary national and international law, as well as against the wider picture and the contexts in which human rights may have effect. Moreover, the topics covered take in a wide range of research fields, including law, politics and criminology.

Emerging Areas of Human Rights in the 21st Century is aimed primarily at undergraduate and postgraduate students, and scholars interested in international law, human rights and politics.

Marco Odello is a Lecturer in law at Aberystwyth University, UK.

Sofia Cavandoli is a Lecturer in law at Aberystwyth University, UK.

Routledge Research in Human Rights Law

Available titles in this series include:

Global Health and Human Rights
Legal and Philosophical Perspectives
John Harrington and Maria Stuttaford

The Right to Development in International Law
The Case of Pakistan
Khurshid Iqbal

The Right to Religious Freedom in International Law
Between group rights and individual rights
Anat Scolnicov

Forthcoming titles in this series include:

Children and International Human Rights Law
The Right of the Child to be Heard
Aisling Parkes

The European Convention on Human Rights and its new Contracting Parties
Democratic transition and consolidation in the European Jurisprudence
James A. Sweeney

Ensuring and Enforcing Economic, Social and Cultural Rights
The Jurisprudence of the UN Committee on Economic, Social and Cultural Rights
Marco Odello and Francesco Seatzu

Human Rights Monitoring Mechanisms of the Council of Europe
Gauthier de Beco

The Human Right to Water
Its Application in the Occupied Palestinian Territories
Amanda Cahill

International Human Rights Law and Domestic Violence
The effectiveness of international human rights law
Ronagh McQuigg

The EU as a 'Global Player' in Human Rights
Jan Wetzel

Human Rights in the Asia-Pacific Region
Towards Institution Building
Hitoshi and Ben Saul (eds.)

Corporate Human Rights Violations
Overcoming Regulatory Hurdles
Surya Deva

Jurisdiction, Immunity and Transnational Human Rights Litigation
Xiaodong Yang

Vindicating Socio-Economic Rights
International Standards and Comparative Experiences
Paul O'Connell

Emerging Areas of Human Rights in the 21st Century

The Role of the Universal Declaration of Human Rights

Edited by
Marco Odello and Sofia Cavandoli

Routledge
Taylor & Francis Group
LONDON AND NEW YORK

First published 2011
by Routledge
2 Park Square, Milton Park, Abingdon, Oxon, OX14 4RN

Simultaneously published in the USA and Canada
by Routledge
270 Madison Avenue, New York, NY 10016

Routledge is an imprint of the Taylor & Francis Group, an informa business

Typeset in Baskerville by Taylor & Francis Books

British Library Cataloguing in Publication Data
A catalogue record for this book is available from the British Library

Library of Congress Cataloging in Publication Data
Emerging areas of human rights in the 21st century : the role of the universal declaration of human rights / edited by Marco Odello and Sofia Cavandoli.
p. cm.
1. Human rights. 2. United Nations. General Assembly. Universal Declaration of Human Rights. I. Odello, Marco. II. Cavandoli, Sofia.
K3240.E44 2011
341.4′8–dc22
2010031807

ISBN 13: 978-0-415-56209-6 (hbk)
ISBN 13: 978-0-203-83172-4 (ebook)

Contents

Contributors

Professor Susan Breau is Professor of International Law at Flinders Law School, Adelaide, Australia. Her research interests are the law of armed conflict and international human rights law. Her latest book co-authored with Kerim Yildiz, Director of the Kurdish Human Rights Project in London is entitled *The Kurdish Conflict: International Humanitarian Law and Post-conflict Mechanisms* (Routledge, 2010). She is also currently the legal advisor to the Recording the Civilian Casualties of Armed Conflict project of the Oxford Research Group in London.

Dr Richard Burchill is the Director of the McCoubrey Centre for International Law and Senior Lecturer at the Law School, University of Hull, UK. He is also a visiting professor at the George C. Marshall European Centre for Security Studies teaching on the programme of Terrorism and Security Studies. His research and teaching interests focus on issues of democracy and the protection of human rights in the context of global governance. His current research is concentrating on the role of international organisations in the promotion and protection of democracy. His publications have appeared in a number of countries including the UK, the US, Canada, New Zealand and Singapore. He is the co-author with A. Conte of *Defining Civil and Political Rights: The Jurisprudence of the United Nations Human Rights Committee*, 2nd edn (Ashgate Publishing, 2009) as well as the editor of *Democracy and International Law: Library of Essays in International Law* (Ashgate Publishing, 2006).

Professor Indira Carr is Professor of Law at Surrey University. Her research interests include various aspects of international trade law and information technology law. She has been working on international corruption for a number of years and her research has been funded by prestigious funding bodies such as the Arts & Humanities Research Council (AHRC) and the British Academy. She is a member of various research panels such as the AHRC and committees such as the Society of Legal Scholars and Transparency International, UK. She is also the Founder Editor of the journal Information and Communications Technology Law and Joint Founder Editor (with Brian Carr) of the journal Asian Philosophy, both published by Taylor & Francis.

Sofia Cavandoli is a Lecturer in law at Aberystwyth University. Sofia is a graduate from the University of East Anglia and holds an LLM in International Law from the University of Hull. Her research interests include various aspects of public international law, international law of human rights and international environmental Law.

Dr Engobo Emeseh is a Lecturer in law at Aberystwyth University. Her broad area of research is environmental law and policy. Her particular areas of interest include environmental regulation and enforcement, corporate social responsibility, environmental governance, and the interface between environmental law and other subject areas such as criminal law, human rights law and international investment law.

Dr Emma McClean is a Lecturer in law at the University of Westminster, London. She is currently working on a monograph on *Human Security and International Law* and has published in the areas of human rights and the United Nations.

Dr Gareth Norris is a Lecturer in criminology at Aberystwyth University. He has a background in psychology and completed the MSc in investigative psychology at the University of Liverpool in 2000. His PhD focused on the concept of the authoritarian personality, and he completed his doctoral thesis at Bond University, Queensland, Australia in 2005. His current research interests include the use of animation during investigations and in court, fear of crime and offender profiling. He has also managed a project in conjunction with the Prison Service in the North West, looking at the barriers to resettlement for ex-offenders, particularly, women, young offenders and those with mental health issues.

Dr Marco Odello is a Lecturer in law at Aberystwyth University. He is a member of the International Institute of Humanitarian Law. He has published articles and contributions in the areas of international law, human rights, humanitarian law and international organisations. Co-author of *La Convenzione Internazionale sui Diritti del Minore e l'Ordinamento Italiano* (ESI, 1994); Mazzarelli and Odello (eds), *L'insegnamento dei Diritti Umani* (EDIUN, 1999); co-author of *Problemas actuales del derecho público en Mexico* (Porrua, 2004).

Professor Diane Rowland is Professor of law at Aberystwyth University. She has published widely in various aspects of IT law and the fourth edition of her book *Information Technology Law* (co-authors Uta Kohl and Andrew Charlesworth) will be published by Routledge in 2011. She is a past Chair and Vice-Chair of the national executive of the British and Irish Law, Education and Technology Association (BILETA) and is also a member of the editorial board of the Journal of Information Law and Technology (JILT), the International Review of Law, Computers and Technology, the Masaryk University Journal of Law and Technology and the IT law editor of the Web Journal of Current Legal Issues.

Professor John Williams is Professor of law at Aberystwyth University. His research interests are in the area of the law and vulnerable adults, with particular reference to older people. This involves considering the impact of social services law, the criminal justice system, health care law and disability law on vulnerable adults. He is currently writing a book, *Older People and the Law*, which will take an overview of how the law impinges on older people.

Introduction

In 1948, the United Nations General Assembly proclaimed the Universal Declaration of Human Rights (UDHR) for all people and all nations.[1] Such a proclamation was one of the first collective expressions of an international community. Fifty-six United Nations Member States from different regions around the world affirmed the inherent dignity of humankind and placed the well-being of the individual at the heart of international law.

Born of a shared condemnation of the atrocities committed during the Second World War, the UDHR provided the world with the first universal statement on the basic principles of inalienable human rights. To this day, the Declaration has been translated into 337 different languages; it has affected and shaped national and international legal systems and it has been central in the promotion of political debates and philosophical discussions. The literature in this area is immense, and it is impossible in just one monograph to take into account the vast array of issues, debates and theories concerning the Declaration's effect on the application and enforcement of human rights.[2]

In 1945 the newly created United Nations had established in the Preamble of its Charter: ' … to reaffirm faith in fundamental human rights, in the dignity and worth of the human person, in the equal rights of men and women and of nations large and small … '.

In keeping to its word, the United Nations endorsed the task of developing an International Bill of Rights to the Commission on Human Rights which was chaired by Eleanor Roosevelt. The Commission, at its first session in 1947, authorised its members to formulate what it termed 'a preliminary draft International Bill of Human Rights'. Different legal, political and philosophical backgrounds shaped the new international document, which was drafted in only two years.[3] Wary of ideological conflicts between Member States, Eleanor Roosevelt purposely formulated the Declaration as a non-binding General Assembly Resolution. By doing so, the declaration passed despite profound disagreements on the nature of certain provisions because it was seen as not creating legal obligations for Member States in international law. Notwithstanding its non-binding status, the Declaration has come to have considerable influence in the international legal arena. Many of the UDHR's provisions are now considered to be binding against Member States because of customary international law.

The UDHR lays down a number of objectives and provides 'a common standard of achievement for all peoples and all nations'. Every 'individual and every organ of society' shall promote 'respect for these rights and freedoms ... by progressive measures ... '. These rights, also, known as first generation rights, include the right to life, to a fair trial, to freedom of expression, opinion and thought. The Declaration condemns torture and slavery and prohibits arbitrary interference with privacy and the family home. The ultimate goal of the Declaration is 'to secure the universal and effective recognition and observance of these rights'. Underlying the entire Declaration is one basic fundamental value. 'All human beings are born free and equal in dignity and rights'.

The adoption of the UDHR in 1948 provided a springboard for the development of international human rights law. The Human Rights Commission, the Human Rights Council,[4] and other related UN bodies and organs, such as the Sub-Commission on Human Rights,[5] the Economic and Social Council, the International Law Commission and the High Commissioner for Human Rights have played a central part in promoting a 'universal respect for and observance of human rights'. Other specialised agencies such as the High Commissioner for Refugees, UNICEF and the International Labour Organisation (ILO) have also contributed to the development of an outstanding number of legal and non-legal documents promulgating provisions that were originally laid out in the UDHR. Specialised treaty bodies, such as the Human Rights Committee and the Committee against Torture,[6] have been created to implement and monitor the application of international human rights law. At the same time, the development of regional organisations such as the Council of Europe, the Organisation of American States and the African Union has led to a further expansion of regional human rights instruments, international human rights courts and supervisory bodies.[7]

These developments have had an unforeseen influence and impact on national legal systems and the concept of state sovereignty.[8] National law is no longer immune from international influence or scrutiny.[9] National borders can no longer be considered obstacles for international action in favour of human rights. Constitutional reforms and national legislation have incorporated fundamental rights and principles which connect the international legal system to the national legal order.[10] This process has been facilitated by the fact that international human rights courts, such as the European Court of Human Rights, and supervisory quasi-judicial bodies[11] at the international level can address human rights violations that occur in national legal systems. The UDHR has set the stage for a system of international accountability that has been unparalleled in history. International criminal tribunals have brought together countries to judge the war crimes of Germany after the Second World War, and later Rwanda and the former Yugoslavia.

Alongside such extraordinary achievements, the international system of human rights has been the subject of much scrutiny. One example of such criticism is the lack of impartiality in the system, being that some states and governments are almost never scrutinised, whilst others are constantly made the object of international blame and criticism. This criticism does not affect the essence and nature of human rights. But essentially the procedure, impartiality and equity of the effective application of human rights norms and standards.[12]

A more substantive point of criticism has been focusing on the so-called 'relativism' of human rights. This criticism is based on anthropological positions[13] that refer to the concept of culture and identify a number of problems in establishing a 'universal' set of values enshrined in the human rights concept.[14] From the political, historical and philosophical perspective, several governments have supported the idea that human rights are a creation of the 'Western civilisation'. This means that they do not correspond to the different legal and philosophical traditions of other states and cultures, and that the international system is using a 'colonialist' approach in expanding and imposing human rights values around the world.

Reflecting on this point of criticism, just because human rights have a primarily Western political, philosophical and religious background, does not mean that these same values are not shared by other cultures and peoples. Ironically, it is usually countries with a very poor human rights track record whose voices are the loudest in raising the issue of cultural relativism.[15]

The international system of human rights has developed so much since the Declaration's inception and is so widespread in both international and national societies that it would be difficult to say that the human rights movement is only based on ideological and biased grounds. There are, of course, possible forms of ideological motivations and political aims, but in general it can be said that the human rights phenomenon has conquered and convinced the great majority of international public opinion, and enjoys support in most parts of the world. It is the responsibility of human rights experts and movements to find the best ways of incorporating human rights values in legal and social systems.[16]

Another aspect of the international human rights system, based on the UDHR, has been the expanding and ever-evolving nature of human rights. Since its adoption, the codification process regarding the definition of new rights and new international principles has never stopped. Universal and regional treaties have been drafted and a considerable number of institutions have been created to enforce and supervise many of the rights included in international agreements.

The 'expanding nature' of human rights is still producing its effects at the beginning of the twenty-first century, more than 60 years after the adoption of the UDHR. Legal developments are based on the codification, application and interpretation of treaties and state practice. Some areas are not fully codified in specific international agreements, but through an expanding interpretation of rights and principles based on the original UDHR new forms of human rights can be identified in the international legal system. Some organisations, governments and scholars believe that the human rights movement must concentrate on ensuring a proper supervision and application of existing rights rather than the creation of new ones. Whilst this is a valid point, one must not forget that with the ever-changing nature of society, the law faces a need for continued evolution and must address new challenges. Not only this but in some situations human rights concerns emerge thanks to the work of civil society and interest groups. Such concerns often require clearer legal provisions in order for them to be dealt with in the form of legal rights. For these reasons, it is important to address the evolution of human rights and look at those emerging in the twenty-first century.

The significance of the Declaration is more relevant than ever today in a world which is threatened by social, economic, racial and religious divides. Principles of fairness, equality and justice that are underlying foundations of the Declaration should be proclaimed and defended by all. The Declaration is there to protect all individuals and confirms human rights as essential for a life of dignity. It is a living document which is there for us all and for future generations. The evolution and growth of human rights has prospered since the Declaration's inception and the progress has been remarkable.

This book is the outcome of a Colloquium which was organised by the Department of Law and Criminology's *International Law Research Forum* at Aberystwyth University on 10 December 2008 in order to commemorate the sixtieth anniversary of the UDHR.

The theme of the Colloquium, 'Emerging Human Rights in the 21st Century: Sixty Years after the UDHR', was chosen in order to examine and reflect on the main developments in international human rights law since the Declaration's inception. Papers presented at the Colloquium concentrated specifically on issues and areas that were not originally mentioned or foreseen in the Declaration but that have recently emerged in the area of human rights as salient topics. Such topics covered a wide range of fields of research including law, politics and criminology.

Each chapter of this edited collection is dedicated to a specific emerging right or issue in the area of international human rights. The chapters cover a diverse array of topical discussions such as the impact of the internet on human rights; the relationship between human rights and environmental protection; the recognition and protection of indigenous peoples in the democratic state; the implication of human rights in relation to humanitarian aid and corruption; an investigation into the rights of incarcerated offenders with mental health issues; an evaluation on whether an international convention on the rights of older people is necessary; a debate on whether a right to democratic governance has emerged; an analysis of the practice of the UN Security Council in relation to the 'dilemma of intervention'.

This is a limited selection of emerging human rights areas, without the pretention of being exhaustive. Our aim in putting this book together was to make some form of contribution, however small, to the ongoing development of international human rights law and research.

We would like to thank the authors who have contributed to this piece of work and the Department of Law and Criminology at Aberystwyth University for making the Colloquium possible. A special thanks to Khanam Virjee and Routledge for believing in this project and for their patience and understanding.

Marco Odello and Sofia Cavandoli
Aberystwyth, 24 May 2010

Notes

1 By its resolution 217 A (III) of 10 December 1948, the General Assembly, meeting in Paris, adopted the Universal Declaration of Human Rights with eight nations abstaining from the vote but none dissenting.

2 Among others, see L Sohn and T Burgenthal, *International Protection of Human Rights* (Indianapolis, IN: Bobbs-Merrill, 1973); H J Steiner, P Alston and R Goodman, *International Human Rights in Context* (3rd edn, Oxford: Oxford University Press, 2007); T Dunne and N J Wheeler (eds), *Human Rights in Global Politics* (Cambridge: Cambridge University Press, 1999); D P Forsythe, *Human Rights in International Relations* (2nd edn, Cambridge: Cambridge University Press, 2006); M Ignatieff, *Human Rights as Politics and Idolatry* (Princeton: NJ, Princeton University Press, 2001); T Evans (ed), *Human Rights Fifty Years on: A reappraisal* (Manchester: Manchester University Press, 1998); C Douzinas, *The End of Human Rights* (Oxford: Hart Publishing, 2000).

3 See M A Glendon, *A World Made New: Eleanor Roosevelt and the Universal Declaration of Human Rights* (New York, NY: Random House, 2001); J Morsink, *The Universal Declaration of Human Rights Origins, Drafting, and Intent* (Philadelphia, PA: University of Pennsylvania Press, 1999).

4 In 2006 the Human Rights Council replaced the Commission on Human Rights, UNGA Res 60/251 (2006).

5 The Sub-Commission on the Promotion and Protection of Human Rights (known as the Sub-Commission on Prevention of Discrimination and Protection of Minorities from 1947 to 1999) has ceased to exist and it was replaced by the Human Rights Council Advisory Committee, composed of 18 experts, in 2007, see UNHRC Res 5/1 (18 June 2007).

6 See R Bernhardt and J A Jolowicz (eds), *International Enforcement of Human Rights* (Berlin: Springer-Verlag, 1987); P Alston (ed), *The United Nations and Human Rights: A Critical Appraisal* (Oxford: Clarendon Press, 1992).

7 For a collection of human rights documents, see I Brownlie and G Goodwin-Gill (eds), *Basic Documents on Human Rights* (6th edn, Oxford: Oxford University Press, 2010). On regional systems, see D Shelton, 'The Promise of Regional Human Rights Systems', in B Weston and S Marks (eds), *The Future of International Human Rights* (Ardsley, NY: Transnational Publishers, 1999); H Steiner, 'International Protection of Human Rights', in M Evans (ed), *International Law* (2nd edn, Oxford: Oxford University Press, 2006).

8 On the issues related to sovereignty and human rights, see S Krasner, *Sovereignty: Organized Hypocrisy* (Princeton, NJ: Princeton University Press, 1999); H Steiner, 'The Youth of Rights' (1991) 104 *Harvard Law Review* 917; R Falk, *On Human Governance: Towards a New Global Politics* (University Park, PA: Penn State Press, 1995); P J Spiro, 'The New Sovereigntists: American Exceptionalism and Its False Prophets' (2000) 79 *Foreign Affairs* 9–15; R Goodman and D Jinks, 'Towards an Institutional Theory of Sovereignty' (2003) 55 *Stanford Law Review* 1979.

9 R Goodman and D Jinks, 'How to Influence States: Socialization and International Human Rights Law' (2004) 54 *Duke Law Journal* 621.

10 See C Heyns and F Viljoen, *The Impact of The United Nations Human Rights Treaties on the Domestic Level* (Dordrecht: Kluwer Law International, 2002); B Conforti and F Francioni (eds), *Enforcing International Human Rights in Domestic Courts* (Dordrecht: Kluwer Law International, 1997); K D Ewing, 'The Human Rights Act and Parliamentary Democracy' (1999) 62 *Modern Law Review* 79; P Alston, *Promoting Human Rights Through Bills of Rights* (Oxford: Oxford University Press, 1999); H Knop, 'Here and There: International Law in Domestic Courts' (2000) 32 *NYUJ Int'l L & Pol'y* 501.

11 Such as the UN Human Rights Council, the specialised treaty bodies like the UN Committee on Human Rights, the UN Committee on the Rights of the Child and the Committee against Torture.

12 See P Alston, 'Promoting the Accountability of Members of the New Human Rights Council' (2005) 15 *J Transnat'l L & Pol'y* 49, 57.

13 American Anthropological Association, Statement on Human Rights, (1947) 49(4) *American Anthropologist* 539; Declaration on Anthropology and Human Rights, adopted

by the AAA membership, June 1999, <www.aaanet.org/stmts/humanrts.htm> (accessed 17 August 2010).

14 See E Hatch, *Culture and Morality: The Relativity of Values in Anthropology* (New York, NY: Columbia University Press, 1983); R Schweder, M Minow and H R Markus (eds), *Engaging Cultural Differences: The Multicultural Challenge in Liberal Democracies* (New York, NY: Russell Sage Foundation, 2002).

15 See R Higgins, *Problems and Process: International Law and How We Use It* (Oxford: Oxford University Press, 1994), p 96.

16 See A Sajó (ed), *Human Rights with Modesty: The Problem of Universalism* (Leiden/Boston, MA: M Nijhoff Publishers, 2004); A A An-Na'im, 'Human Rights in the Muslim World' (1990) 3 *Harvard Human Rights Journal* 13; R Coomaraswamy, *Report on Cultural Practices in the Family that are Violent Towards Women*, Commission on Human Rights, UN Doc E/CN.4/2002/83 (31 January 2002).

1 'Virtual world, real rights?': Human rights and the internet

Diane Rowland

1.1 Introduction

In a world of Facebook, Twitter and YouTube, where millions of people read and write blogs, participate in internet games, sell goods on eBay and find out about the world via Wikipedia, for many people it has become difficult to imagine a world without the internet. Yet, despite its current ubiquity, the internet, and specifically the web, is a comparatively recent development. When the Universal Declaration of Human Rights (UDHR) was signed there could have been no anticipation of the changes which the advent of global computer networks would bring in terms of global interconnectivity and its implications for life some 60 years later. As this chapter is being written, the fortieth anniversary of the internet itself has just been marked[1] and, before embarking on a more substantive discussion, it is useful to reflect on the way in which this medium has changed and has the ability to change communication and human relationships. As with many technological developments, the internet had a slow start; although email, something which is now seen as a basic communication tool, was possible in the early 1970s, it did not really take off until the early 1990s simply because there was not a sufficiently large critical mass of email users. What really changed the face of the medium in terms of its utility as a mass communication device was the advent of what was then called the 'world wide web' now referred to merely as 'the web'. This term is often now used as synonymous with the internet even though in fact it is a specific application, but without it, arguably the internet might not enjoy its current ubiquity as it has enabled easier access, easier navigation and easier location of information. In the current technological environment, it is difficult to appreciate that, only 15 years ago, there were, in total, only some 600–700 websites on the internet, but within only a very few years familiar presences such as Amazon, Google and Wikipedia were established, the number of users increased rapidly and is currently approaching 2 billion. This is the type of phenomenal growth for which the overused word 'exponential' is an accurate and apposite description.

The effect of these changes has been of sufficient significance to be described as heralding 'a new and more democratic information age'.[2] It is a challenge in a short chapter such as this to convey the impact these developments in information and communications technology with their 'huge and growing importance … for facilitating in practice the free flow of information that lies at the heart of the right to freedom of expression',[3] have had in relation to the recognition, exercise and development of human rights into the twenty-first century. However, two key words are probably 'enhancement' and 'awareness' – in very simple terms there could be said to be more of all types and usages of information; more information to allow individuals to find out about their own rights, more information about abuse of other's rights, more opportunities to participate, to speak and to listen, but also more opportunities for violations.

Although the example of Jamie McCoy referred to further below shows that Information and Communications Technology (ICT) may have the capacity to be empowering for those previously excluded from society, it is a moot point how representative a picture this paints. The phrase the 'digital divide' reflects the fact that there are sections of global society which are excluded from the 'never-ending conversation' on the internet and despite the relentlessly upbeat messages emanating from summit meetings on the information society,[4] the small print suggests that the digital divide is still of significant proportions. Nonetheless, it is almost certainly the case that the majority of readers of this collection now conduct many of their relationships, at least partially, online and do this via a range of communication methods which may include email, instant messaging and social networking sites. The relationships fostered in this way may be continuations of relationships in real life but an increasing number are with people who have been encountered in cyberspace – and are rarely if ever met in real life. In addition, the internet provides the functionality via websites, wikis and blogs to publish material to the world at large; material which covers an incredible spectrum of material from inane chat to erudite literary comment. More and more people use MMOGs,[5] such as Second Life,[6] as a leisure activity. Very few internet users have not also used the internet market place and shopped online. The virtual space denoted by the generic term, the internet, has thus become a massive phenomenon which encompasses a whole range of activities. The significant question in this context is why should a mere communications medium have any impact on the shape, interpretation and application of the law in general or human rights in particular? On the other hand, there is a school of thought which suggests that the internet creates a parallel universe with its own culture and ethos and, if this is an accurate or at least appropriate description, what implications does this have for the application of legal regimes and more specifically human rights?

Ever since the word 'cyberspace' was coined and applied to activities, communications and relationships made possible by the internet there have been discussions about its nature and its manifestation. A number of lawyers, courts and legal commentators have been willing to espouse the notion of a separate space, community or virtual world variously termed cyberspace or metaverse. Interestingly both the terms cyberspace and metaverse were originally coined in works of fiction. 'Cyberspace' appeared in the novel *Neuromancer*[7] in which it was defined as a 'consensual hallucination experienced daily by billions of legitimate operators in every nation ... A graphic representation of data abstracted from the banks of every computer ... '. The term 'metaverse' – literally 'beyond the universe' was first used in the novel *Snow Crash*.[8] Cyberspace has been described judicially as 'a word that recognises that the interrelationships created by the Internet exist outside conventional geographic boundaries'[9] and as a 'unique medium ... located in no particular geographical location but available to anyone, anywhere in the world, with access to the Internet'.[10] Although to date little legal reasoning has depended on the 'existence' of cyberspace or even on the concept of a virtual world, there have been many comments which suggest connotations of space and location; cyberspace is 'its own thriving city' for instance.[11] Although some commentators may wish to downplay the implications of this by referring to the 'cyberspace fallacy'[12] or pointing out that 'the internet is merely a simple computer protocol ... ',[13] the reality is that to most users it is much more than that, if indeed they consciously consider it in those terms at all. As Hunter remarks the 'place may be inchoate and virtual but no less real in our minds'.[14] Whereas it would be quite possible to reject the whole concept of cyberspace as a fantasy or mass delusion, the fact remains that many people talk about cyberspace as if it were real and it is difficult to escape the conclusion that things having both social and political significance and consequences can happen 'out there'. It could legitimately be viewed as merely a pragmatic response to acknowledge that the construction of these so-called 'virtual worlds' within the already virtual environment of cyberspace has the capacity to generate a whole new generation of human rights issues.

The purpose of the following discussion is not to perform an exhaustive analysis of human rights issues on the internet but to focus on the way in which the right to freedom of expression is being shaped by the ongoing developments in ICT (and the potential impact of these developments on other fundamental human rights such as privacy).

1.2 Freedom of expression

Some of the early cases which could be said to relate to human rights issues on the internet resulted in the first judicial consideration of the nature of cyberspace. This was not so much because of any perceived need to understand the technical aspects of the way in which cyberspace manifests itself but rather to appreciate the things that happen there – whether these be the facilitation of personal interactions, the formation of contracts, the perpetration of crime, the playing of games – since the courts have had to adjudicate on disputes concerning such matters. Although decided more than 10 years ago now and so in some ways almost of legal historical significance in relation to internet jurisprudence, the case of *ACLU v Reno*[15] remains an important case in terms of the discussion of the nature of cyberspace. The case was concerned with a challenge to attempts in the US to introduce legislation, known as the Communications Decency Act (CDA), intended to protect minors, which would have had, *inter alia*, the effect of restricting access by adults to material on the internet.

In his judgment, Judge Dalzell made some important points about the removal of barriers to entry to the marketplace of ideas which was facilitated by the internet:

> Four related characteristics of Internet communication have a transcendent importance … First, the Internet presents very low barriers to entry. Second, these barriers to entry are identical for both speakers and listeners. Third, as a result of these low barriers, astoundingly diverse content is available on the Internet. Fourth, the Internet provides significant access to all who wish to speak in the medium, and even creates a relative parity among speakers … [16]

He went on to conclude that the internet 'has achieved, and continues to achieve, the most participatory marketplace of mass speech that this country – and indeed the world – has yet seen'[17] and that it is 'a far more speech-enhancing medium than print, the village green, or the mails'.[18] This apparently rose-tinted view of the internet was tempered by the recognition that:

> Some of the dialogue on the Internet surely tests the limits of conventional discourse. Speech on the Internet can be unfiltered, unpolished and unconventional, even emotionally charged, sexually explicit and vulgar – … But we should expect such speech to occur in a medium in which citizens from all walks of life have a voice. …
>
> … the Internet may fairly be regarded as a never-ending worldwide conversation. … the most participatory form of mass speech yet developed …

The interactive nature of communications forums on the internet, blurring as they do the distinction between 'speakers and listeners' means that, once the initial boundary of entering cyberspace has been crossed, a speaker who might otherwise have had access to only a few local listeners has a potentially global audience and is also able to 'listen' to responses from an equally wide setting. This apparent democratising trend has continued apace with the development of Web 2.0, a rather misleading name which suggests a new version of the web but is instead one which has grown organically from the original, now often denoted as 'Web 1.0'. Web 2.0 is characterised by two-way involvement; participants are simultaneously readers and writers, speakers and listeners. New applications allow and encourage such two-way communication, whether public or semi-public, private or semi-private, by means of wikis, social networking sites, blogs and so on, leading to a proliferation of user-generated content, sometimes described as putting the 'me' back in media. Neither is this participation confined to leisure and pleasure pursuits. The growth of internet auction sites such as eBay has revolutionised informal buying and selling and commercial operators such as Amazon invite user-generated content in the form of customer reviews. There is anecdotal evidence that these are at least as influential in marketing terms as more apparently authoritative reviews in traditional outlets. The interactivity which these applications facilitate all appears to give the average user the opportunity to disseminate his or her thoughts and creative output in a way which would have been denied to all but a few when output was usually restricted to those fortunate enough to get a contract with a publisher, a speaking engagement or who could afford to pay for their own publication. Clearly, these aspects of the environment provided by the internet are speech-enhancing and of itself this could be said almost to move beyond a right of free expression to a right to communicate with others. In addition, the rise and rise of weblogs or 'blogs' can provide a voice for those who might otherwise be disenfranchised or not have access to a platform to express their views. A good example of this is provided by <www.jamiesbigvoice.blogspot.com/> referred to in the introduction. Jamie McCoy was a homeless man with no formal education living on the streets of London when, in 2005, he started to participate in a project in a hostel for the homeless which provided access to basic computers and internet access. This rapidly became a significant blog commenting on the social, economic and political issues surrounding homelessness. So this might appear to provide anecdotal empirical evidence for the democratising effect of the internet which was postulated in *ACLU v Reno*.

It is thus beyond doubt that the internet and more specifically now, Web 2.0 applications continue to provide the democratisation of speech which was alluded to in the early case of *ACLU v Reno*. But as might be suspected and expected, this both misrepresents and idealises the case. Nonetheless, this should not obscure the fact that, notwithstanding problems of the so-called digital divide, the internet does reduce and, for some, virtually eliminate barriers to the marketplace of speech; anyone with access to the internet can post content which in theory can be accessed on a global scale. Whereas in real life the saying goes that a cat may look at a king – in cyberspace a cat can talk to a king, at least, in principle. In addition, the cat and the king may be anywhere in the world and neither may the king have any idea that he is being addressed by a cat because, with apologies to the New Yorker, on the internet no one knows you're a cat.[19]

1.3 Freedom of speech or freedom of communication?

Conventional justifications for the existence of a right to freedom of expression are contained in arguments based on self-fulfilment, seeking after truth and participation in democratic debate. The extent to which these are factors of the nature of the internet are open to debate. It may be the case, for instance that open debate is fostered and encouraged but, as discussed further below, the use of the internet to spread dissonance rather than harmony could also have a chilling effect on speech. Barendt suggests that 'more weight might be accorded to the argument from self-fulfilment,[20] given the ease and increasing frequency of internet use' and it was evident in the 2008 US presidential elections that the internet and Web 2.0 in particular were being used directly for political debate by both the electorate and those seeking office. The web, as noted by Søraker appears to be 'a perfect vehicle for promoting the fundamental ideals of deliberative democracy'.[21]

It remains, though, a moot point as to whether the right to freedom of speech also embraces a right to communicate. What distinguishes a right to communicate from a right of free expression? Although freedom of expression usually refers to the right to receive as well as to impart information, something rather more active is presumably envisaged in communication. Web 2.0 applications with their focus on user-generated content, are at once interactive, participative and collaborative and so allow users to act simultaneously as speakers and listeners, in principle, therefore providing a fertile environment for nurturing a right to communicate. However, the size of the internet is now vast; the more information is available and the more people there are that use the internet, the less likely the individual user is to be heard over the 'din of cyberspace'.[22] As an indication of its size, it is currently estimated that there are over 20 billion web pages[23] and these are only those in the so-called 'surface web', i.e. ones which are indexed and can be located by users via search engines, etc. This is only the tip of the iceberg in the sense that there are also unquantifiable numbers of pages in the so-called 'deep web' – the 'dynamic' pages which lie behind web-based databases on ticket booking sites, B2C sales sites, etc for which some sort of access or permission protocol is required. Unless the user is extremely internet-savvy and can optimise their content to match the way in which search engines operate, an individual website or blog, unless on a very niche subject area, is very unlikely to be anywhere near the top of the list returned by Google or other search engine. Although the technology has been heralded as being speech-enhancing, the current size of the internet means that one individual is perhaps doing no more than merely whispering in a crowd and so, although the internet may provide both the freedom to speak and disseminate views, and also a potentially global audience, the reality may be that few actually 'hear' the message. So whilst there is clearly a democratising effect, in that more people are able to publish their views on everything from French cookery to fly fishing,[24] the success of the spread of the medium suggests that the number of readers or recipients of that expression may be extremely small.[25]

However, that is not necessarily to say that the democratising effect is therefore illusory, but the power to effect democratic change is one which is due, not only to the enhancement of speech but also to the coercive effects of collective pressure. Nonetheless, there have been some notable examples where the power of the medium to foster participation on matters of public interest and effect democratic change has been very efficient. An example is provided by the lifting of the 'superinjunction' placed on the *Guardian* newspaper to prevent it reporting the Minton report.[26] In brief, the order papers for the House of Commons business for the relevant week contained a question to be answered by a minister. However, the terms of the injunction prevented publication of the question itself as well as who asked it and who might answer it. In addition, it was forbidden to explain why parliamentary business could not be reported, which itself was an unprecedented occurrence. After the *Guardian* had stated that it was unable to publish details of Commons business, this fact was taken up on a variety of online media: blogs, social networking sites, Twitter, etc with the end result being that, far from the matter remaining shrouded in secrecy, it was very much brought out into the open. It is difficult to be categoric that the eventual lifting of the injunction would not have happened in the absence of the ability to discuss and protest about the issue via web-based media, but it is clearly plausible that this discussion played a significant part in the events as they unfolded.

The phrase 'the right to communicate' suggests on its face a right, akin to the right to freedom of expression which might feasibly form part of a bundle of rights guaranteed by charters and bills of rights. If, in fact, such a right can be identified in the way in which online discourse has progressed in response to advancing technological change, it is perhaps more accurate to view it as a 'bottom up' right fostered by the way in which the web has been developed by technical pioneers, rather than one bestowed on individuals by governments or intergovernmental bodies.

1.4 Access to knowledge and the digital divide

The discussion in the previous section focused on the empowering and democratising effect of the internet, but this of course is not a uniform effect and there are still many people in the world who have neither access to nor hope of access to the internet. For them, the fact that the internet reduces the barriers to access to the marketplace of ideas is meaningless. Recent figures show that, far from diminishing, the digital divide – the phrase which encompasses the schism between the technological haves and have nots – is still considerable and has arguably even been accentuated by the advent of superfast broadband.[27] An examination of the number of internet users as a percentage of the total population shows some stark differences. While the Scandinavian countries lead in terms of connectedness (Iceland and Norway each have more than 90% of the population with internet access), a vast number of countries have an internet penetration of less than 5%, and even less than 1%. This may be an eloquent illustration of the extent of the international digital divide, but it nevertheless masks the extent of what could be termed the domestic digital divide within individual jurisdictions. The fact that, even within the developed world, many may be excluded from the ICT revolution is probably reflected in the fact that the percentage of those with internet access in the US is estimated at only 74.1%; this is still significant but lower than for instance Israel (77%) and South Korea (77.3%).[28]

Although a large proportion of the world's population is clearly not currently in a position to benefit from the changing nature of ICT, the positive benefits of access to the internet have been seized upon at both national and international level, notwithstanding that a large proportion of the world's population cannot benefit from these developments. Governments promote the use of and access to ICT as a means of apparently encouraging participation in the democratic process, improving education,[29] and so on. As international summit meetings began to acknowledge the significance of ICT for global society, discussions and documents often presented a relentlessly positive approach. In 2000, the Okinawa Charter on Global Information Society promulgated in the G8 summit of that year, although recognising the challenge posed by the digital divide and emphasising the importance of implementing a coherent strategy to address the issue, nevertheless focused primarily on the power of ICT, *inter alia*, to strengthen democracy and promote human rights.[30] Similar positive messages about the use of ICT were evident in the Geneva Declaration following the United Nations' establishment of the World Summit on the Information Society in 2003 (WSIS).[31] As pointed out by Hamelink, 'the general feeling is that the information society can yield an unprecedented win-win situation and can contribute to a better life for all its citizens'.[32] The WSIS initiative spawned the Internet Governance Forum, which meets annually to discuss issues relating to internet governance; the documents published after such events continue to promulgate the benefits of universal connectivity and focus almost exclusively on positive aspects of increased internet access, even though acknowledging that the perceived benefits in terms of democratic participation and freedom of expression can only be enjoyed by an asymmetrical proportion of the global population.[33]

In tandem with moves to erode the digital divide, the access to knowledge movement (A2K) also seeks to spread the benefits of the technological revolution more uniformly. This movement is often associated with the challenge to the global expansion of intellectual property rights which again tends to disadvantage those countries at the 'wrong' end of the digital divide, but many of its proponents have also been instrumental in drawing attention to the huge deficit between such states in terms of access to the perceived benefits of internet access. However, there is considerable discussion amongst those working in this area as to the most effective way forward and there is significant potential for tension between the cyberlibertarian approach, which, recognising that the diffuse and amorphous world of cyberspace transcends international boundaries and creates obvious difficulties in enforcing external regulation, advocates self-regulation and minimal interference by both states and the international community.[34] A more traditional human rights approach, on the other hand, would be more likely to espouse action by states and international bodies to both safeguard and police human rights on the internet.[35]

1.5 Regulation of the internet and its content

Although the international fora referred to in the previous section have created a number of initiatives designed to increase access to the internet, significantly governments of all persuasions remain very wary of the internet – or at least its unfettered use by ordinary citizens. There are very few states which have not tried to control specific or more general use of the internet or content which is posted on it. This may be either overtly by legislation or more covertly by tracking internet use, etc which obviously has implications for privacy of communications. The case of *ACLU v Reno* referred to earlier was the start of ongoing litigation in the US courts challenging the constitutionality of successive pieces of legislation presented as protecting children's use of the internet but which could have outlawed adult material which was lawfully available offline.[36] China has an extremely well-developed system of internet censorship and surveillance achieved by a combination of technology (the so-called 'Great Firewall'[37]) backed up by legislation.[38] At the time of writing, Google (which had previously established a separate search engine google.cn) announced that it would cease operating in China, unless it was not subject to such censorship.[39] But it is not only states with a tradition of fettering freedom of expression which are targeting the internet; there is also an ongoing movement in Australia[40] vociferously challenging ongoing government proposals to censor the internet.[41] Given that Internet Service Providers (ISPs) are the gatekeepers of the free marketplace of ideas represented by an idealised vision of the internet, one way to control what could be an otherwise anarchic medium is to target regulation at the ISPs.[42] In consequence, some states impose licence conditions on ISPs and require compliance with codes of practice detailing what is or is not acceptable content. Such regulation varies in its severity[43] but may also be accompanied by potential liability for the ISP which provides the conduit for unauthorised content, neglecting the almost impossible task for ISPs of monitoring, let alone scrutinising all the content to which they provide access. Other states may try to require all communications to be routed through government-controlled servers or attempt to block access to content which does not accord with the political or religious ethos in the state. Many in the latter category are those at the far end of the digital divide who have very few citizens with access to the internet and yet attempt to exert strenuous and disproportionate control over the medium.[44] Very few of these measures are completely successful because of the nature of the internet; as it is a network there are always a number of different ways of getting from A to B, some may be more circuitous perhaps but still provide a way of getting to the destination. So if one route is blocked whether by state intervention or network failure or for any other reason, the communication can be routed round the blockage. In consequence in a number of states, most often those which historically have exerted tight control over the media, there has been a vicious reaction to liberalisation of views and political opinions which might not chime with the prevailing administration in a particular jurisdiction. This has resulted in reprisals against bloggers, internet users and web content providers, especially those who use these forms of communication to engage in political and social commentary about the state in question. The organisation 'Reporters without Borders' reports that in 2009, 151 bloggers and cyberdissidents were arrested, one blogger died while in prison[45] and that there are at present 114 cyberdissidents in prison in a total of 12 states. Of these, more than half are in China, as a result of trials dating back to 1999.[46] At the time of writing the most recent trial, on 20 January 2010, resulted in a Vietnamese court imposing custodial sentences amounting to a total of 33 years on four people – a human rights lawyer and three pro-democracy activists – for 'activities aimed at overthrowing the people's administration' contrary to Article 79 of the Vietnamese Penal Code (1999).[47] The defendants had originally been charged under Article 84 with the lesser offence of conducting propaganda against the state, but, for reasons which were not given, the charge was changed to the more serious one; the death penalty can be imposed for breaches of Article 79. Such activity against internet users is in marked contrast to the aspirational statements about the importance of the internet for political participation and freedom of expression.

But in addition to the obligation not to interfere with the freedom of expression of their citizens, states also need to protect their citizens from the actions of others. The internet may be speech-enhancing but it provides a forum not only for useful, interesting, creative and intelligent content but also for scurrilous, vituperative, defamatory and obscene content. Communication on the internet is still primarily (although no longer exclusively) text-based and yet it can have the immediacy of speech. In addition this 'speech' often comes with none of the facial indications or body language which allow the listener in a more traditional encounter to ascertain whether the message is meant seriously, humorously or whatever. The major concern of those who would restrict internet content as a protectionist measure is not the casual offender but the organised production of hate speech through exactly the same channels as other information: websites, social networking sites, etc. The internet is a brilliant facilitator of communication across borders and is able to unite in hatred bigots just as easily as it can locate lost school friends. Its functionality also provides a perfect means of propagating such information often protected by a cloak of anonymity. At what point should free expression on the internet be fettered when it might be damaging to individuals or specific racial or religious groups? Although there may be powerful arguments in support of legal intervention, Barendt suggests that 'it is far from clear that this is justifiable in a society with any serious commitment to the principles of free speech',[48] suggesting that even though hate speech might be abhorrent to most people it is not established that it necessarily gives credence to racist attitudes and that driving it underground might be counterproductive. Although in a free speech utopia it might be best countered by strong public advocacy of the benefits of multiculturalism, realistically it appears that some legal intervention is likely to be considered appropriate.[49] However, a particular challenge in relation to hate speech on the internet is that the requisite legal definition and the legal response to it are frequently culturally and jurisdictionally dependent. The French Constitution for instance has a number of provisions on hate speech including section R645–1 of the French Criminal Code, which prohibits the offering for sale of Nazi propaganda and artefacts. In the internet context this led to the case of *Yahoo!, Inc v La Ligue Contre Le Racisme et L'Antisemitisme* (LICRA). LICRA brought a complaint against Yahoo! in France citing the above section as Yahoo! auction sites offering Nazi memorabilia for sale could be accessed in France via either Yahoo.com or Yahoo.fr. The order of the French court required Yahoo! to 'take all necessary measures to dissuade and render impossible any access via Yahoo.com to the Nazi artefact auction service and to any other site or service that may be construed as constituting an apology for Nazism or a contesting of Nazi crimes'.[50] Yahoo! then brought an action in the US courts as to whether the order of the French court could be enforced in the US.[51] In deciding that the order could not be enforced, the court was at pains to point out that the case was not about whether promoting the symbols or propaganda of Nazism was morally acceptable, rather the question was:

> whether it is consistent with the Constitution and laws of the United States for another nation to regulate speech by a United States resident within the United States on the basis that such speech can be accessed by Internet users

> in that nation. In a world in which ideas and information transcend borders and the Internet in particular renders the physical distance between speaker and audience virtually meaningless, the implications of this question go far beyond the facts of this case.[52]

Even this one example demonstrates how difficult it is likely to be to achieve a consensus on the global scale required for uniform internet governance; the internet may be increasingly globalised but the legal response remains local, not global. The futility of such actions is summed up by Greenberg's comment on the Yahoo! case that states are unable to:

> deal with the complex cultural and legal issues that arise when material posted lawfully on servers in one country violates the law when viewed by web surfers in another country. The courts in each country attempt to walk the fine line between preserving their sovereignty and preserving the principle of international comity. The results are less than satisfying on all sides. Perhaps the most disappointing element of this dispute is that after more than three years of litigation, the parties are no better off than when they started ... [53]

So in purely pragmatic terms, suppression of hate speech on the internet is an almost intractable problem from both a technological and a legal viewpoint. Arguably, this is reflected in the UK's recent publication of draft regulations that will exempt ISPs from liability for hate speech based on religion or sexuality made available via their networks.[54]

1.6 Is the internet different?

The courts have often appeared to struggle with defining the appropriate basis for control of internet content, and what standard should be applied. The mantra of technological neutrality namely 'what is illegal offline remains illegal online' is often and uncritically repeated together with its corollary 'what is legal offline should be legal online' – but this neatly sidesteps the fact that the same standards are not necessarily applied to other media such as traditional print and broadcast media. The difference between the internet and other forms of communication is often presented as merely one of quantity – more content can be streamed to more people in less time, and so on. While this is undeniable it certainly does not paint the entire picture and, second, it could be suggested that extreme quantitative differences could be sufficient to constitute a qualitative difference. So are there analogies which can be made with other communication media to arrive at an appropriate solution or is the internet a *sui generis* method of communication? The analogy with radio and television was firmly rejected in *ACLU v Reno* as, unlike broadcast media, the internet user does not come across content completely – rather there has to be some sort of active seeking.[55] As the statistics above indicate, like the needle in the haystack, even if there are pages with inappropriate content they may be extremely difficult to locate. Nonetheless, even though overzealous application of the law of defamation can have an extremely chilling effect on speech, some recent Canadian cases on defamation on the internet have proceeded on the basis that the internet is a ubiquitous medium with a global reach. The Court of Appeal of Alberta in *Angle v LaPierre*[56] suggested that publications on the internet were indiscriminate in nature and had global reach – this meant in its view that there were bound to be people who had read content which was not intended for them, or at least that this could happen, with the consequent result that no defendant could take advantage of any defence of qualified privilege. The court seemed to infer that this would be its view even if evidence was brought that no one outside the target audience had actually accessed the information. In contrast in the earlier UK case of *Dow Jones v Jameel*,[57] Jameel failed in his claim relating to a publication in the *Wall Street Journal* because the evidence was that only five people had accessed the article in question; three of these were Jameel and his advisors and the other two had no idea who Jameel was and had swiftly navigated away from the site. In other rights areas, notably property rights, the courts struggle with the intangible nature of the internet and its manifestations and property rights over so-called 'virtual property'; not merely intellectual property but to rights over websites, 'property' in MMOGs such as Second Life and so on. American cases have wrestled with the use of actions in trespass to deal with unauthorised access to online databases. In *eBay v Bidders Edge*[58] the court found that the analogy of harm favoured by eBay of 'sending in an army of 100,000 robots a day to check the prices in a competitor's store' was inappropriate[59] and instead allowed the injunction on the basis that eBay's server and its contents were private property.[60] However, a website can be stored on any server without the awareness of the user, i.e. the collection of software files containing the intangible code which represents the website is essentially quite separate from the physical medium which is the server. It is thus difficult to see how such an argument is tenable although it has been affirmed in later US cases. It is thus clear that courts struggle sometimes with the nature of the internet; instead of trying to get a handle on its unique features they focus on ways in which it can be compared with existing modes of communication. Whilst this may be understandable it does not always produce a coherent rational or logical outcome.

1.7 Conclusion

Can the internet be regarded as a new medium without parallel to other forms of communication? Is it realistic to regard it as a mere computer protocol, or is it rather something much more elemental than that in the way it shapes and fosters relationships online? The answers to these questions may depend on the reader's subjective view of the internet and its role in twenty-first century society. But in particular in the context of this chapter, the question which has to be addressed relates to the manner in which the internet has affected the way in which human rights, specifically the right to freedom of expression, can be exercised and enjoyed or, conversely, the manner in which it can be violated and abused. That there are manifest changes seems clear but it remains a moot point whether the advent of the internet has changed the direction of human rights development. It is difficult to assess the extent to which the sheer magnitude of communications across geographical, social and political borders has had a profound effect. Overall it seems that the community of internet users ('netizens') are able to spread both serious and trivial matter with equal alacrity. In terms of the spread of news, the activities of citizen journalists, especially in countries with no tradition of either press freedom or a pluralist press, has provided a valuable tool by which the world has been made aware of the enormity and severity of the actual conditions in their countries, albeit sometimes with serious consequences to themselves. Use of the internet has also been instrumental in assisting pro-democracy campaigns in many parts of the world, but as documented above this has led to a number of authoritarian governments taking action against users of the internet. Given the rapid way in which netizens can be mobilised via Web 2.0 applications, it is clear that rumour and scandal can be spread as rapidly as good news and bonhomie and that the former could wreak great damage. Whether such dissemination and consequent damage actually occurs may depend on who are the movers and shakers in cyberspace; the followers and followed in Twitter terminology. Notwithstanding the erosion of barriers to speaking, as in real life, some voices will be listened to rather more attentively and their suggestions acted upon rather more assiduously than others.

Historically, the scope of exceptions to free speech has depended on the particular cultural political and social environment in individual states. The internet has threatened the ability of individual states to exert their preferred level of control over the delicate balance of conflicting interests. Cyberspace famously is without borders: at least in the usually accepted territorial sense. Whereas anonymity and pseudonymity have provided shields to enable users both to advance unpopular or critical views without fear of reprisal, fears of the abuse of anonymity have led to presumptions that all those who do not wish to identify themselves must inevitably be engaged in nefarious pursuits. In relation to hate speech, history does not demonstrate that suppression of extreme and dangerous behaviour has been particularly successful at controlling, much less eradicating it. Further, those who advocate a cyberutopia characterised by absolute freedom of expression deny the interests of those who hear the message which should arguably be accorded as much consideration as the interests of those who speak. There are many potential justifications for restricting speech on this basis. These are well-rehearsed in the standard texts and include the fact that hate speech has no basis in self-fulfilment, truth-seeking or democratic participation. A controversial view but one which perhaps works quite well for the internet is to rationalise it by considering the primary right not to be that of the speaker but rather the audience's right to hear. The speaker's right then may be equally important but is a derivative right arising out of the right of reception of ideas.[61]

In summary, it may be that the internet has not fundamentally changed the landscape of human rights but rather has enhanced certain issues and created challenges for the courts in terms of coherence of approach and their ability to grapple with the nature of this medium and what happens there. In terms of the future, it will be interesting to see how emergent communities in MMOGs such as Second Life, where the potential for crossover between real life and the virtual world is most pronounced, deal with rights issues.[62] Second Life has many communities, a number of which may exhibit anarchic or dystopian tendencies, but others of which may attempt to establish utopian standards with regard to freedom of expression but which may lead the 'inhabitants' to a zero tolerance approach to policing these spaces in order to maintain these standards. The Universal Declaration of Human Rights suggested that the 'the advent of a world in which human beings shall enjoy freedom of speech ... has been proclaimed as the highest aspiration of the common people';[63] in the twenty-first century it appears that the fight for freedom of expression is being fought largely online as 'the internet has become a means of expression of choice for political dissidents, democracy activists, human rights defenders and independent journalists'.

Notes

1 There is some dispute about what constitutes the actual 'birthday' of the internet. *National Geographic* suggests it is 2 September 1969, which apparently marks communication between two computers in the same laboratory (see <http://news.nationalgeographic.com/news/2009/08/090831-internet-40th-video-ap.html> (accessed 17 August 2010)) whereas the *Guardian*, although pointing out that it is 'impossible to say for certain when the internet began', marked the occasion on 29 October, which is the anniversary of the first communication between two computers at remote sites (see <www.guardian.co.uk/technology/2009/oct/23/internet-40-history-arpanet> (accessed 17 August 2010)).

2 E Barendt, *Freedom of Speech* (2nd edn, Oxford: Oxford University Press, 2005), p 451.

3 See Joint Declaration by UN Special Rapporteur on Freedom of Opinion and Expression, the OSCE Representative on Freedom of the Media and the OAS Special Rapporteur on Freedom of Expression (2005), <www.osce.org/documents/rfm/2005/10/26809_en.pdf> (accessed 17 August 2010).

4 See below, para 1.4.

5 Massively multiplayer online games. Although often seen as a recent development, these applications have evolved from the early MUDs and MUSHs of the early 1990s (see <www.mud.co.uk> (accessed 17 August 2010)) but technological developments have made them far more accessible to the average internet user.

6 <www.secondlife.com> (accessed 17 August 2010).

7 W Gibson, *Neuromancer* (London: Gollancz, 1984). Interestingly, this was written after the birth of the internet but before the advent of the web.

8 N Stephenson, *Snow Crash* (London: Penguin, 1994) (originally published in 1992).

9 *Dow Jones v Gutnick* [2002] HCA 56, para 80.

10 *Reno v ACLU* 521 US 844, 851.

11 *Playboy Enterprises, Inc v Chuckleberry Pub, Inc* 939 F Supp 1032, 1037.

12 C Reed, *Internet Law* (2nd edn, Cambridge: Cambridge University Press, 2004), p 218.

13 M Lemley, 'Place and cyberspace' (2003) 91 *Cal L Rev* 521, 523.

14 D Hunter, 'Cyberspace as place and the tragedy of the digital anticommons' (2003) 91 *Cal L Rev* 439, 452.

15 *ACLU v Reno* 929 F Supp 824 (ED Pa, 1996).

16 *Ibid*, 877.

17 *Ibid*, 881.

18 *Ibid*, 882.
19 <www.cartoonbank.com/invt/106197> (accessed 17 August 2010).
20 Op. cit., Barendt, fn 2, p 453.
21 Johnny Hartz Søøraker, 'Global freedom of expression within non textual frameworks' (2008) 24 *The Information Society* 40.
22 929 F Supp 824, 872.
23 28.13 billion on 17 August 2010.
24 Cf. District Judge Dalzell in *ACLU v Reno I* 929 F Supp 824, 872.
25 Precise statistics are difficult to find for the actual numbers of blogs, blog readers and users of social networking sites and other web 2.0 applications but for some idea of the potential users and audiences, see e.g. <http://thefuturebuzz.com/2009/01/12/social-media-web-20-internet-numbers-stats/> (accessed 17 August 2010); <http://popacular.com/gigatweet/> provides a continuous count of the number of tweets being submitted to Twitter (accessed 17 August 2010); <www.caslon.com.au/weblogprofile1.htm> (accessed 17 August 2010) contains an interesting consideration of the amount of readership of blogs and concludes that the average readership for a blog is 250 and that many have far fewer readers than that, leading to the suggestion that 'nanoaudiences are the logical outcome of continued growth in blogs'.
26 See <www.guardian.co.uk/world/2009/oct/16/carter-ruck-abandon-minton-injunction> (accessed 17 August 2010) and <www.guardian.co.uk/world/2009/oct/16/trafigura-carter-ruck-the-guardian> (accessed 17 August 2010).
27 For statistics on internet usage by country, see generally <http://internetworldstats.com/stats.htm> (accessed 17 August 2010); <http://en.wikipedia.org/wiki/List_of_countries_by_number_of_Internet_users> (accessed 17 August 2010) provides an accessible list of internet users by country from the same source.
28 For a more detailed consideration of the extent and effect of the digital divide, see e.g. the World Bank Working Paper, 'E-Ready for What? E-Readiness in Developing Countries: Current Status and Prospects toward the Millennium Development Goals' (Washington DC: World Bank, May 2005), <www-wds.worldbank.org/WBSITE/EXTERNAL/EXTWDS/0,detailPagemenuPK:64187510~menuPK:64187513~pagePK:64187848~piPK:64187934~searchPagemenuPK:64187283~siteName:WDS~theSitePK:523679,00.html> (accessed 17 August 2010).
29 See e.g. <www.tes.co.uk/article.aspx?storycode=394625> (accessed 17 August 2010).
30 Okinawa Charter on Global Information Society (2000), <www.g8.utoronto.ca/summit/2000okinawa/gis.htm> (accessed 17 August 2010).
31 <www.itu.int/wsis/docs/geneva/official/dop.html> (accessed 17 August 2010).
32 C J Hamelink, 'Did WSIS achieve anything?' (2004) 66 *Gazette: The International Journal for Communication Studies* 281, 282.
33 The 2009 IGF meeting was held in Egypt on 15–19 November with the theme 'Internet Governance: Creating an opportunity for all'. For details of outcomes, see <www.intgovforum.org/cms/index.php/component/content/article/314-2009-meeting>.
34 See e.g. the seminal works D R Johnson and D Post, 'Law and borders – the rise of law in cyberspace' (1996) 48 *Stan L Rev* 1367 and Lawrence Lessig, *Code and Other Laws of Cyberspace* (New York, NY: Basic Books, 1999).
35 A more detailed exploration of the inherent tension between these two approaches is beyond the scope of this chapter, but see further Molly Beutz Land, 'Protecting Rights Online' (2009) 34 *Yale J Int'l L* 1 and references cited therein.
36 See also *ACLU v Reno II* 217 F 3d 162 (3rd Cir 2000), *Ashcroft v ACLU* 535 US 564 (2002) and *Ashcroft v ACLU* 124 S Ct 2783 (2004).
37 See further R Clayton, S J Murdoch and R N M Watson, 'Ignoring the Great Firewall of China' (2007) 3 *Journal of Law and Policy for the Information Society* 271.
38 See e.g. <www.amnestyusa.org/business/Undermining_Freedom_of_Expression_in_China.pdf> (accessed 17 August 2010); <www.rsf.org/IMG/pdf/Voyage_au_coeur_de_la_censure_GB.pdf> (accessed 17 August 2010).

39 See <http://googleblog.blogspot.com/2010/01/new-approach-to-china.html> (accessed 17 August 2010); <www.out-law.com/page-10663> (accessed 17 August 2010).

40 See <http://nocleanfeed.com/> (accessed 17 August 2010).

41 For news reports and details of the Australian proposals, see e.g. <www.theinquirer.net/inquirer/opinion/1566179/australia-try-censor-internet> (accessed 17 August 2010); <http://globalvoicesonline.org/2009/12/21/australia-pushes-internet-censorship-twitter-erupts/> (accessed 17 August 2010); Renée Watt and Alana Maurushat, 'Clean Feed: Australia's Internet Filtering Proposal' [2009] *UNSWLRS* 7, <www.austlii.edu.au/au/journals/UNSWLRS/2009/7.html> (accessed 17 August 2010).

42 Cf. op. cit., Hartz Søraker, fn 21.

43 See e.g. the regulatory framework in Singapore, <www.mda.gov.sg/Policies/PoliciesandContentGuidelines/Internet/Pages/default.aspx> (accessed 17 August 2010).

44 See e.g. details of the position in North Korea and Myanmar provided by the OpenNet Initiative (ONI), <http://opennet.net/research/profiles/north-korea> (accessed 17 August 2010) and <http://opennet.net/research/profiles/burma> (accessed 17 August 2010). ONI is operated by a consortium of research groups from four universities, Harvard, Toronto, Oxford and Cambridge, which aim 'to investigate, expose and analyze Internet filtering and surveillance practices in a credible and non-partisan fashion'. For more details, see <http://opennet.net/about-oni> (accessed 17 August 2010).

45 <www.rsf.org/Wars-and-disputed-elections-The.html> (accessed 17 August 2010). Similar details are reported on <http://opennet.net> (accessed 17 August 2010).

46 <http://en.rsf.org/spip.php?page=article&id_article=1290> (accessed 17 August 2010). For a general resume of repressive government activity relating to the internet, see <www.rsf.org/en-pays225-Internet.html> (accessed 17 August 2010).

47 See <www.amnesty.org.uk/news_details.asp?NewsID=18582> (accessed 17 August 2010); <www.rsf.org/Court-sentences-four-netizens-and.html> (accessed 17 August 2010); <www.reuters.com/article/idUSTRE60J38G20100120> (accessed 17 August 2010).

48 Op. cit., Barendt, fn 2, p 171.

49 See generally R Delgado and J Stefanic 'Four Observations about Hate Speech' (2009) 44 *Wake Forest L Rev* 353 and J Weinstein and I Hare (eds), *Extreme Speech and Democracy* (Oxford: Oxford University Press, 2009).

50 High Court of Paris (22 May 2000) Interim Court Order No 00/ 05308, 00/ 05309.

51 *Yahoo! v LICRA* 169 F Supp 2d 1181 (ND Cal 2001). See also discussion in e.g. Marc H Greenberg, 'A return to Lilliput: the *LICRA v Yahoo!* case and the regulation of online content in the world market' (2003) 18 *Berkeley Tech LJ* 1191. Note, however, that a later hearing held by a majority that the US District Court lacked personal jurisdiction over the French defendants, 433 F 3d 1199 (9th Cir 2006).

52 169 F Supp 2d 1181, 1186.

53 *Ibid*, 1205.

54 See the draft statutory instrument, Electronic Commerce Directive (Hatred against Persons on Religious Grounds or the Grounds of Sexual Orientation) Regulations 2010, <www.opsi.gov.uk/si/si2010/draft/ukdsi_9780111490402_en_1> (accessed 17 August 2010).

55 929 F Supp 824, paras 75–89.

56 2008 ABCA 120.

57 [2005] EWCA Civ 75.

58 100 F Supp 2d 1058 (ND Cal 2000).

59 *Ibid*, 1065.

60 *Ibid*, 1070. In the subsequent case of *Register.com Inc v Verio Inc*, 126 F Supp 2d 238, 250 (SDNY 2000), the same reasoning was adopted and the decision was subsequently affirmed by 356 F 3d 393 (2nd Cir 2004).

61 See further L Alexander, *Is there a right of freedom of expression* (New York: Cambridge University Press, 2005).

62 For discussion of some of the relevant issues, see e.g. B M Chin, 'Regulating your Second Life: Defamation in Virtual Worlds' (2006) 72 *Brook L Rev* 1303, A Adrian

'No one knows you are a dog: Identity and reputation in virtual worlds' (2008) 24 *CLSR* 366 and P Sinclair 'Freedom of Speech in the Virtual World' (2009) 19 *Alb LJ Sci & Tech* 231.

63 European Parliament Resolution on Freedom of Expression on the Internet (July 2006) Recital C.

Bibliography

Adrian, A, 'No one knows you are a dog: Identity and reputation in virtual worlds' (2008) 24 *CLSR* 366.

Alexander, L, *Is there a right of freedom of expression* (New York: Cambridge University Press, 2005).

Barendt, E., *Freedom of Speech* (2nd edn, Oxford: Oxford University Press, 2005), p 451.

Beutz Land, M, 'Protecting Rights Online' (2009) 34 *Yale J Int'l L* 1.

Chin, B M, 'Regulating your Second Life: Defamation in Virtual Worlds' (2006) 72 *Brook L Rev* 1303.

Clayton, R, Murdoch, S J and Watson, R N M, 'Ignoring the Great Firewall of China' (2007) 3 *Journal of Law and Policy for the Information Society* 271.

Delgado, R and Stefanic, J, 'Four Observations about Hate Speech' (2009) 44 *Wake Forest L Rev* 353.

Gibson, W, *Neuromancer* (London: Gollancz, 1984).

Greenberg, M H, 'A return to Lilliput: the *LICRA v Yahoo!* case and the regulation of online content in the world market' (2003) 18 *Berkeley Tech LJ* 1191.

Hamelink, C J, 'Did WSIS achieve anything?' (2004) 66 *Gazette: The International Journal for Communication Studies* 281.

Hartz Søraker, J, 'Global freedom of expression within non textual frameworks' (2008) 24 *The Information Society* 40.

Hunter, D, 'Cyberspace as place and the tragedy of the digital anticommons' (2003) 91 *Cal L Rev* 439.

Johnson, D R and D Post, 'Law and borders – the rise of law in cyberspace' (1996) 48 *Stan L Rev* 1367.

Lemley, M, 'Place and cyberspace' (2003) 91 *Cal L Rev* 521.

Lessig, L, *Code and Other Laws of Cyberspace* (New York, NY: Basic Books, 1999).

Reed, C, *Internet Law* (2nd edn, Cambridge: Cambridge University Press, 2004).

Sinclair, P, 'Freedom of Speech in the Virtual World' (2009) 19 *Alb LJ Sci & Tech* 231.

Stephenson, N, *Snow Crash* (London: Penguin, 1994) (originally published in 1992).

Watt, R and Maurushat, A, 'Clean Feed: Australia's Internet Filtering Proposal' (2009) *UNSWLRS* 7.

Weinstein, J and Hare, I, (eds) *Extreme Speech and Democracy* (Oxford: Oxford University Press, 2009).

World Bank, 'E-Ready for What? E-Readiness in Developing Countries: Current Status and Prospects toward the Millennium Development Goals', Working Paper (Washington DC: World Bank, May 2005).

2 The dilemma of intervention: Human rights and the UN Security Council

*Emma McClean**

2.1 Introduction

The refrain of 'never again' ensured the inclusion of human rights provisions in the United Nations (UN) Charter at San Francisco in 1945. Three years later the Universal Declaration of Human Rights (UDHR) was adopted by the UN General Assembly (GA), inspired by 'opposition to the barbarous doctrines of Nazism and fascism',[1] which consolidated the Charter pledge to promote 'universal respect for, and observance of, human rights and fundamental freedoms for all'.[2] While the UN Charter and the UDHR bring human rights into the purview of legitimate international concern, the refrain of 'never again' continues to reverberate. The Rwandan genocide, the massacre at Srebrenica and the ethnic cleansing in Kosovo in the 1990s along with, for example, the humanitarian crises in Darfur, Sudan and the Democratic Republic of Congo (DRC) today bring into sharp relief the 'dilemma of intervention' facing the UN. This intervention dilemma was characterised by UN Secretary-General (SG) Annan as a choice between the 'defence of sovereignty' and the 'defence of humanity'[3] and directly engages the issue of humanitarian intervention by the UN Security Council (UNSC).[4]

Against the backdrop of the 'internationalisation of human rights'[5] that began with the UN Charter and the UDHR (see below, para 2.2), this chapter examines UNSC practice in responding to human rights violations, such as genocide and ethnic cleansing, with a particular emphasis on humanitarian intervention by the UNSC, in order to evaluate how the UNSC has resolved the tension between human rights and sovereignty (see below, para 2.3). The third part of the chapter (see below, para 2.4) explores whether the responsibility to protect as presently articulated by the UN resolves the intervention dilemma in favour of human rights by galvanising the UNSC to authorise the use of force to respond to human rights violations. In this respect it is argued that the responsibility to protect – from endorsement by the UN at the 2005 World Summit to the 2009 Report of the SG, *Implementing the Responsibility to Protect* – fails to move beyond the decisive dichotomy of human rights versus sovereignty that mired the humanitarian intervention debate and, moreover, represents a missed opportunity to develop UNSC practice with respect of responding to genocide, ethnic cleansing and other human rights violations.

2.2 The internationalisation of human rights

The protection of human rights in international law is a relatively new phenomenon dating from the end of the Second World War and the creation of the UN. The delegates at San Francisco charged with drafting the UN Charter proclaimed 'respect for human rights and fundamental freedoms' as a purpose of the UN in Article 1(3) and pledged as an organisation to promote 'universal respect for, and observance of, human rights and fundamental freedoms for all' in Article 55(c). However, a number of delegates expressed concern that the human rights provisions, especially the promotional role envisaged under Article 55, could be construed as permitting the UN to intervene in the domestic affairs of Member States and thus insisted on including the principle of non-intervention in Article 2(7) of the Charter.[6] In light of this drafting history, human rights are placed in a subordinate, even antithetical, position relative to the principle of non-intervention and sovereignty more generally. Moreover, the Charter human rights provisions do not create specific legal obligations for the UN or UN Member States in respect of human rights.

The UN embarked on a 'programme of codification'[7] in the field of human rights by entrusting to the former Commission on Human Rights the task of drafting an international bill of rights, a task that was subsequently divided into three parts, namely preparation of a declaration, followed by a convention, and finally 'measures of implementation'.[8] The logic of this division of labour was to accommodate concerns voiced by the US and the UK, with the former reluctant to accept 'legally binding commitments' and the latter 'sceptical of the value of a declaration'.[9] Thus it is unsurprising that when the Commission submitted a declaration to the GA for consideration towards the end of 1948, the general understanding was that the declaration was not legally binding, which no doubt contributed to the unanimous adoption of what became known as the UDHR. Indeed, all UN Member States, including the nine that abstained, insisted that the UDHR, in the words of the British delegate, 'could not impose specific obligations'.[10]

The clear injunction that the UDHR has no legal value was tempered somewhat by claims, such as that made by Argentina, that the UDHR is 'a document which involves moral obligations'.[11] Indeed, the moral and political reach of the UDHR is evident upon considering the practice of referencing the UDHR in appropriate GA Resolutions.[12] Moreover, the preambles of the nine core UN human rights treaties all make explicit reference to the UDHR as do the regional human rights treaties, while national constitutions have also drawn inspiration from the UDHR. The UDHR has also served as an effective rallying cry for non-governmental organisations and civil society generally. For instance, activists framed the self-determination debate in the decolonisation period in terms of human rights, relying in part on the UDHR, which helped transform self-determination into a legal right recognised in common Article 1 of the International Covenant on Civil and Political Rights (ICCPR) and the International Covenant on Economic, Social and Cultural Rights (ICESCR).[13] Seen in this light it is easy to appreciate Cassese's characterisation of the UDHR as the 'lodestar' of the international human rights system.[14]

The UN did not rest on the laurels of the UDHR. Between 1946 and 1966 when the ICCPR and ICESCR opened for ratification, the UN produced a total of 34 human rights instruments of which 18 are international treaties, including the International Convention on the Elimination of All Forms of Racial Discrimination (CERD) 1965 which is counted as a core UN human rights treaty. These documents spanned subjects such as stateless persons, freedom of association and collective bargaining and genocide, prompting the observation that the UN has been prolific in the 'adoption of new international norms for the protection of human rights'.[15] Nonetheless, it was the ICCPR and the ICESCR that sealed the role of the UN as the progenitor of international human rights law. As comprehensive treaties spanning the spectrum of civil, cultural, economic, political and social rights, the ICCPR and ICESCR impose specific obligations on State Parties, namely 'to respect and to ensure to all individuals' the civil and political rights enumerated in the ICCPR and 'to take steps' to progressively realise the socio-economic rights protected under the ICESCR.[16] In addition to the two Covenants, along with the CERD the UN counts the Convention on the Elimination of All Forms of Discrimination against Women 1979, the Convention against Torture and other Cruel, Inhuman or Degrading Treatment or Punishment 1984, the Convention on the Rights of the Child 1989, the International Convention on the Protection of the Rights of all Migrant Workers and Members of their Families 1990, the Convention on the Rights of Persons with Disabilities 2006 and the International Convention for the Protection of all Persons from Enforced Disappearance 2006[17] as the nine core human rights treaties, each of which imposes specific legal obligations on State Parties.

The standard-setting activities of the UN in the field of human rights have unequivocally brought human rights within the purview of legitimate international concern and in doing so have internationalised human rights. More particularly for present purposes, the legal obligations imposed under the various human rights treaties have, according to Finnemore, changed perceptions and expectations on government performance in the field of human rights. She argues that events 'once seen as unfortunate (but inevitable) tragedies'[18] are now not only seen as humanitarian crises but are also seen as requiring intervention by the international community.[19] Indeed, according to a recent poll, world public opinion holds that the UN has the responsibility to protect people from genocide and other severe human rights abuses, even if this means acting against the will of the government concerned.[20] Seen in this light, the internationalisation of human rights places human rights in direct conflict with state sovereignty, in particular the principle of non-intervention found in Article 2(7) of the UN Charter. Given the drafting history of the Charter human rights provisions noted above, it falls to consider whether the internationalisation of human rights has penetrated UNSC practice and, if so, how the UNSC has resolved the tension between human rights and sovereignty.

2.3 The UN Security Council and human rights violations

The UNSC does not have an explicit Charter mandate in respect of human rights. Under Article 24(1) the UNSC is charged with primary responsibility for the maintenance of international peace and security. In discharging this responsibility the UNSC, upon making a determination under Article 39 that a threat to the peace, breach of the peace, or act of aggression exists, may authorise enforcement action under Chapter VII of the Charter. Enforcement action comprises measures not involving the use of force under Article 41, such as the imposition of sanctions, or measures involving the use of force under Article 42. Paragraph 2.3 assesses whether the UNSC takes into account human rights issues, specifically violations such as genocide and ethnic cleansing, when making an Article 39 determination before moving to examine UNSC responses to human rights violations, with an emphasis on the authorisation of the use of force.

2.3.1 Human rights violations and 'threat to the peace'

The UN Charter requires the UNSC to act in accordance with the principles and purposes of the UN, including the promotion and protection of human rights and thus, human rights guide the UNSC in furtherance of its Charter mandate to maintain international peace and security.[21] Indeed, several delegates at San Francisco saw the threat to the peace rubric in Article 39 as encompassing human rights violations which was confirmed in 1946 when the UNSC declared itself ready to take measures 'as may become necessary to maintain international peace and security' in relation to the repressive activities of the Franco government in Spain.[22] As White observes, this response confirmed 'the view that Article 2(7) was inapplicable in cases of international concern'[23] such as human rights violations. The UNSC followed this brief engagement with human rights issues under the rubric of threat to the peace with a series of resolutions in the 1960s and 1970s condemning the apartheid and racially discriminatory regimes in South Africa and Southern Rhodesia. In 1965 the UNSC declared the proclamation of independence from the UK by 'a racist settler minority' in Southern Rhodesia as illegal, the continuation of which constituted a 'threat to international peace and security'.[24] The apartheid regime in South Africa similarly prompted an Article 39 determination of the existence of a threat to the peace.[25]

While the UNSC debates on the situation in Southern Rhodesia were infused with the language of self-determination,[26] the South African situation provides a particularly clear illustration of the penetration of human rights into UNSC practice. For instance, Resolution 181 (1963) referred to 'world public opinion' in respect of apartheid before noting that the situation 'is seriously disturbing international peace and security' and calling on the South African government to abandon such policies.[27] By Resolution 473 (1980) the UNSC not only 'reaffirmed' that apartheid was a crime against 'the conscience and dignity of mankind' which was also incompatible with the UDHR but apartheid also 'seriously disturbs international peace and security'.[28] Nonetheless these situations do not provide a precedent for the proposition that human rights issues *per se* constitute a threat to the peace, potentially triggering enforcement action under Chapter VII. For example, Resolution 232 (1966) in respect of the situation in Southern Rhodesia speaks of the failure of the UK, as the 'administering power' to 'bring the rebellion in Southern Rhodesia to an end', a concern echoed during the UNSC debates in terms of the effect of the illegal regime on neighbouring states.[29] Similarly, Resolution 418 (1977) in respect of South Africa emphasises the military build-up by South Africa, including the potential of nuclear capability, and its 'persistent' attacks on neighbouring states. Indeed, it was the legal responsibility of the UK in respect of Southern Rhodesia that removed the situation from the grasp of Article 2(7) while the aggressive stance by South Africa and stock-piling of arms ensured the inapplicability of Article 2(7) by giving the situation an 'international dimension'. The insistence on an 'international dimension' permeates subsequent UNSC practice in relation to human rights violations.[30]

For instance in Resolution 688 (1991) the UNSC made an Article 39 determination that the repression of the Iraqi civilian population, in particular the Kurdish population in northern Iraq, by the Iraqi government constituted a threat to international peace and security.[31] In order to do so the UNSC emphasised the transboundary impact of the repression, namely refugee flows into neighbouring states, thereby giving the human rights issue an international dimension. In doing so the Resolution unequivocally brought human rights concerns within the purview of Chapter VII of the Charter and was proclaimed by contemporary commentators as ushering in a new era of human rights protection by the UNSC.[32] Nonetheless, Resolution 688 did not displace the understanding that human rights issues properly reside within the domestic jurisdiction of states and therefore beyond the reach of the UNSC. This is readily apparent in the terms of Resolution 688 which recalls the provisions of Article 2(7) which also featured prominently in the UNSC debate. States supporting the Resolution welcomed the inclusion of Article 2(7) and discussed the transboundary effects of the repression of the Iraqi population, bolstered by letters from Turkey and Iran detailing the refugee flow, along with the competence of the UNSC to address human rights issues in order to disengage the application of Article 2(7).[33] It was this latter aspect that Zimbabwe and Cuba primarily based their objection to Resolution 688. Having dismissed, along with the Yemen, the elevation of the repression of the civilian population to the status of a threat to the peace by virtue of the transboundary impact, Zimbabwe and Cuba asserted that other UN organs, such as the GA with specific responsibility for human rights, was the appropriate avenue to address the repression.[34] These arguments were reiterated by China which, along with India, abstained from the Resolution. In refraining from vetoing the Resolution, China stressed the exceptional nature of the situation and warned against viewing Resolution 688 as precedent setting.[35]

Resolution 688 was swiftly followed by a number of resolutions determining that the situations, for example, in the former Yugoslavia (1991), Somalia (1992), Haiti (1993), Rwanda (1994), Sierra Leone (1997) and East Timor (1999) constituted threats to international peace and security. For instance Resolution 713 (1991) spoke of the heavy loss of life in the former Yugoslavia and the consequences for neighbouring states and the region before making an Article 39 determination[36] while in Resolution 733 (1992) in respect of the situation in Somalia the UNSC, after noting the 'rapid deterioration of the situation', 'the heavy loss of life' and the 'consequences on stability and peace in the region' made an Article 39 determination that a threat to the peace existed.[37] By the end of the year the situation in Somalia had deteriorated to the point whereby the UNSC, in Resolution 794 (1992), directly equated the 'magnitude of the human tragedy' with a threat to the peace.[38] In doing so the UNSC gave concrete expression to the 1992 Presidential Statement of the UNSC which recognised that '[n]on-military sources of instability in the economic, social, humanitarian and ecological fields have become threats to peace and security'.[39] Yet, claims that Resolution 794 established a precedent that human rights violations constitute a threat to the peace,[40] are diluted upon considering that, at the material time, Somalia as a state had disintegrated. It was this aspect that prompted China to vote in favour of the resolution as concerns as to domestic jurisdiction and the application of Article 2(7) were outweighed by the state failure,[41] while other states, including Russia, emphasised the unique character of the situation and stressed the need to avoid setting a precedent that would make inroads on the principle of non-interference in Article 2(7), concerns which were ultimately reflected in the terms of Resolution 794.[42]

These characteristics – the exceptional or unique character of the situation and a concern not to set a precedent – along with an insistence on transboundary effects of the human rights issue, imbue UNSC practice in relation to human rights issues in the 1990s. For instance, Resolution 841 (1993) in respect of the situation in Haiti following the military coup that toppled the democratically elected government saw the UNSC refer to refugee flows and 'the unique and exceptional circumstances' of the situation when making an Article 39 determination that a threat to the peace exists.[43] Similarly, Resolution 918 (1994) in relation to Rwanda noted the 'magnitude of the human suffering caused by the conflict', alongside refugee flows, in determining a threat to the peace and stressed that the situation in Rwanda was a 'unique case' in Resolution 929 (1994).[44] The UNSC deemed the situation in Sierra Leone a threat to international peace and security in Resolution 1132 (1997) on the basis of the continued violence and loss of life, deteriorating humanitarian conditions and the consequences for neighbouring states.[45] However, the UNSC's approach to making an Article 39 determination where human rights are an issue appears to change towards the end of the 1990s. For instance refugee flows and other transboundary effects of the relevant human rights issue are conspicuously absent from Resolution 1203 (1998) in respect of the situation in Kosovo. Here the UNSC, while reaffirming the sovereignty of the former Yugoslavia noted, amongst others, the grave humanitarian situation and the need to prevent 'the impending humanitarian catastrophe' when determining that the 'unresolved situation in Kosovo' constitutes a threat to peace and security in the region.[46] This Resolution must be seen in the context of previous resolutions on the situation in the former Yugoslavia, such as Resolution 713 (1991) noted above, which condemn the adverse humanitarian impact of armed conflict on neighbouring states.

A year later, in Resolution 1264 (1999) the UNSC was sufficiently appalled by the 'worsening humanitarian situation in East Timor' and concerned at reports of 'systematic, widespread and flagrant violations of international humanitarian and human rights law' to make an Article 39 determination that a threat to the peace exists.[47] As Welsh observes this Resolution marks a 'change in language within the Council in respect of threats to international peace and security' insofar as the UNSC did not emphasise the uniqueness of the situation in an effort to avoid bestowing precedential value on the Resolution.[48]

UNSC practice in the following decade confirms the erosion of the 'unique case' and reinforces the 'gradual shift away from reliance on the transboundary implications of a situation'[49] when determining that a threat to the peace exists. For instance while the UNSC expressed concern over the humanitarian situation in the DRC and reaffirmed the sovereignty of the DRC in Resolution 1291 (2000), it also spoke of deep concern at 'all violations and abuses of human rights and international humanitarian law' when determining that a threat to the peace existed.[50] Indeed, the UNSC has since made repeated references to violations of human rights law when making Article 39 determinations, for example, in respect of the situation in Ivory Coast, Liberia and Sudan.[51] Such references to international human rights law speak of a 'greater willingness' by the UNSC to 'describe action as consistent with both the Charter and contemporary expectations of the international community's obligations'.[52] This greater willingness to refer to human rights law prompted Tomuschat to observe that the Council has lost its fear of the phrase 'human rights'[53] and speaks to Finnemore's argument, noted above, as to changing expectations of government performance. Nonetheless, human rights violations are not an 'autonomous issue'[54] for the UNSC when making an Article 39 determination. For instance, while an emphasis on the transboundary effects of the human rights violations is notably absent from the resolutions and debates in respect of the DRC, Liberia and the Ivory Coast, the resolutions also noted, for example, the exploitation of natural resources, child soldiers and disarmament, when making the Article 39 determination that a threat to peace exists.[55] Moreover, the human rights violations occurred in a time of armed conflict, supporting Chesterman's observation that UNSC enforcement powers under Chapter VII are 'unlikely to be invoked in response to a humanitarian crisis unless it occurs in a time of conflict'.[56] Indeed, the armed conflict context provides the international dimension necessary to disengage the application of Article 2(7) and, in this way, the UNSC resolves the tension between human rights and sovereignty when making an Article 39 determination.

The evolution of the meaning of threat to the peace to include human rights violations in times of armed conflict is evidenced in a series of four thematic UNSC resolutions on the protection of civilians in armed conflict. The first of these resolutions, Resolution 1265 (1999) spoke of the willingness of the UNSC to respond to situations of armed conflict, including enforcement action, where civilians are being targeted or humanitarian assistance to civilians is deliberately obstructed,[57] which the UNSC reaffirmed the following year in Resolution 1296 (2000). Here the UNSC also explicitly stated that:

> the deliberate targeting of civilian populations or other protected persons and the committing of systematic, flagrant and widespread violations of international humanitarian and human rights law in situations of armed conflict may constitute a threat to international peace and security.[58]

While the most recent resolution on the protection of civilians in armed conflict, Resolution 1738 (2006) focuses on the protection of journalists in armed conflict, it also reaffirms the link between human rights violations in armed conflict and threats to international peace and security and, in doing so, confirms the balance drawn between human rights and sovereignty evident in existing UNSC practice.[59] Moreover, each of the four resolutions mirrors the increased reference to international human rights law in situation specific resolutions, such as Resolution 1291 (2000) noted above, in that the resolutions recall the obligations of states under international humanitarian law, international human rights law and international refugee law towards civilians.[60] However, the third resolution, Resolution 1674 (2006) endorses the responsibility to protect populations from genocide, war crimes, ethnic cleansing and crimes against humanity[61] and in doing so appears, as is discussed below, to broaden the threat to the peace rubric to include the proposition that human rights violations, such as genocide and ethnic cleansing, *will* constitute a threat to the peace.

2.3.2 UN Security Council responses to human rights violations

On the basis of an Article 39 determination that a threat to the peace exists, the UNSC may authorise enforcement action under Article 41 and/or Article 42 of the UN Charter which, as noted above, govern measures not involving the use of force and measures involving the use of force respectively. Thus the determination in Resolution 232 (1966) that the situation in Southern Rhodesia constituted a threat to the peace provided the jurisdictional trigger for the imposition of mandatory economic sanctions under Chapter VII, a practice which the UNSC followed in Resolution 418 (1977) in respect of South Africa. Nonetheless the paralysis of the UNSC, engendered by Cold War rivalries, guaranteed that 'for the first 45 years the UN was firmly associated with the principle of non-intervention'.[62]

With the end of the Cold War, the UNSC consolidated the fledging practice of imposing sanctions under Chapter VII of the Charter as a response to human rights violations. For instance Resolution 713 (1991) which spoke of the heavy loss of life in the former Yugoslavia imposed a 'general and complete embargo on all deliveries of weapons and military equipment' under Chapter VII, while Resolution 733 (1992), after noting 'heavy loss of life', imposed a similar arms embargo against Somalia.[63] During the 1990s the UNSC imposed mandatory sanctions for example, against Haiti (Resolution 841 (1993)), Rwanda (Resolution 918 (1994)) and Sierra Leone (Resolution 1132 (1994)). However, while the imposition of sanctions was requested by Haiti and welcomed by Sierra Leone in these instances, Rwanda vigorously opposed the introduction of an arms embargo under the terms of Resolution 918. Rwanda, which held a non-permanent seat on the UNSC at the time, argued that the arms embargo would infringe the right to self-defence which, although Resolution 918 recalls the commitment of the UNSC 'to the unity and territorial integrity of Rwanda', was rejected by the UNSC.[64] This is unsurprising for two years previously the UNSC rejected an attempt by Bosnia-Herzegovina, as a new state emerging from the former Yugoslavia, to tailor the terms of the arms embargo imposed under Resolution 713 to account for its right to self-defence. An application to the International Court of Justice to construe Resolution 713 and relevant subsequent resolutions in a manner consistent with the right to self-defence was also unsuccessful and the arms embargo remained in place against the entire territory of the former Yugoslavia.[65]

The UNSC was more receptive to the argument of tailoring sanctions in order to alleviate the adverse humanitarian impact on the civilian population of the targeted state. The adverse humanitarian impact of sanctions was particularly evident in respect of Iraq during the 1990s. Here the UNSC imposed sanctions pursuant to Resolution 661 (1990) and not, importantly for present purposes, under Resolution 688 which, as noted above, determined the existence of a threat to the peace on the basis of the repression of the civilian population, and remained in place until May 2003.[66] While the plight of the Iraqi population during this time is well-documented, suffice to note that the SG indicted the regime and sanctions more generally as a 'blunt instrument' and supported efforts to develop 'smart' or 'targeted' sanctions as a means to alleviate the humanitarian impact.[67] Targeted sanctions, such as travel restrictions on specified individuals, were subsequently imposed in Sierra Leone and Angola[68] and also, notably, in relation against Al-Qaida and the Taliban where human rights violations were not a factor when making the Article 39 determination that a threat to the peace existed.[69] In short, from the end of the Cold War the UNSC not only consolidated the practice of responding to human rights violations by imposing sanctions, the UNSC also developed its general sanctions practice to take account of human rights concerns irrespective of whether human rights violations were a factor in Article 39 determinations. This demonstrates a willingness on the part of the UNSC to resolve the tension between human rights and sovereignty in favour of human rights, particularly given the rejection of arguments as to the adverse impact of sanctions on the right to self-defence.

The end of the Cold War also saw the UNSC authorising the use of force in response to human rights violations, precipitating claims of an era of 'new interventionism'.[70] For example, Resolution 794 (1992) established a Unified Task Force (UNITAF), led by the US, which was authorised to 'use all necessary means' to establish a secure environment for humanitarian relief in Somalia.[71] This, coupled with the unequivocal connection between human rights violations and international peace and security made in Resolution 794, produced claims of an emerging norm of humanitarian intervention by the UNSC.[72] As noted above, such claims are diluted in light of the broader context of Resolution 794, in particular the disintegration of Somalia as a state which rendered consent to the use of force superfluous. Indeed two years later, when the UNSC debated the expansion of the mandate of the UN Assistance Mission in Rwanda (UNAMIR) to include humanitarian assistance and protection, there was marked reluctance to authorise the use of force and Resolution 918 merely charged UNAMIR with '[contributing] to the security and protection of displaced persons, refugees and civilians at risk in Rwanda, including through the establishment and maintenance, where feasible, of secure humanitarian areas', and, to this end, was authorised to use force in self-defence.[73] While states welcomed Resolution 918,[74] the inefficacy of such a mandate as a response to human rights violations was clearly illustrated when the United Nations Protection Force (UNPROFOR), with a similar mandate to use force only in self-defence, proved unable to prevent the massacre at Srebrenica in July 1995.[75]

However, deployment of UNAMIR was delayed from the outset in part due to the recalcitrance of states to contribute troops and other resources to the proposed mission. It was only when faced with a report by the SG characterising the situation in Rwanda as genocide that the UNSC responded with Resolution 929 (1994). Here the UNSC authorised a multinational force, led by France, under Chapter VII of the Charter to use 'all necessary means' in furtherance of the humanitarian mandate set out in Resolution 918, namely the protection of civilians. Nonetheless, the debates on Resolution 929 were infused with concerns as to the authorisation of force with Brazil and China stressing the availability of other avenues, such as the rapid deployment of UNAMIR under the original mandate, while Russia reluctantly agreed to the authorisation of the use of force seeing that it was 'imperative in the prevailing conditions'.[76]

It was against the backdrop of the failures at Srebrenica and in respect of Rwanda that, on the 24 March 1999, NATO began an air campaign against the former Yugoslavia motivated in part to avert ethnic cleansing in Kosovo.[77] With the UNSC deadlocked under the threat of veto from Russia and China, UNSC authorisation was not sought for Operation Allied Force. In previous UNSC debates Russia and China had made it clear that the situation in Kosovo fell within the terms of Article 2(7) and, while willing to acquiesce to the imposition of mandatory sanctions, considered the use of force inappropriate. For instance Russia and China refrained from vetoing Resolution 1203 (1998), which endorsed agreements between the former Yugoslavia and the Organisation for Security and Cooperation in Europe for a verification mission in Kosovo, precisely because it did not authorise the use of force.[78] Russia also emphasised the availability of political and diplomatic avenues to resolve the situation, in addition to questioning the Article 39 determination that the situation in Kosovo constituted a threat to the peace.[79] The absence of an explicit UNSC authorisation for the use of force prompted Russia, China, India and Belarus to condemn Operation Allied Force as illegal and to seek a UNSC resolution on the matter, giving credence to the conclusion that Operation Allied Force was an illegal but legitimate response to prevent ethnic cleansing.[80]

The situation in East Timor, which came before the UNSC later the same year, offers a useful point of contrast to the intransigence of the UNSC in relation to Kosovo. Here in Resolution 1264 (1999) the UNSC authorised an Australian-led multinational force, INTERFET, to 'take all necessary measures' to facilitate humanitarian assistance amongst other tasks.[81] The Resolution and deployment of INTERFET was in response to violence which had erupted in East Timor after an overwhelming affirmative vote for independence from Indonesia by the East Timorese. However, the willingness of the UNSC to intervene in this instance and, indeed, the capacity to do so – in contrast to Rwanda – is somewhat tempered in light of the request for UN cooperation by Indonesia. With parallels to Resolution 841 in respect of Haiti, it is evident from the terms of Resolution 1264 that the deployment of INTERFET was contingent upon the consent of Indonesia.[82] Indeed, it was the insistence on consent which enabled the provisions of Article 2(7) to be circumvented.

In the following decade the issues of consent, recourse to other avenues, and resources which were evident in the UNSC debates on East Timor, Kosovo and Rwanda respectively, pervaded UNSC practice on the use of force to respond to human rights violations. For instance consent featured predominantly in UNSC debates on the situation in Darfur, Sudan. Indeed, Weiss observed that the UNSC equivocated over the consent of Sudan when discussing the authorisation of the use of force,[83] a position that was ultimately reflected in the terms of Resolution 1706 (2006). Here the UNSC authorised the use of force to protect the civilian population and, in doing so, invited the Sudanese government to consent to the deployment of the proposed peace operation.[84] Further, the UNSC response to the situation in Darfur illuminates a graduated approach to human rights violations with sanctions imposed in 2004, followed by the creation of peacekeeping mission to, amongst others, monitor a cease-fire agreement in 2005, and referral to the International Criminal Court (ICC) and the adoption of Resolution 1706 providing for the use of force to respond to human rights violations in 2006.[85] Such an approach, with parallels to Kosovo where Russia insisted on the exhaustion of diplomatic and political avenues such as sanctions, is also apparent in the UNSC's response to the human rights violations in the DRC. Here the UNSC imposed sanctions, established a peacekeeping mission MONUC, with a mandate to, amongst others, monitor a ceasefire agreement, which was then expanded to include the use of force 'to protect the civilian population'.[86] The debates on the expansion of the mandate of MONUC emphasised the issue of resources, with Canada expressing concern over a mismatch between the mandate and resources 'needed to guarantee its success'.[87] Thus while the concern over resources in respect of the proposed peace operation in Rwanda was intimately tied to political willingness, in the case of the DRC resources were mapped onto the success of the peace operation.

In short, the UNSC approaches the dilemma of intervention on a case-by-case basis, with consent, availability of other avenues, and resources as factors in the decision to authorise the use of force to respond to human rights violations. This approach is in keeping with the discretion of the UNSC under the Charter which recognises that the UNSC response, including the use of force, 'involves political evaluation of highly complex and dynamic situations'.[88] Nonetheless, there is a discernible change in the language employed by the UNSC when authorising the use of force in response to human rights violations which speaks to the heightened position of human rights within UNSC practice, namely the use of the formula 'to protect the civilian population' which is often accompanied by references to the pertinent thematic resolution(s) on the protection of civilians in armed conflict.[89] In this respect it is notable that the UNSC debates on Darfur were infused with references to the responsibility to protect, as endorsed by the UNSC in Resolution 1674 (2006). As such, the next part of the article explores whether the responsibility to protect galvanises the UNSC to authorise the use of force to respond to human rights violations, thereby resolving the intervention dilemma in favour of human rights.

2.4 The responsibility to protect: In defence of humanity?

When the International Commission on Intervention and State Sovereignty (ICISS) proclaimed the responsibility to protect, it was hailed as 'the most sophisticated attempt at establishing a moral guideline for international action in the face of humanitarian emergency'.[90] For present purposes, ICISS proposed to change the contours of the intervention dilemma in two main ways, first, through the re-fashioning of sovereignty as responsibility and, second, by issuing guidelines for military intervention.[91] According to ICISS the re-calibration of sovereignty as responsibility is founded on an understanding of sovereignty as implying dual responsibility, one externally 'to respect the sovereignty of other states' and another internally 'to respect the dignity and basic rights of all the people within the state'.[92] This latter responsibility is grounded on the impact of international human rights law and, in echoes of Finnemore's argument noted above, ICISS concluded that 'sovereignty as responsibility has become the minimum content of good international citizenship'.[93] This understanding of sovereignty provides the essence of the responsibility to protect namely that the responsibility to protect lies first and foremost with states and a secondary responsibility falls to the international community when a state is unwilling or unable to 'protect their own citizens from avoidable catastrophe'.[94] The guidelines for military intervention are a key element of this international responsibility and, in this respect, ICISS set down six criteria under the rubric of the 'responsibility to react' which determine when, how and by whom military intervention is to be authorised.[95]

The first criterion, right authority, etches out a role for the UNSC in authorising the use of force based on the Charter mandate as the organ with primary responsibility for international peace and security, while the just cause threshold of large scale loss of life or large scale ethnic cleansing triggers the responsibility to react. The remaining four criteria – right intention, reasonable prospects of success, force as a last resort and proportional means – are precautionary principles designed to 'strictly limit the use of coercive military force for human protection purposes'.[96] However, these guidelines are conspicuously absent from Resolution 1674 (2006) in which the UNSC endorsed the responsibility to protect populations from genocide, war crimes, ethnic cleansing and crimes against humanity. More specifically, the UNSC endorsed the responsibility to protect as set down in the Outcome Document of the 2005 World Summit. Here UN Member States, amongst others, declared themselves prepared:

> to take collective action, in a timely and decisive manner, through the Security Council, in accordance with the Charter, including Chapter VII, on a case-by-case basis and in cooperation with relevant regional organisations as appropriate, should peaceful means be inadequate and national authorities are manifestly failing to protect their populations from genocide, war crimes, ethnic cleansing and crimes against humanity.[97]

The exclusion of guidelines for military intervention from the UN responsibility to protect was confirmed in the 2009 Report of the SG, *Implementing the Responsibility to Protect.* Here the SG merely noted 'the hard truth that no strategy for fulfilling the responsibility to protect would be complete without the possibility of collective enforcement measures, including through sanctions or coercive military action in extreme cases'.[98] In this regard the SG acknowledged the role of the UNSC in authorising such collective measures but only when, in accordance with the terms of the Outcome Document, 'should peaceful means be inadequate' *and* 'national authorities are manifestly failing to protect their populations from genocide, war crimes, ethnic cleansing and crimes against humanity'. Hence, in addition to the omission of guidelines for military intervention, there are three other key differences between the UN and ICISS articulations of the responsibility to protect. First, the international responsibility is transformed into one of 'simple preparedness'[99] under the Outcome Document which also introduces a higher threshold – 'manifestly failing' – for the transfer of responsibility from states to the UN than envisaged by ICISS. Finally, the UN narrowed the broad just cause threshold under ICISS to the more specific tetralogy of 'genocide, war crimes, ethnic cleansing, and crimes against humanity'. In short, under the UN responsibility to protect, the UNSC *may* respond to the tetralogy of specified human rights violations[100] with military force if peaceful means are inadequate and the state concerned has manifestly failed to protect its population.

The UNSC response to Darfur, widely regarded as the test-case for the responsibility to protect,[101] exposes a number of inherent flaws with the UN responsibility to protect to galvanise the UNSC to respond to genocide, war crimes, ethnic cleansing and crimes against humanity. The first of these is indeterminacy as to what triggers the responsibility to protect. In the debates on Darfur the UNSC resisted calls to describe the unfolding humanitarian crisis as genocide and opted for the familiar formula that violations of international human rights law and international humanitarian law, in part, constituted a threat to the peace.[102] In doing so the UNSC acted in accordance with the Charter which gives the UNSC discretion to make an Article 39 determination. Nonetheless, the reluctance of the UNSC to characterise the situation in Darfur as genocide indicates a lack of 'Security Council buy-in'[103] to the UN responsibility to protect, particularly as regards the apparent broadening of the threat to the peace rubric. This broader notion – namely that the enumerated human rights violations *will* constitute a threat to the peace – demands substantive Article 39 determinations by the UNSC, with attendant issues of definition and fact-finding. As borne out in respect of Darfur, the UNSC is ill-suited to such activities which, moreover, are arguably outside the Charter mandate of the UNSC.

A further flaw is exposed upon considering that the UN responsibility to protect equivocates as to when enforcement action is an appropriate response to genocide, war crimes, ethnic cleansing and crimes against humanity. By emphasising that the UNSC is prepared to take enforcement action on a 'case-by-case basis' the UN responsibility to protect explicitly guards against bestowing any degree of automaticity to an Article 39 determination – however formulated. In doing so the UN responsibility to protect recognises the discretion accorded to the UNSC under the Charter as to whether, if at all, to take enforcement action under Chapter VII. That said, between 2003 and 2007, the UNSC imposed sanctions in respect of the situation in Darfur, referred the situation to the ICC and authorised the use of force to protect the civilian population, responses made on foot of specific Article 39 determinations that were based, in part, on violations of international human rights law.[104] Yet, the multiplicity of the UNSC response to the situation in Darfur reveals another flaw in the UN responsibility to protect, namely, ambiguity as to what type of enforcement action is an appropriate response to genocide, war crimes, ethnic cleansing and crimes against humanity. Such ambiguity is encapsulated in the injunction that 'peaceful means are inadequate' which, according to the SG in his 2009 Report, refers to the measures under Article 41 of the Charter.[105] In this light, it is understandable that the UNSC responded to the situation in Darfur by imposing sanctions followed by referral to the ICC, before authorising the use of force. This graduated approach to enforcement measures is in line with existing UNSC practice and invokes the ICISS requirement that the use of force is a last resort. In this respect the International Crisis Group (ICG) concluded that this criterion was not met in the context of Darfur precisely because of the plethora of UNSC responses.[106] Yet, Wheeler observes that 'during the time that policy-makers are trying to achieve a halt to the abuses through non-violent means, massacres and expulsions might be continuing on the ground' and thus the requirement of last resort does not necessarily entail the exhaustion of peaceful means.[107] The SG echoed this in the understanding of the inadequacy of peaceful means under the UN responsibility to protect, stressing that the UNSC 'would not and should not wait until all other possible tools had been tried and failed before considering more robust collective measures'.[108] While the emphasis on a graduated response in respect of Darfur is unfortunate it also 'impeded a clear and coherent strategy' prompting de Waal to conclude that 'it is unsurprising that little progress was made'.[109] In short, the indeterminacy of the UN responsibility to protect, though in line with the Charter frame on international peace and security and UNSC practice, has undermined the effectiveness of the UN responsibility to protect in Darfur.

The final flaw in the UN responsibility to protect to galvanise the UNSC to respond to genocide, war crimes, ethnic cleansing and crimes against humanity, pertains to the injunction that 'national authorities are *manifestly failing* to protect their populations' from the specified human rights violations. While, as noted previously, this sets a particularly high threshold for the transfer of responsibility from a state to the UN, it was not a factor in the decision to impose sanctions in respect of the situation in Darfur, which is in line with UNSC practice as set out above. In contrast, the requirement of manifest failure did play a significant role in the decision to authorise the use of force, in part motivated by concerns as to encroaching on state sovereignty. In this respect it is recalled that the UNSC invited the Sudanese government to consent to the peacekeeping mission proposed under Resolution 1706. Moreover, when such consent was not forthcoming the UN proposed a hybrid mission in conjunction with the African Union (UNAMID) which, with the consent of Sudan, was subsequently deployed with a mandate to 'take the necessary actions' to protect the civilian population.[110] In short, the requirement of manifest failure appears to apply to the authorisation of the use of force which, in turn, can be circumvented by obtaining the consent of the state concerned. In this respect, it is noteworthy that the only situation in which consent was not sought or obtained by the UNSC was in respect of Somalia which, at the material time, had disintegrated as a state.

Furthermore, the UNSC debates on the authorisation of the use of force emphasised the consent of Sudan to the deployment of the peace operation as critical to the success of the mission. In this respect the ICG observed that a 'non-consensual deployment would be desperately difficult … and the overall security situation for civilians in the region could well worsen'[111] difficulties which would be compounded by operational challenges to deployment in terms of terrain, troop numbers and other logistical questions.[112] Yet de Waal observes that 'very little attention was paid to the operations and strategic goal' of UNAMID in the UNSC debates leading up to the adoption of Resolution 1769 (2007). This is illustrative of the issue of operational capacity which the UNSC debates in respect of the DRC saw as intimately linked to the success of the mission. Indeed, the Brahimi Report on UN peacekeeping noted the potential for a 'large mismatch' between the objective of a civilian protection mandate and resources, concluding that '[i]f an operation is given a mandate to protect civilians. … it also must be given the specific resources needed to carry out that mandate'.[113] Nonetheless, UNAMID has been plagued by operational difficulties relating to resources,[114] testimony to de Waal's conclusion that the debate on the responsibility to protect focuses on 'when and whether to intervene, not how to do so and with what aim in mind'.[115]

2.5 Conclusion

Darfur is widely regarded as the 'test case' for the responsibility to protect. On this basis the responsibility to protect, as presently articulated by the UN, fails to galvanise the UNSC to respond to human rights violations, such as genocide, war crimes, ethnic cleansing and crimes against humanity, in large part due to the retention of UNSC discretion and the emphasis on consent. To the extent to which these elements, as argued above, are consistent with the mandate of the

UNSC under the Charter and existing UNSC practice, the UN responsibility to protect fails to move beyond the decisive dichotomy of human rights versus sovereignty that plagued the humanitarian intervention debate. As such it is unsurprising that the UN responsibility to protect has been criticised as 'moving away from the boldness' of ICISS, particularly as regards the guidelines for military intervention.[116] While much has been written on the promise of such guidelines, specifically in relation to injecting the rule of law into UNSC decision-making,[117] it is arguable that the ICISS guidelines would not have prompted the UNSC to respond with the authorisation of the use of force in respect of Darfur. For instance, the exercise in semantics as to whether the humanitarian crisis constituted genocide illustrates the inherent indeterminacy of the 'just cause' threshold, while the ICG concluded that the requirements of last resort and reasonable prospects of success were not met for the purposes of military intervention due to the plethora of UNSC responses and operational difficulties in respect of deployment.[118] In this latter respect, the UN responsibility to protect represents a missed opportunity to develop UNSC practice as regards the modalities of peace operations with a civilian protection mandate. Thus while international human rights law and norms have penetrated UNSC practice in responding to human rights violations, specifically in respect of the imposition of sanctions, and provided the foundation for the articulation of the responsibility to protect, the intervention dilemma remains unchanged.

Notes

* Emma McClean, Lecturer in Law, University of Westminster.

1 Charles Malik, quoted in J Morsink, 'World War Two and the Universal Declaration' (1993) 15 *Human Rights Quarterly* 357, 357.

2 Article 55 (c) of the UN Charter.

3 UN SG, *We the Peoples: The role of the United Nations in the 21st Century* (New York, NY: United Nations, 2000), para 48.

4 The phrase humanitarian intervention by the UNSC relates to the authorisation of the use of force for humanitarian purposes by the UNSC.

5 T Buergenthal, 'The Normative and Institutional Evolution of International Human Rights' (1997) 19 *Human Rights Quarterly* 703, 703.

6 L M Goodrich and E Hambro, *The Charter of the United Nations: Commentary and Documents* (1st edn, Boston, MA: World Peace Foundation, 1946), p 190.

7 I Brownlie, *Principles of Public International Law* (6th edn, Oxford: Oxford University Press, 2003), p 534.

8 J P Humphrey, 'The UN Charter and the Universal Declaration', in Evan Luard, *The International Protection of Human Rights* (London: Thames and Hudson, 1979), pp 39, 47.

9 L M Goodrich, *The United Nations* (London: Stevens, 1960), p 246.

10 Cited in H Lauterpacht, *International Law and Human Rights* (London: Stevens and Sons Limited, 1950), p 416.

11 *Ibid*, pp 401–2.

12 See for example, UNGA Res 265 (III) (14 May 1949), para 2.

13 J Von Bernstorff, 'The Changing Fortunes of the Universal Declaration of Human Rights: Genesis and Symbolic Dimensions of the Turn to Rights in International Law' (2008) 19(5) *European Journal of International Law* 903, 912.

14 A Cassese, *International Law* (2nd edn, Oxford: Oxford University Press, 2005), p 382.

15 H Hannum, 'Human Rights', in Oscar Schachter and Christopher C Joyner (eds), *United Nations Legal Order (Vol 1)* (Cambridge: Cambridge University Press, 1995), p 319.

16 Article 2(1) of the ICCPR; Article 2(1) of the ICESCR.

17 The International Convention for the Protection of all Persons from Enforced Disappearance is not yet in force.

18 M Finnemore, 'Paradoxes in Humanitarian Intervention', Symposium on Norms and Ethics of Humanitarian Intervention (14 April 2000, revised September 2000), <www.cgpacs.uci.edu/research/working_papers/martha_finnemore_humanitarian_intervention.pdf> (accessed 22 October 2009). This is borne out in UNSC practice, for instance, during the cold war '"of the three main instances that most closely resemble "humanitarian interventions" – India in East Pakistan (1971), Vietnam in Cambodia (1978) and Tanzania in Uganda (1979) – only the former two were discussed within the Council, and in both cases humanitarian rationales for military action were hotly contested'. Jennifer M Welsh, 'The Security Council and Humanitarian Intervention', in Vaughan Lowe and others (eds), *The United Nations Security Council and War: The evolution of thought and practice since 1945* (Oxford: Oxford University Press, 2008), p 537.

19 *Ibid*, Finnemore.

20 Chicago Council on Global Affairs and WorldPublicOpinion.org, 'Publics Around the World say UN has Responsibility to Protect Against Genocide' (2007), <www.thechicagocouncil.org/> (accessed 22 October 2009).

21 Article 24(2) reads in part: 'In discharging these duties the Security Council shall act in accordance with the Purposes and Principles of the United Nations'. See also Bruno Simma and others (eds), *Charter of the United Nations: A Commentary* (2nd edn, Oxford: Oxford University Press, 2002), p 771.

22 UNSC Res 7 (26 June 1946), preamublar para 3.

23 N D White, *The Law of International Organisations* (Boulder, CO: Lynne Rienner, 2005), p 91.

24 UNSC Res 217 (20 November 1965), preamublar paras 3 and 1.

25 UNSC Res 418 (4 November 1977), preamublar para 1.

26 See generally, UN, *Repertoire of the Practice of the Security Council 1966–68* (New York, NY: Department of Political and Security Council Affairs, 1968), pp 113–24; UNSC Res 232 (16 December 1966), para 4.

27 UNSC Res 181 (7 August 1963), preamublar paras 3 and 8.

28 UNSC Res 473 (13 June 1980), para 3.

29 UNSC Res 232 (16 December 1966), preamublar para 2. See generally, op. cit., UN, *Repertoire 1966–68*, fn 26, pp 113–24.

30 On the link between human rights and international concern, see op. cit., White, fn 23, pp 92–4.

31 UNSC Res 688 (5 April 1991), para 1.

32 T J Farer and F D Garer, 'The United Nations and International Security after the Cold War', in Adam Roberts and Benedict Kingsbury (eds), *United Nations, Divided World* (2nd edn, Oxford: Oxford University Press, 1993), pp 289–91. On the evolution of the meaning of threat to the peace, see generally K Wellens, 'The UN Security Council and New Threats to the Peace: Back to the Future' (2003) 8(1) *Journal of Conflict and Security Law* 15.

33 UN, *Repertoire of the Practice of the Security Council 1989–1992* (New York, NY: Department of Political Affairs, 2007), pp 689–92.

34 *Ibid*, pp 692–3.

35 *Ibid*, pp 693–4.

36 UNSC Res 713 (25 September 1991), preamublar para 3.

37 UNSC Res 733 (23 January 1992), preamublar para 3.

38 UNSC Res 794 (3 December 1992), preamublar para 3.

39 Security Council Summit Statement Concerning the Council's Responsibility in the Maintenance of International Peace and Security (31 January 1992) S/23500, cited

in Simon Chesterman, *Just War or Just Peace? Humanitarian Intervention and International Law* (Oxford: Oxford University Press, 2001), p 128.

40 C Tomuschat, *Human Rights: Between Idealism and Realism* (1st edn, Oxford: Oxford University Press, 2003), pp 130–1; op. cit., Simma and others, fn 21, p 724.

41 Op. cit., UN, *Repertoire 1989–1992*, fn 33, pp 330–1.

42 Op. cit., UN, *Repertoire 1989–1992*, fn 33, p 331; UNSC Res 794 (1992), preamublar para 2.

43 UNSC Res 841 (16 June 1993), preamublar paras 9 and 10.

44 UNSC Res 918 (17 May 1994), preamublar paras 18 and 8; UNSC Res 929 (22 June 1994), preamublar para 9.

45 UNSC Res 1132 (8 October 1997), preamublar paras 8 and 9.

46 UNSC Res 1203 (24 October 1998), preamublar paras 14, 11 and 15.

47 UNSC Res 1264 (15 September 1999), preamublar paras 7, 13 and 14.

48 Op. cit., Welsh, fn 18, p 551.

49 Op. cit., Chesterman, fn 39, p 151.

50 UNSC Res 1291 (24 February 2000), preamublar paras 16, 3 and 18.

51 For instance, UNSC Res 1509 (19 September 2003), preamublar paras 4 and 21 (Liberia); UNSC Res 1528 (27 February 2004), preamublar paras 6 and 17 (Ivory Coast); UNSC Res 1556 (30 July 2004), preamublar paras 8 and 21 (Sudan).

52 Op. cit., Welsh, fn 18, p 551.

53 C Tomuschat, *Human Rights: Between Idealism and Realism* (2nd edn, Oxford: Oxford University Press, 2008), p 156.

54 Op. cit., Tomuschat, fn 40, p 130.

55 UNSC Res 1291 (2000), preamublar para 4; UNSC Res 1509 (2003), preamublar para 12; UNSC Res 1528 (2004), preamublar para 4.

56 Op. cit., Chesterman, fn 39, p 140.

57 UNSC Res 1265 (17 September 1999), para 10.

58 UNSC Res 1296 (19 April 2000), para 5.

59 UNSC Res 1738 (23 December 2006), para 9. Correct as of December 2009.

60 UNSC Res 1265 (1999), para 4; UNSC Res 1296 (2000), preamublar para 7 and para 19; UNSC Res 1674 (28 April 2006), para 6; UNSC Res 1738 (2006), para 5.

61 UNSC Res 1674 (2006), para 4.

62 A Roberts, 'The United Nations and Humanitarian Intervention', in J Welsh (ed), *Humanitarian Intervention and International Relations* (Oxford: Oxford University Press, 2004), p 71.

63 UNSC Res 713 (1991), para 6; UNSC Res 733 (1992), para 5.

64 UNSC Res 918 (1994), preamublar para 16.

65 Op. cit., UN, *Repertoire*, fn 33, pp 519–22; *Application of the Convention on the prevention and Punishment of the Crime of genocide (Bosnia-Herzegovina v Yugoslavia)* (Provisional Measures) [1993] ICJ Rep 3.

66 UNSC Res 1483 (22 May 2003).

67 UN SG, 'Supplement to An Agenda for Peace: Position paper of the Secretary-General on the occasion of the 50th anniversary of the United Nations' (3 January 1995), A/50/60-S/1995/1, para 70.

68 UNSC Res 1132 (1997) (Sierra Leone); UNSC Res 1521 (22 December 2003) (Liberia).

69 UNSC Res 1267 (15 October 1999).

70 See for example, M Glennon, 'The New Interventionism: The Search for a Just International Law' (1999) *Foreign Affairs* (May/June) 2.

71 UNSC Res 794 (1994).

72 Op. cit., Tomuschat, fn 40, pp 130–1.

73 UNSC Res 918 (1994), para 3 (a).

74 New Zealand saw Resolution 918 as a modest first step to address the humanitarian situation. UN, *Repertorie of the Practice of the Security Council 1993–1995* (Advance Version) 55, <www.un.org/en/sc/repertoire/> (accessed 8 October 2009).

75 See generally UN SG, *Report of the Secretary General pursuant to General Assembly Resolution 53/35: The Fall of Serbrencia* (15 November 1999), UN Doc A/54/549, <www.un.org/peace/srebrenica.pdf> (accessed 9 October 2009).
76 Op. cit., UN, *Repertoire 1993–1995* (Advance Version), fn 74, p 72.
77 On the aims of NATO's intervention, see op. cit., Chesterman, fn 39, p 211.
78 UN, *Repertorie of the Practice of the Security Council 1996–1999* (Advance Version), <www.un.org/en/sc/repertoire/> (accessed 9 October 2009).
79 *Ibid.*
80 See for example, A Hehir, 'NATOs "Humanitarian Intervention" in Kosovo: Precedent or Aberration?' (2009) 8(3) *Journal of Human Rights* 245.
81 UNSC Res 1264 (1999), para 3.
82 *Ibid*, preamublar para 2.
83 T G Weiss, *Humanitarian Intervention: Ideas in action* (Cambridge: Polity, 2007), p 56.
84 UNSC Res 1706 (18 August 2006), para 1.
85 UNSC Res 1564 (18 September 2004) (sanctions); UNSC Res 1590 (24 March 2005) (establishment of the United Nations Mission in Sudan); UNSC Res 1593 (31 March 2005) (referral to the ICC).
86 UNSC Res 1279 (30 November 1999) (establishment of MONUC); UNSC Res 1616 (29 July 2005) (sanctions); UNSC Res 1856 (22 December 2008) (extension of mandate to include 'protection of civilians').
87 UN, *Repertoire of the Practice of the Security Council 2004–2007* (Advance Version), <www.un.org/en/sc/repertoire/> (accessed 9 October 2009).
88 *Prosecutor v Tadic* (Interlocutory Appeal on Jurisdiction) ICTY (2 October 1995), para 39.
89 See for example UNSC Res 1709 (2006), preamublar para 2; UNSC Res 1856 (2008), preamublar para 12.
90 G Day and C Freeman, 'Operationalising the Responsibility to Protect – the Policekeeping Approach' (2005) 11 *Global Governance* 139.
91 On the contributions of the responsibility to protect to the debate, see Gareth Evans, 'From Humanitarian Intervention to the Responsibility to Protect' (2006) 24 *Wisconsin International Law Journal* 703.
92 ICISS, *The Responsibility to Protect* (Ottawa: International Development Research Centre, 2001), para 1.35.
93 *Ibid.*
94 *Ibid*, p viii.
95 There are three dimensions to the responsibility to protect: the responsibility to prevent, react and rebuild.
96 Op. cit., ICISS, fn 92, para 4.32.
97 UNGA Res 60/1, '2005 World Summit Outcome' (16 September 2005), A/RES/60/1, para 139.
98 UN SG, 'Implementing the Responsibility to Protect' (12 January 2009), UN Doc A/63/677, para 56.
99 A J Bellamy, 'Whither the Responsibility to Protect? Humanitarian Intervention and the 2005 World Summit' (2006) *Ethics and International Affairs* 143, 197.
100 Op. cit., Cassese, fn 14, p 99.
101 See for example, Kithure Kindiki, *Intervention to Protect Civilians in Darfur: Legal dilemmas and policy imperatives*, ISS Monograph Series (Pretoria: ISS, 2007).
102 UNSC Res 1564 (2004), preambular, para 9.
103 Op. cit., Evans, fn 91.
104 UNSC Res 1564 (2004); UNSC Res 1593 (2005); UNSC Res 1769 (31 July 2007).
105 Op. cit., UN SG, fn 98, para 49.
106 ICG, 'Getting the UN into Darfur', Africa Briefing No 43 (12 October 2006), p 17.
107 N Wheeler, *Saving Strangers: Humanitarian Intervention in International Society* (Oxford: Oxford University Press, 2002), p 35.
108 Op. cit., UN SG, fn 98, 22.

109 A de Waal, 'Darfur and the Failure of the Responsibility to Protect' (2007) 83(6) *International Affairs* 1039, 1043.
110 UNSC Res 1769 (2007), para 15 (a).
111 Op. cit., ICG, fn 106, p 17.
112 *Ibid.*
113 UNGA, *Report of the Panel on United Nations Peace Operations* (21 August 2000), UN Doc A/55/305, para 63.
114 See for example, The Darfur Consortium, 'Putting People First: The Protection Challenge Facing UNAMID in Darfur', <www.darfurconsortium.org/darfur_consortium_ actions/reports/2008/Putting_People_First_UNAMID_report.pdf> (accessed 9 October 2009).
115 Op. cit., De Waal, fn 109, p 1045.
116 Op. cit., Welsh, fn 18, p 558.
117 See for example, I Johnstone, 'Security Council Deliberations: The Power of the Better Argument' (2003) 14 *European Journal of International Law* 437.
118 Op. cit., ICG, fn 106, pp 15–17.

Bibliography

Bellamy, A J, 'Whither the Responsibility to Protect? Humanitarian Intervention and the 2005 World Summit' (2006) *Ethics and International Affairs* 143.

Brownlie, I, *Principles of Public International Law* (6th edn, Oxford: Oxford University Press, 2003).

Buergenthal, T, 'The Normative and Institutional Evolution of International Human Rights' (1997) 19 *Human Rights Quarterly* 703.

Cassese, A, *International Law* (2nd edn, Oxford: Oxford University Press, 2005).

Chesterman, S, *Just War or Just Peace? Humanitarian Intervention and International Law* (Oxford: Oxford University Press, 2001).

Day, G and Freeman, C, 'Operationalising the Responsibility to Protect – the Police-keeping Approach' (2005) 11 *Global Governance* 139.

de Waal, A, 'Darfur and the Failure of the Responsibility to Protect' (2007) 83(6) *International Affairs* 1039.

Evans, G, 'From Humanitarian Intervention to the Responsibility to Protect' (2006) 24 *Wisconsin International Law Journal* 703.

Farer, T J and Garer, F D, 'The United Nations and International Security after the Cold War', in Roberts, A and Kingsbury, B (eds), *United Nations, Divided World* (2nd edn, Oxford: Oxford University Press, 1993).

Glennon, M, 'The New Interventionism: The Search for a Just International Law' (1999) *Foreign Affairs* (May/June) 2.

Goodrich, L M, *The United Nations* (London: Stevens, 1960).

Goodrich, L M and Hambro, E, *The Charter of the United Nations: Commentary and Documents* (1st edn, Boston, MA: World Peace Foundation, 1946).

Hannum, H, 'Human Rights', in Schachter, O and Joyner, C C (eds), *United Nations legal Order (Vol 1)* (Cambridge: Cambridge University Press, 1995).

Hehir, A, 'NATOs "Humanitarian Intervention" in Kosovo: Precedent or Aberration?' (2009) 8(3) *Journal of Human Rights* 245.

Humphrey, J P, 'The UN Charter and the Universal Declaration', in Luard, E, *The International Protection of Human Rights* (London: Thames and Hudson, 1979).

ICG, *Getting the UN into Darfur* (Africa Briefing No 43, 2006).

ICISS, *The Responsibility to Protect* (Ottawa: International Development Research Centre, 2001).

Johnstone, I, 'Security Council Deliberations: The Power of the Better Argument' (2003) 14 *European Journal of International Law* 437.

Kindiki, K, *Intervention to Protect Civilians in Darfur: Legal dilemmas and policy imperatives*, ISS Monograph Series (Pretoria: ISS, 2007).

Lauterpacht, H, *International Law and Human Rights* (London: Stevens and Sons Limited, 1950).

Morsink, J, 'World War Two and the Universal Declaration' (1993) 15 *Human Rights Quarterly* 357.

Roberts, A, 'The United Nations and Humanitarian Intervention', in Welsh, J (ed), *Humanitarian Intervention and International Relations* (Oxford: Oxford University Press, 2004)

Simma, B and others (eds) *Charter of the United Nations: A Commentary* (2nd edn, Oxford: Oxford University Press, 2002).

Tomuschat, C, *Human Rights: Between Idealism and Realism* (1st edn, Oxford: Oxford University Press, 2003).

Tomuschat, C, *Human Rights: Between Idealism and Realism* (2nd edn, Oxford: Oxford University Press, 2008).

UN, *Repertoire of the Practice of the Security Council 1989–1992* (New York: Department of Political Affairs, 2007).

UNGA, *2005 World Summit Outcome* (16 September 2005), UN Doc A/60/1.

UNGA, *Report of the Panel on United Nations Peace Operations* (21 August 2000), UN Doc A/55/305.

UN SG, 'Implementing the Responsibility to Protect' (12 January 2009), UN Doc A/63/677.

UN SG, *Report of the Secretary General pursuant to General Assembly Resolution 53/35: The Fall of Srebrenica* (15 November 1999), UN Doc A/54/549.

UN SG, 'Supplement to an Agenda for Peace: Position paper of the Secretary-General on the occasion of the 50th anniversary of the United Nations' (3 January 1995), UN Doc A/50/60-S/1.

UN SG, *We the Peoples: The role of the United Nations in the 21st Century* (New York, NY: United Nations, 2000).

Von Bernstorff, J, 'The Changing Fortunes of the Universal Declaration of Human Rights: Genesis and Symbolic Dimensions of the Turn to Rights in International Law' (2008) 19 (5) *European Journal of International Law* 903.

Weiss, T G, *Humanitarian Intervention: Ideas in action* (Cambridge: Polity, 2007).

Wellens, K, 'The UN Security Council and New Threats to the Peace: Back to the Future' (2003) 8(1) *Journal of Conflict and Security Law* 15.

Welsh, J M, 'The Security Council and Humanitarian Intervention', in Lowe, V and others (eds), *The United Nations Security Council and War: The evolution of thought and practice since 1945* (Oxford: Oxford University Press, 2008).

Wheeler, N, *Saving Strangers: Humanitarian Intervention in International Society* (Oxford: Oxford University Press, 2002).

White, N D, *The Law of International Organisations* (Boulder, CO: Lynne Rienner, 2005).

3 The contribution of the Universal Declaration of Human Rights to the promotion and protection of democracy in international law

Richard Burchill and Sofia Cavandoli

3.1 Introduction

This chapter puts forth the proposition that the Universal Declaration of Human Rights (UDHR) holds an important place with regard to the promotion and protection of democracy in international law. Our argument is that the UDHR serves as a foundation for understanding the meaning, content and parameters of democracy as an international legal principle. Commentators have attempted to claim that the adoption of the UDHR in 1948 gave rise at that time to an international right to democratic governance.[1] Clearly, the reality of the international system from 1948 showed that such a right was non-existent as international law and took minimal notice of the structures or processes of government and governance. International law's attention to governance took a major turn with the end of the Cold War. In both practice and rhetoric, international law was utilised to engage in the promotion and protection of democracy. While there has been widespread evidence of support expressed for democracy in both international law and relations, determining the meaning of what is at stake remains a critical issue to be addressed.

We will assert that the UDHR provides substantial guidance for defining democracy in international law as it contains the core elements of a definition of democracy that covers procedures, substance and a normative basis. The UDHR does not establish a detailed framework for democracy as democratic practices will vary and a degree of pluralism in understanding democracy is necessary. What the UDHR does provide is the parameters for understanding what constitutes democracy in international law as well as normative support for the pursuit of more effective democratic systems. As the UDHR is not a legally binding document its contribution to the promotion and protection of democracy in international law does not come in the form of legal obligations but rather as normative support that has widespread acceptance. This chapter will begin with a brief discussion of international law and the promotion and protection of democracy in order to highlight the definitional issues that are at stake. The next section will discuss the drafting of the UDHR focussing on debates concerning the nature of government and governance before undertaking an assessment as to how the final version of the UDHR supports an understanding of democracy.

The adoption of the UDHR was a revolutionary development in international law as it marked the first significant effort to restrain the exercise of government by reference to the promotion and protection of human interests over state interests. The development of an international law of democracy in the post-Cold War period has also marked a major development in the nature of international law and relations. In both cases these developments can be seen as efforts 'to promote social progress and better standards of life in larger freedom',[2] ideas and practices that are central to an appropriate understanding of democracy.

3.2 International law and democracy

In discussing the issue of democracy in international law it is necessary to establish what is actually being talked about. Democracy is a term that has been used by many to describe a seemingly infinite amount of government forms and processes over a considerable amount of time.[3] At the same time, in debates about democracy it is clear that there are limits upon the ideas, principles and practices that are being discussed. Even within these limits substantial disagreement remains as to what is the most appropriate way of understanding democracy. At the heart of any system of governance claiming to be democratic is the belief that individuals should be part of the processes that impact their lives. Equally it has been recognised that a process for participation alone is not enough to ensure democracy as there must also be the equal opportunity for all to realise their full potential. This can take a variety of forms and manifests itself through a range of institutional structures. At the core is the belief that the exercise of government has to be responsive to the needs and desires of society for the purposes of supporting, rather than limiting, the ongoing quest for greater empowerment and emancipation. Of course establishing a comprehensive and universally applicable definition of democracy is a task that political theorists have been grappling with for thousands of years and one that we cannot resolve here. However, as international law has become involved in the promotion and protection of democracy as a practice and standard of principle in the processes of governance, it is necessary to establish margins for determining the boundaries of democracy for these purposes.

Establishing the meaning of democracy in international law is a delicate issue as it brings into question fundamental principles and practices of the international system. Any discussion of democracy as something that is part of international law will bring into question how government is structured and how governance is carried out. Crawford and Marks explain that international law has long maintained:

> an attitude of official indifference with respect to national political organization. It adopted a *de facto* approach to statehood and government, an approach which followed the facts of political power and made few enquiries into how that power was established.[4]

This observation is not surprising as international law has long been understood as only being a system for organising the relations between sovereign states. However, the creation of the UN brought about a number of changes regarding international law's role in the international system and extended the system beyond just regulating relations between states. While international law maintained this primary purpose it also took on a stronger normative agenda directed at the actual material conditions being experienced by individuals and societies. The creation of the UN system shifted international law from being primarily a descriptive system that observed what states did as being the extent of legal obligations, to one that attempted to be more prescriptive about what occurred in the international system which included the practice and processes of government.[5]

While the activities of the UN extended international law's concern to the process of governance, primarily through international human rights law, the ideological restraints of the Cold War meant this did not extend to international law expressly or actively setting limits on how governments were constituted. There were some exceptions to this general trend such as the condemnation of colonisation and the apartheid regimes of South Africa. The 1960 Declaration on Decolonisation[6] adopted by the General Assembly (GA) condemned the practice of colonial rule through reference to the importance of self-determination and self-government. In subsequent practice, however, the focus was on the removal of colonial rule as an end in itself and the nature of governance that followed was not subjected to any further scrutiny.[7] The 1970 Declaration on Principles of International Law Concerning Friendly Relations[8] made direct reference to the nature of governance by suggesting that the exercise of self-determination was effective when the resultant state possesses 'a government representing the whole people belonging to the territory without distinction as to race, creed or colour'.[9] This Declaration was clearly aimed at the existence of apartheid in South Africa and there is little evidence of this aspect of the Declaration being applied to other situations where questions may have been raised about a government that did not represent the people. Outside colonial control and explicitly racist governments, international law's concern with the nature of governance was limited. As the American Law Institute's Restatement of the Foreign Relations Law of the United States accurately explained, 'international law does not generally address domestic constitutional issues, such as how a national government is formed'.[10] Even within the system of international human rights law little attention was given to the wider context of governance.[11]

The end of the Cold War brought significant changes to the international system including international law's position regarding democracy. The move towards increased concern with, and evidence of, democratic practice led Thomas Franck in 1992 to put forth the argument that the international system was experiencing the emergence of a right to democratic governance.[12] Franck's argument was based on the evolution of the practice of self-determination, the growth of state practice involving the holding of elections as a means of choosing domestic governments, the increase in requests to the UN for observing elections in order to bestow international legitimacy, and finally the growth of participatory rights in international human rights law. In his work, Franck was clear that the evidence pointed to an *emerging* right, not one that was fully established at that time. He also admitted that the type of democracy he was discussing was relatively limited in scope, confined primarily to the holding of elections and the protection of a small group of civil and political rights. He also recognised that this minimalist definition of democracy was likely to be the most the international system would agree upon for determining the boundaries and extent of democracy. Franck's observations on this emerging right to democratic governance quickly gave rise to a wide range of claims that democracy was a central feature to international law and for the most part these claims relied upon a minimalist definition whereby democracy was primarily understood as the conduct of elections. Any questions about the wider context of governance or the extent to which elections actually empowered societies were marginalised.

This gave rise to a problematic issue for international law, because:

> [i]n no setting is the meaning of democracy a technical issue, on which a scholar may hope authoritatively to pronounce. Rather, the significance attached to 'rule by the people' is always and everywhere a political struggle, with winners and losers and exceptionally high stakes.[13]

For the most part it was clear that the focus of international law regarding democracy was on the technical issues which worked to limit the political struggle involved at the heart of any claim of democracy. The minimalist approach of international law is not surprising as it corresponds with prominent trends in the literature from political theory where there is a tendency to confine democracy to verifiable events.[14] It has been asserted that a basic procedural definition of democracy is the only way forward for it overcomes the problems of ambiguity and imprecision which come from trying to define democracy through source or purpose.[15] However, as Marks explains confining democracy to procedures constrains 'the efforts of those seeking to transform relations of domination'.[16] This poses a particular dilemma for international law for even though it has a long history of supporting patterns of domination, it has equally taken a concern with the actual material conditions being experienced by individuals and society. By adhering to a minimalist conception of democracy, it was clear that international law's promotion and protection of democracy was not leading to an improvement of the actual conditions experienced by individuals.[17]

A leading explanation for why minimalist conceptions have been prominent in international law is related to the prominence of the global spread of free market economic models. While the advancement of political systems marked by elections and constitutional guarantees was seen as a positive development in the international system, it is equally apparent that free market models of economic and social organisation have taken a higher priority.[18] A strong adherence to free market models has a direct correlation with the conception of democracy that is pursued as it is the market which is left to determine social and economic organisation distancing individuals from the ability to participate or influence the decisions that impact their lives.[19] A fuller discussion of the impact of free market thinking upon international law's understanding of democracy is not possible here but it remains a matter that influences how democracy is understood in international law.[20] The influence of minimalist conceptions of democracy has resulted in simplistic understandings in international law that have not satisfactorily addressed the full range of considerations involved in understanding governance and legitimacy.[21]

Given the nature of democracy as a continual political struggle, it may not be possible to establish a more concrete definition but at the same time it may be possible to put forth a 'guiding orientation that can help generate a basis for specifying relations between different normative concerns'.[22] As democracy has become an active consideration for international law, it is necessary to establish some indication as to its meaning and content. International law's attention to democracy today differs from the Cold War period where democracy had become a meaningless descriptor adopted by any type of government. Today the matter has changed. The UN Secretary General explained at the opening of the 1993 World Conference on Human Rights that the UN's support for democracy is 'not merely a statement of principle, even less a concession to a fashion of the moment, but the realization that democracy is the political system which best allows for a free exercise of individual rights'.[23] In order to ensure that international law's efforts for the promotion and protection of democracy is effective and appropriate it is imperative to establish the boundaries involved. This is critical to international law, for as Beetham explains 'It is only by grasping the underlying principles involved that we are able to assess how far a given institution is democratic in practice, and what else might be required to make it so'.[24] If international law is to be an effective system in the processes of global organisation it needs to be able to assert the limits of what is involved with regards to particular aspects of international behaviour.

Democracy as an idea has consistently been invoked as a desire by individuals for the opportunity to participate in decision making processes that affect their own lives. This desire is based on the belief that active and widespread participation provides the best way forward in social organisation and ensures that individuals are not treated as a means to an end desired by someone else. This is an expansive understanding of democracy that takes us well beyond the existence of specific procedures and, following Beetham's line of thinking, it is necessary to examine the underlying principles involved. A minimal conception of democracy that focuses primarily on elections accommodates a number of the principles central to democracy. However, because democracy is more than just a process, its promotion and protection need to uphold 'the idea of equal human worth or dignity'. At the core of democracy is the belief that individuals 'should be free and equal in the processes of deliberation about the conditions of their own lives and in the determination of those conditions, so long as they do not deploy this framework to negate the rights of others'.[25] Identifying the core principles of democracy involves addressing both procedures and norms for ensuring 'not only "one man, one vote", but also "one man, one equal right to live as fully humanly as he may wish"'.[26] It is the belief here that the UDHR upholds these core principles to serve as a foundation for determining the boundaries of democracy in international law.

By taking such an expansive approach to understanding democracy, one is not exempt from scrutiny and criticism. Political theory has argued that democracy and normative considerations such as human rights are often incompatible. Such theories, however, have not been able to survive critical examination that demonstrates democracy is about procedures and substantive rights.[27] The minimalist approach to democracy has been more about simplicity than any sort of convincing argument of appropriateness. A range of scholars have demonstrated the paradox of minimalist forms of democracy that have resulted in supposed political equality but with massive social and economic inequalities, something no democratic system can accept as appropriate.[28] Of course international law has to ensure that its understanding of democracy is related to actual events on the ground, which results in an emphasis on elections. Equally, however, democracy needs to have a vision that is grounded in experience but at the same time possesses a vision that is not limited by experience if 'democracy is not to be drained of its critical and emancipatory potential'.[29] Democracy needs to be understood as:

> less a matter of forms and events than an affair of relationships and processes, on open-ended and continually recontextualized agenda of enhancing control by citizens of decision-making which affects them and overcoming disparities in the distribution of citizenship rights and opportunities.[30]

Or as Sen has explained, 'It is necessary to avoid confining attention only to appropriate procedures' as it is both processes and the actual opportunities individuals have which determine the existence of freedom.[31] This is why we are adopting the UDHR as a foundation for defining democracy in international law as it provides an understanding of democracy that addresses procedures and principled commitments regarding the nature of governance. By using the UDHR as a foundation for defining democracy in international law we are able to identify and discuss 'democracy's essential ingredients'.[32]

3.3 The drafting of the UDHR and democracy

The UDHR was at the time of its acceptance a monumental event in international law. Even though it was a non-binding document not intended to create legal obligations upon Member States it did represent one of the first attempts to articulate how societies and states were to be governed. It symbolised recognition in the international system that pure power was not to be the only consideration for determining how governance was pursued and that individuals and societies were deserving of respect and protection and that international law would take a direct interest in these matters. The UDHR has not necessarily met all of the expectations originally attached to it as the document and the international system for the promotion and protection of human rights which have evolved from it have had to compete with other priorities in the international system.

As the Second World War drew to a close, ideas regarding how the international system would be organised did suggest a particular place for the promotion and protection of democracy.[33] But as efforts towards the creation of the new United Nations organisation progressed, particular references to democracy were dropped and the new system of international organisation was to be based on the 'principle of the sovereign equality of all peace-loving states' with no mention of particular systems of governance. The nature of a state's government along with its commitment to democracy and human rights was not a factor for determining who participated in the new international organisation and future membership to the UN required a state to be 'peace-loving' with no definition of what this actually meant.[34] At the same time the impact of events during the Second World War did ensure that the protection of human rights featured as an item in the agenda of the new organisation.[35] The final version of the Charter included references to ensuring faith in human rights, contributing to social progress and improving standards of life for all. It further provided that the UN and the Member States would take action for the promotion and protection of human rights.[36] The Economic and Social Council was given the responsibility for setting up a Commission to address the protection of human rights,[37] which occurred in 1946 and the first objective for this newly constituted Commission was to draw up an International Bill of Rights, of which the UDHR would be the cornerstone of this process.

A full account of the drafting process of the UDHR is documented elsewhere[38] and due to space restraints it is only possible to highlight some of the key issues raised regarding the nature and form of governance. The term democracy appears only once in the UDHR in reference to a 'democratic society' in Article 29, however the issue of how governance should be constituted was a prominent theme during the drafting process. This process was clearly influenced by varying philosophical views and even more critically by the emerging ideological divide that would come to characterise the Cold War. While at times it appeared all sides were speaking the same language concerning democracy, the underlying ideological viewpoints created numerous obstacles when it came to including any direct reference to it or provisions explicitly protecting democracy or democratic governance.[39]

The first draft document of the International Bill of Rights, from which the UDHR emerged, was prepared by John Humphreys of the UN Division of Human Rights. In this draft there was a direct mention of democracy, along with references to protecting participation and measures for ensuring that government would be accountable to the people. Humphreys' draft Article 30 read that:

> Everyone has the right to take an effective part in the government of the State of which he is a citizen. The State has a duty to conform to the wishes of the people as manifested by democratic elections. Elections shall be periodic, free and fair.

This one article provided substantial limitations upon the nature of government and equally set out important normative guidance. The wording used by Humphreys is significant as the provision is not just about a right to participate in government but also that participation has to be 'effective'. At the same time reference to the nature of government, conforming to the wishes of the people, was expressed in weaker terms than what emerged from the final version of the UDHR which clearly states the will of the people shall be the basis of the authority of government. The first draft also contained provisions on the right to petition government in order to redress grievances and a right to resist oppression and tyranny,[40] elements which never made it to substantive provisions in the final draft but represent further the idea that government is to be directed towards the will and desires of the people it serves and that it is for the people to determine the extent to which this actually occurs and not those who are in power.

The inclusion of provisions in the first draft of the UDHR dealing with the nature of governance and how this was manifested stimulated a good deal of discussion and a variety of proposals on this matter.[41] The Drafting Committee took the initial suggestions to derive a provision that read:

> The State can derive its authority only from the will of the people and has a duty to conform to the wishes of the people. These wishes shall be manifested particularly by democratic elections, which shall be periodic, free, and 'by secret ballot'.[42]

From this proposal the UK suggested an even briefer provision that only included a reference to the right of everyone to take part in the government either directly or through freely chosen representatives; purposely leaving out any mention of the nature of government or even elections.[43] In a desire to shorten the document even further, reference to the will of the people as being the basis of government was almost edited out at a later stage in drafting.[44] Reference to the will of the people did remain but any specific reference to 'democracy' in the document was removed and this gave rise to further debates about the necessity of clearly including provisions addressing democracy. Support for explicit protection was justified on the grounds that the effective protection of human rights depended upon the existence of a democratic society.[45] But equally, variations in opinion as to what constituted a democratic society reflected the varying ideological positions.[46]

In the final version of the UDHR, Article 21 provided that everyone has the right to take part in government, everyone has the right to access to public services and most significantly it includes the statement:

> The will of the people shall be the basis of the authority of government; this will shall be expressed in periodic and genuine elections which shall be by universal and equal suffrage and shall be held by secret vote or by equivalent free voting procedures.

It was a revolutionary concept for international law to include in an international instrument a statement declaring how governance was to be constituted. At the same time, as the debates about the drafting make clear, most states felt that they did conform to the will of the people in one way or another. Even the question of holding elections in principle did not raise a great deal of controversy even though the particulars of this matter were widely discussed.[47] Article 21 received 'broad formal support' despite the clear disagreements over the details.[48] It is likely that this broad formal support was a direct result of removing all of the initial references to any right for opposing a government. For some representatives any mention to the will of the people being the authority of government required the inclusion of a right 'to oppose government and to promote its replacement by legal means'.[49] This was opposed widely as the US and UK saw the inclusion of a right to resist oppression as opening the way for non-democratic forces to threaten established governments[50] and the USSR used the point to argue that fascist movements would be legitimated.[51]

The other area where the nature of government was debated came in relation to the restriction clauses in the UDHR, in particular final Article 29(2) which provides that any limitations upon the exercise of rights must be:

> solely for the purpose of securing due recognition and respect for the rights and freedoms of others and of meeting the just requirements of morality, public order and the general welfare in a democratic society.

Much of the debate in relation to this clause revolved around the nature and basis of human rights with discussions about natural rights or rights endowed by a god of some kind.[52] This led to discussions about the origins of rights, as being either endowed by nature or provided for by the state. Morsink views this debate as being of 'crucial importance' for the UDHR because it attempts to balance rights and duties and recognises that human rights, even if of natural origin are not unlimited.[53] The main focal point of the discussion was the continual insistence by the USSR for inclusion of a clause that read rights were to be exercised 'in accordance with just requirements of the democratic state', a point that was rejected.[54] The resultant 'democratic society' indicator was preferred as it would ensure that governments would be barred from invoking any limitations clauses when they did not have a genuine mandate of the people.[55]

In its final form the UDHR does not make an emphatic statement about the nature of governance and at the time of its acceptance it was felt that a wide range of governmental forms could achieve the expectations of the document. However, not every state in 1948 approved the UDHR during its acceptance in the GA. In a rather ironic twist, the Soviets and other like-minded states abstained, mainly due to the failure to include a direct mention of the role of the democratic state in relation to human rights and also the failure to include an outright condemnation of fascism.[56] The Soviet view was clearly influenced by the limitations placed upon the state in the UDHR and its ability to act as a source for empowering individuals over and above the state. A similar line of reasoning placed South Africa in the abstention group as it felt that the document was contrary to that state's view on the nature of government and participation in government as understood under the influence of apartheid.[57] Even though the European colonial powers of the time approved the UDHR, the final provisions regarding the authority of government would have a major impact upon their world positions as it would eventually also have on communist and apartheid regimes.[58]

3.4 The UDHR and defining democracy

As mentioned previously, at the time of its adoption the UDHR was not intended to be an instrument creating legal obligations, only a statement of principles. This remains the case today even though its significance as a statement of principles is substantial. As a non-binding declaration the UDHR had no immediate impact upon the nature of government in international law. This is not a fault of the UDHR or even of the international system for the promotion and protection of human rights, but rather a reality of the international system whereby the nature of government remained outside the realm of legal considerations. However, the end of the Cold War brought about significant changes to the international system whereby democracy quickly became the leading normative value of political legitimacy.[59] A major part of these changes in the system was the extent to which international law, in a variety of ways, took a direct concern with the nature of governance and began to actively engage with the promotion and protection of democracy and the UDHR was central to these efforts.

To view the UDHR as a foundation for democracy in international law it is crucial to adopt an interdependent approach to understanding the document. This requires looking at the individual provisions in relation to each other and as part of the wider context of the document as a whole.[60] By taking an expansive and holistic view of the UDHR it is possible to construct the parameters of democracy as well as establish objectives for systems of government and governance. This analysis of the UDHR draws on David Beetham's work which investigates the relationship between democracy and human rights. At the heart of Beetham's analysis is the assertion that civil and political rights are integral to the basic functioning of a democratic system and that socio-economic rights are crucial for the effective exercise of democracy.[61] As the UDHR covers the full expanse of rights as well as indicators for the wider context within which governance is conducted, it provides a solid foundation for international law's definition of democracy. This is not an attempt to argue the UDHR creates legal obligations of democracy, rather it is more of a methodological issue for determining the parameters of a particular area of international legal regulation where controversy exists over content and meaning.

The Preamble of the UDHR provides an extensive political statement highlighting core notions of freedom, dignity and equality as inherent features of humankind. Such notions are equally foundational elements of democracy for without them any system of governance would not be effective in ensuring individuals are able to participate in the processes impacting upon their lives or have the opportunity to realise their full potential.[62] The Preamble also sets out that the effective protection of human rights is essential if 'man is not to be compelled to have recourse, as a last resort, to rebellion against tyranny and oppression' making clear that the processes of governance have to correspond to the needs and desires of individuals and societies. The Preamble is not directed towards any particular system of governance but it does in many ways encompass the ideals of democracy.[63] It is very much in line with the core principles of democracy set out above through its recognition of freedom, dignity and equality as well as expressing the belief that human beings should not be subject to control and oppression that is not justified.

Article 21 of the UDHR is the most 'vocal' in its endorsement of democracy as it provides practical and principled foundations for the nature and processes of government. It reads:

(1) Everyone has the right to take part in the government of his country, directly or through freely chosen representatives.
(2) Everyone has the right of equal access to public service in his country.
(3) The will of the people shall be the basis of the authority of government; this will shall be expressed in periodic and genuine elections which shall be by universal and equal suffrage and shall be held by secret vote or by equivalent free voting procedures.

The first paragraph deals with the open and expansive nature of democracy by ensuring that everyone has the right to participate in government. At the time of drafting, this provision was directed narrowly at the actual central government of a state, however, as understandings of government and governance have expanded, so has the applicability of this Article and now it can be seen as supporting the importance of participation in all forms of governance.

The second paragraph deals with the right of access to public services for all. This covers the principle that government works for the benefit of society and that this applies to all in society and not just a select few. As already discussed, it is the final paragraph that has been the most significant in developing international law's support for democracy, in expressing the principle that the source of authority of government comes from the people. This rather basic proposition, while having a long tradition in democratic theory, contrasts significantly with the long established general position in international law that government needs only to exercise effective control over society. In this understanding 'effective' has not been subject to any specific criteria such as the will of the people. Article 21 has been described as a 'revolution within a revolution'. Not only has it recognised the idea of equal and inalienable rights of the individual in relation to his/her state, it has also set the minimum standard for the structure and functioning of a government by explicitly requiring it to be based on the will of the people and for there to be democratic participation in public life.[64]

The importance of Article 21 for understanding the meaning of democracy is supported by the remainder of the UDHR. Article 1 provides 'All human beings are born free and equal in dignity and rights'. This has been described as 'the keystone, cornerstone and credo of the whole declaration as well as the basis, foundation and framework of the rights enumerated in its various articles'.[65] Although Article 1 is a statement of principle rather than a specific right, the drafters chose to include it at the start of the document in order to highlight and emphasise the importance of the concept of humanity. It was felt that after the intolerance and brutality of the Second World War, the notion of humanity needed to be powerfully reasserted, rather than merely presumed. By declaring that 'all human beings are born free and equal in dignity and rights', Article 1 emphasises the Enlightenment idea that rights exist by virtue of the human condition. Individuals have rights because they are human beings, not because of their social status or because they have been given them by the state. The concept of human dignity is one of the most important and innovative elements introduced into international law by the UN Charter and the UDHR. Within both documents and more prominently in the Universal Declaration it is viewed as the foundation of all human rights. Although a clear definition of dignity is not given, the document sets out that in order for dignity to be preserved, a meaningful political programme must be in place within each country in order to establish conditions under which human beings can equally enact their responsibilities as citizens of the world.[66]

As well as dignity, freedom and equality are what every human being is due, whether or not he/she is in fact accorded them. Individuals must be free to participate in society and participation is integral to the nature of governance in any society. Freedom in this case is synonymous with autonomy. A human being is autonomous when they are able to deliberate, judge, choose and act upon different possible courses of action in private as well as public life without infringing the rights of others.[67] A democratic society allows for people to pursue their own interests and activities free from the fear of arbitrary use of political authority or coercive power. Equality is also an essential feature of democratic society. The importance of equality has been espoused since democracy's inception in ancient Greece.[68] In a democratic society, to be equal does not necessitate that each individual should possess the same characteristics and abilities as one another; equality entails having equal status as a member of society.[69] These two notions are necessary in a democratic society in order to ensure that all are able to enjoy the benefits of participation in that society and the standards by which they are treated by those in authority.

As a corollary to equality is the concept of non-discrimination and Article 2 of the declaration provides that everyone is entitled to the rights in the UDHR without distinction of any kind including 'race, colour, sex, language, religion, political or other opinion, national or social origin, property, birth or other status. Furthermore, no distinction shall be made on the basis of the political, jurisdictional or international status of the country or territory to which a person belongs. Democracy has as a basic principle the equal worth of each individual in society regardless of race, gender, personal belief or style of life. Articles 1 and 2 provide substantial guidance for determining the full extent to which any system of governance represents a true understanding of democracy that extends beyond basic procedures as they articulate core principles to be associated with an understanding of democracy.

Key rights for the purposes of participation are included in the Declaration, such as freedom of thought, opinion and expression along with the right to assembly and association. Article 19 of the Declaration articulates one of the most important aspects of democracy: freedom of expression. It was identified as a key component of human rights when the Human Rights Commission was originally mandated to draft the declaration. In a liberal democracy, freedom of opinion or expression allows for both the personal autonomy and self-realisation of the individual and guarantees the democratic process of the society. A free responsible citizen is protected from any outside intervention in order to enable him/her to form and express his/her opinions without any outside threat or coercion.[70] Article 20 provides for freedom of association and assembly which is a fundamental notion of civil society. Together with freedom of expression they form the core of the category of political rights. They are the legal basis for an active civil society enabling rational-collective will-formation, the publicity of public affairs, and also for any participatory or representative democratic processes.[71]

The UDHR covers a number of rights directly concerned with the actual material conditions being experienced by individuals. The document contains a number of personal integrity rights such as the right to life, freedom from slavery, the right not to be tortured, and recognition as a person and equality before the law. The protection of personal integrity rights such as these is essential for any society and clearly the basic respect they ensure for human beings is at the heart of emancipation and empowerment. These personal integrity rights are associated with both the participation rights discussed above and socio-economic rights which are also included in the UDHR. The effective realisation and protection of socio-economic rights along with civil and political rights strengthens the democratic system as a whole. Included in the UDHR are the rights to social security, just and favourable conditions of employment, and other social benefits. There is also a specific article on the right to education which is a critical element of democracy as it allows for the effective exercise of rights, ensures individuals are able to engage in public debate as well as serving to support assertions of self-rule. For understanding democracy beyond the minimalist conception, Article 25 provides a crucial aspect protecting the right of everyone to a standard of living adequate for health and well-being. While it is rather trite to say that individuals need to be alive in order to engage in political participation, it is a point that still needs to be reinforced in the face of the influence exerted by free market models upon conceptions of democracy. As free market models have influenced the organisation of society and understandings of democracy, the actual material conditions being experienced by individuals have not been adequately considered. It is too often argued that social welfare is an economic matter to be determined by the market and not something directly controlled by government. But if any democratic system is to be effective, it cannot sustain and hold as legitimate, widespread social and economic inequalities that lead to marginalisation.[72] In attempting to support international law's efforts for providing emancipation and empowerment for the poor and marginalised, the UDHR has been given a central role for understanding what is required.[73] Attention to the actual material conditions being experienced requires an understanding of governance that extends beyond the confines of the state. The UDHR recognised this understanding through Article 28 which states that 'everyone is entitled to a social and international order in which the rights and freedoms set forth in this Declaration can be fully realized'. This is a crucial aspect in establishing frameworks understanding the promotion and protection of democracy as well as human rights in the current process of globalisation.

The final element of the UDHR that contributes its foundation for defining democracy in international law comes through its limitation clauses. This comes primarily in Article 29(2) in relation to the appropriate extent of any limitations on the rights in the UDHR. By establishing that any limitation on the exercise of rights has to be for the wider purpose of the general welfare in a democratic society, the boundaries for the exercise of authority and power are set down. At the time of drafting it is unlikely this phrase caused much concern as all participants were claiming their systems were based upon a democratic society. However, in today's international system this phrase has a more defined meaning, whereby the extent of limitations upon rights cannot be merely whatever the ruling authority deems to be acceptable. Limitations upon rights are legitimate but they must be for the purpose of securing or furthering the core principles of democracy. Related to this is the restriction set out in Article 30 which provides that 'Nothing in this Declaration may be interpreted as implying for any State, group or person any right to engage in any activity or to perform any act aimed at the destruction of any of the rights and freedoms set forth herein'. This restriction is important for establishing the parameters of a democratic society itself, for too often understandings of democracy assert that whatever the democratic process decides must be legitimate, even if it involves the denial of rights to certain sections of society. Such an understanding of democracy has been severely discredited, at the same time it is essential to reassert that the democratic process, under the pretext of being indicative of 'the will of the people' cannot legitimately deny the exercise of rights to individuals in society.

3.5 The UDHR as the foundation for an international law of democracy

Understanding the UDHR as a foundation for defining democracy is a contemporary interpretation of the document that is tied in with developments relating to international law's attention to the promotion and protection of democracy. It is primarily through the UN that the UDHR has been utilised as a foundation for understanding the nature and elements of democracy in the context of international law.[74] The GA has taken an active role in expressing its support for democracy in a variety of ways since the late 1980s.[75] The expressions of the GA are not indicative of international legal obligations but they do demonstrate an expression of a rhetoric that supports the promotion and protection of democracy. In this rhetoric the UDHR plays a foundational role. The most emphatic statement of this nature has been the view that there exists 'indissoluble links between the principles enshrined in the Universal Declaration of Human Rights and the foundations of any democratic society'.[76] When dealing with the matter of democracy, the GA has described it as a universal value based on the freely expressed will of the people to determine their own political, economic, social and cultural systems and their full participation in all aspects of their lives.[77] When expressing its backing for UN activities supporting elections, the GA recalls the importance of the UDHR's provisions for the 'right freely to choose representatives through periodic and genuine elections which shall be by universal and equal suffrage and held by secret vote or by equivalent free voting procedures'.[78] The GA has also endorsed the UDHR's position that 'the will of the people shall be the basis of the authority of government' and it has further reminded states of this obligation.[79]

The GA's reference to the will of the people being the basis of authority of government as being a central feature of democracy is resituating the organisation's stance on government and the issue of national sovereignty. There has been a discernable shift in the GA's rhetoric on this point. In resolutions from the early 1990s the GA would express support for elections as part of the democratisation process in a state. It would also adopt another resolution calling for respecting national sovereignty based on Article 2(7) of the UN Charter. While with the former resolutions the GA indicated clear support for democracy, the latter resolutions make no reference to democracy or the will of the people – elections are viewed as only an event occurring within a state with no wider implications involved.[80] The GA's position of democracy as just one possible model for state sovereignty changed as the UN's position on the matter took a major turn with the 2000 Millennium Declaration. In this statement, agreed by the heads of state and government, it is expressed that no effort will be spared to support democracy and human rights along with direct reference to the UDHR as the basis for these efforts.[81] The position was developed further through the 2005 World Summit Outcome, another document agreed to at the level of head of state and government. In the Summit Outcome document the UN affirms 'democracy is a universal value based on the freely expressed will of people to determine their political, economic, social and cultural systems and their full participation in all aspects of their lives'.[82] Democracy is included alongside human rights as part of the 'universal and indivisible core values and principles' of the UN.[83] The Summit Outcome also links democracy with socio-economic development stating the need for 'solid democratic institutions responsive to the needs of the people'.[84] From this explicit support for democracy as part of the principles of the UN, the GA began expressing a view of state sovereignty that was now determined by a reference to democracy. It viewed national sovereignty as being understood as situated within the principles and practice of democracy as set out in the

UDHR.[85] The UDHR has also been invoked in particular country situations where the maintenance of international peace and security has included the promotion of democracy[86] or where the UN has had a role in supporting the return of democracy.[87] There is also a direct reference to the UDHR in resolutions calling for a more democratic and equitable international order.[88]

In other areas of UN activity the UDHR features as a central part of efforts in support of democracy. The UN Secretary General has issued a guidance note on democracy which describes the UDHR as the normative fabric through which democratic principles are woven.[89] The UN's Electoral Assistance Division quotes Article 21(3) of the UDHR on the first page of its website indicating the centrality of this provision to its work.[90] The UDHR as a single document encompasses the necessary parameters of this normative fabric as it covers civil and political rights, recognises the importance of socio-economic rights, the core principles of freedom and equality and ensures the connection between the individual and society is based on a substantive understanding whereby the needs and interests of both must be accommodated in a substantive understanding of democracy.[91]

The UDHR is not a complete statement and a variety of features central to substantive understandings of democracy, such as minority rights, are absent. But as a general statement of the broad parameters concerned, the UDHR serves as the foundation for understanding the necessary principles and processes for the promotion and protection of democracy in international law.

Notes

1 C Cerna, 'Universal democracy: an international legal right or the pipe dream of the West?' (1995) 27 *New York University Journal of International Law and Politics* 290.
2 Universal Declaration of Human Rights, UNGA Res 217A (III) (10 December 1948), Preamble.
3 The work of David Held, *Models of Democracy* (3rd edn, Cambridge: Polity, 2006), clearly demonstrates the wide range of ideas and practices that fall under the term 'democracy'.
4 J Crawford and S Marks, 'The global democracy deficit: an essay in international law and its limits', in D Archibugi, D Held and M Köhler (eds) *Re-imagining Political Community: Studies in Cosmopolitan Democracy* (Cambridge: Polity, 1998), p 72.
5 J Crawford, 'Democracy and international law' (1993) 64 *British Yearbook of International Law* 119–23.
6 UNGA Res 1514 (XV) (14 December 1960).
7 A James, *Sovereign Statehood: The Basis of International Society* (London: Allen and Unwin, 1986), pp 160–1; R Higgins, *Problems and Processes: International Law and How We Use It* (Oxford: Oxford University Press, 1994), pp 40, 43.
8 UNGA Res 2625 (XXV) (24 October 1979).
9 UNGA Res 2625 (XXV), section entitled 'The Principle of equal rights and self-determination of peoples'.
10 Restatement Third, Foreign Relations Law of the United States, para 203.
11 B Roth, *Governmental Illegitimacy in International Law* (Oxford: Oxford University Press, 1999), p 321.
12 T Franck, 'The Emerging Right to Democratic Governance' (1992) 86 *American Journal of International Law* 46.

13 As quoted in E Stein, 'International integration and democracy: no love at first sight' (2001) 95 *American Journal of International Law* 493, fn 20.
14 For example see Bollen who states that providing a definition of democracy that everyone finds acceptable is impossible, K Bollen, 'Political democracy: conceptual and measurement traps', in D Beetham (ed), *Defining and Measuring Democracy* (London: Sage, 1994), p 5.
15 S Huntington, *The Third Wave: Democratization in the Late Twentieth Century* (Norman, OK: Oklahoma University Press, 1991), pp 6–7.
16 S Marks, *The Riddle of All Constitutions: International Law, Democracy and the Critique of Ideology* (Oxford: Oxford University Press, 2000), p 61.
17 See S Marks, 'Guarding the gates with two faces: international law and political reconstruction' (1999) 6 *Indiana Journal of Global Legal Studies* 457; J Macey and G Miller, 'The end of history and the new world order: the triumph of capitalism and the competition between liberalism and democracy' (1992) 25 *Cornell International Law Journal* 277.
18 C Nyamu, 'Human Rights, Democracy and Free Markets: Is it a Package?' (1999) *ASIL Proceedings* 121–3.
19 M Goodhart, *Democracy as Human Rights: Freedom and Equality in the Age of Globalization* (London: Routledge, 2005), p 220.
20 For a fuller account of the impact free market thinking has on democracy, see *ibid*, Goodhart, and for how this influences international law see op. cit., Marks, fn 16.
21 J D'Aspermont, 'Legitimacy of Governments in the Age of Democracy' (2006) 38 *New York University Journal of International Law and Politics* 880.
22 See op. cit., Held, fn 3, p 261.
23 B Boutros-Ghali, 'Human rights the common langue of humanity', in D Bhaskara Rao (ed), *World Conference on Human Rights* (New Delhi: Discovery Publishing, 2003), p 17.
24 D Beetham, *Democracy and Human Rights* (Cambridge: Polity, 1999), p 3.
25 See op. cit., Held, fn 3, p 264.
26 C B Macpherson, *Democratic Theory: Essays in Retrieval* (Oxford: Oxford University Press, 1973), p 51.
27 See C Brettschneider, *Democratic Rights: The Substance of Self-Government* (Princeton, NJ: Princeton University Press, 2007).
28 See op. cit., Marks, fn 16; op. cit., Beetham, fn 24; J Donnelly, 'Human rights, democracy and development' (1999) 21 *Human Rights Quarterly* 608.
29 S Marks, '"The Emerging Norm": Conceptualizing "Democratic Governance"' (1997) 91 *ASIL Proceedings* 376.
30 See op. cit., Marks, fn 16, p 110.
31 A Sen, *Development as Freedom* (Oxford: Oxford University Press, 1999), p 17.
32 Report of the High Commissioner for Human Rights submitted in accordance with Commission Resolution 2001/41, UN Doc E/CN.4/2003/59, 27 January 2003, para 3.
33 See G Simpson, *Great Powers and Outlaw States: Unequal Sovereigns in the International Law Order* (Cambridge: Cambridge University Press, 2004), p 264.
34 *Ibid*, pp 266–9.
35 See J Morsink, *The Universal Declaration of Human Rights: Origins, Drafting and Intent* (Philadelphia, PA: University of Pennsylvania Press, 2000), p 2; M A Glendon, *A World Made New: Eleanor Roosevelt and the Universal Declaration of Human Rights* (New York, NY: Random House, 2001), Chapter 1.
36 Articles 55 and 56 of the UN Charter.
37 *Ibid*, Article 68.
38 See op. cit., Morsink, fn 35; op. cit., Glendon, fn 35.
39 See op. cit., Glendon, fn 35, p 184.
40 E/CN.4/AC.1/3, Articles 28 and 29.
41 The proposals are contained in UN Doc E/CN.4/21, 1 July 1947.
42 UN Doc E/CN.4/21, 1 July 1947, p 79.

43 UN Doc E/CN.4/99, 24 May 1948, pp 5–6.
44 See op. cit., Morsink, fn 35, p 59.
45 See statements by Chile, UN Doc E/CN.4/SR.51, p 3; France, UN Doc E/CN.4/SR.51, p 10.
46 See statements by Yugoslavia, UN Doc E/CN.4/SR.51, p 4; USSR, UN Doc E/CN.4/SR.51, p 7; Belgium UN Doc E/CN.4/SR.51, p 3.
47 See UN Doc A/C.3/SR.131 (11 November 1948); UN Doc A/C.3/SR.133 (12 November 1948).
48 A Rosas, 'Article 21', in A Eide *et al* (eds), *The Universal Declaration of Human Rights – A Commentary* (Oslo: Scandinavian University Press, 1992), p 34.
49 Views of Columbia and Costa Rica, UN Doc A/C.3/SR.131 (11 November 1948), p 449
50 See statements in J Morsink, 'The Philosophy of the Universal Declaration' (1984) 6 *Human Rights Quarterly* 324–2.
51 UN Doc A/C.3/SR.131 (11 November 1948), p 449.
52 See op. cit., Morsink, fn 50.
53 See op. cit., Morsink, fn 50, p 317.
54 UN Doc E/CN.4/SR.74, p 15.
55 T Opsahl, 'Articles 29 and 30', in A Eide *et al* (eds), *The Universal Declaration of Human Rights – A Commentary* (Oslo: Scandinavian University Press, 1992), p 460.
56 See op. cit., Morsink, fn 35, pp 21–4.
57 See op. cit., Morsink, fn 35, pp 27–8.
58 See op. cit., Glendon, fn 35, p 184; op. cit., Rosas, fn 48, p 302.
59 See D Held, 'Democracy and Globalization', in D Archibugi, D Held and M Köhler, (eds) *Re-imagining Political Community: Studies in Cosmopolitan Democracy* (Cambridge: Polity, 1998), p 12; also op. cit., Held, fn 3, pp ix–xi.
60 See M Scheinin, 'The Right to Self-determination under the Covenant on Civil and Political Rights', in Pekka Aikio and Martin Scheinin (eds), *Operationalizing the Right of Indigenous Peoples to Self-Determination* (Turku/Abo: Institute for Human Rights, Abo Akademi University, 2000), pp 181–6.
61 See op. cit., Beetham, fn 24, Chapter 5, p 89.
62 See opening Statement by Mehr Khan-Williams, The Deputy High Commissioner for Human Rights to the Expert Seminar on Democracy and the Rule of Law, Office of the High Commissioner for Human Rights, Geneva, 28 February–2 March 2005.
63 Goodhart explains democracy is about 'a principled commitment to making the promise of freedom and equality real and meaningful for everyone', op. cit., fn 19, p 216. The Preamble of the UDHR sets out a similar commitment.
64 See op. cit., Rosas, fn 48, p 299.
65 T Lindholm, 'Article 1', in A Eide *et al* (eds), *The Universal Declaration of Human Rights – A Commentary* (Oslo: Scandinavian University Press, 1992), pp 31–56, esp p 41.
66 K Dicke, 'The Founding Function of Human Dignity in the Universal Declaration of Human Rights', in D Kretzmer and E Klein, *The Concept of Human Dignity in Human Rights Discourse* (Kluwer Law International, 2002), p 111, esp p 120.
67 See op. cit., Held, fn 3, p 300.
68 Aristotle, *The Politics* (Harmondsworth: Penguin Publishers, 1981), pp 362–4, 'Ruling and being ruled in turn, is one element in liberty, and the democratic idea of justice is in fact numerical equality, not equality based on merit; and when this idea of what is just prevails, the multitude must be sovereign, and whatever the majority decides is final and constitutes justice. For they say there must be equality for each of the citizens'.
69 R H Tawney, *Equality* (London: Allen & Unwin Publishers, 1964), p 46.
70 See J Kortteinen, K Myntti and L Hannikainen, 'Article 19', in G Alfredsson and A Eide, *The Universal Declaration of Human Rights: A Common Standard of Achievement* (The Hague/London: Kluwer, 1999).
71 See M Scheinin, 'Article 20', in G Alfredsson and A Eide, *The Universal Declaration of Human Rights: A Common Standard of Achievement* (The Hague/London: Kluwer, 1999), p 417.

72 C B Macpherson, *The Life and Times of Liberal Democracy* (Oxford: Oxford University Press, 1977), pp 86–91.
73 See Report of the Secretary General, Legal Empowerment of the Poor and Eradication of Poverty, UN Doc A/64/133 (13 July 2009), para 12.
74 On the United Nations' efforts, see Edward Newman and Roland Rich (eds), *The UN Role in Promoting Democracy: Between Ideals and Reality* (Tokyo: United Nations University Press, 2004).
75 For an overview of activity see G Fox and B Roth, 'Introduction: the spread of liberal democracy and its implications for international law', in G Fox and B Roth (eds), *Democratic Governance and International Law* (Cambridge: Cambridge University Press, 2000), p 1.
76 See for example UNGA Res 50/133, Support by the United Nations System of the efforts of Governments to promote and consolidate new or restored democracies (20 December 1995), and subsequent resolutions of the same title.
77 UNGA Res 55/96, Promoting and consolidating democracy.
78 Article 21(3) of the UDHR; also UNGA Res 54/173, Strengthening the role of the United Nations in enhancing the effectiveness of the principle of periodic and genuine elections and the promotion of democratization, UN Doc A/RES/54/173 (15 February 2000).
79 See GA 64/155, Strengthening the role of the United Nations in enhancing periodic and genuine elections and the promotion of democratization (18 December 2009), A/RES/64/155, and other resolutions of a similar title.
80 See UNGA Res 48/124, Respect for the Principles of National Sovereignty and Non-Interference in the Internal Affairs of States in their Electoral Processes, UN Doc A/Res/48/124 (14 February 1994).
81 UNGA Res 55/2, United Nations Millennium Declaration, UN Doc A/RES/55/2, paras 24–5.
82 UNGA Res 60/1, 2005 World Summit Outcome Document, UN Doc A/RES/60/1, para 135.
83 *Ibid*, para 119.
84 *Ibid*, para 24(b).
85 See for example UNGA Res 60/164, Respect for the principles of national sovereignty and diversity of democratic systems in electoral processes as an important element for the promotion and protection of human rights (16 December 2005), UN Doc A/RES/60/164.
86 UNGA Res 46/7, The situation of democracy and human rights in Haiti (11 October 1991).
87 UNGA Res 55/280, United Nations Electoral Observer Mission for the general elections in Fiji in August 2001 (25 July 2001), UN Doc AA/RES/55/280.
88 See for example UNGA Res 59/193, Promotion of a democratic and equitable international order (20 December 2004), UN Doc A/RES/59/193, and all other resolutions of a similar title.
89 <www.un.org/democracyfund/Docs/UNSG%20Guidance%20Note%20on%20Democracy.pdf> (accessed 2 June 2010).
90 <www.un.org/Depts/dpa/ead/> (accessed 2 June 2010).
91 See A Eide and G Alfresdsson, 'Introduction', in A Eide *et al* (eds), *The Universal Declaration of Human Rights – A Commentary* (Oslo: Scandinavian University Press, 1992), pp 12–13.

Bibliography

Aristotle, *The Politics* (Harmondsworth: Penguin Publishers, 1981).
Beetham, D, *Democracy and Human Rights* (Cambridge: Polity, 1999).

Bollen, K, 'Political democracy: conceptual and measurement traps', in Beetham D, (ed), *Defining and Measuring Democracy* (London: Sage, 1994).

Boutros-Ghali, B, 'Human rights the common langue of humanity', in Bhaskara Rao, D (ed), *World Conference on Human Rights* (New Delhi: Discovery Publishing, 2003).

Brettschneider, C, *Democratic Rights: The Substance of Self-Government* (Princeton, NJ: Princeton University Press, 2007).

Cerna, C, 'Universal democracy: an international legal right or the pipe dream of the West?' (1995) 27 *New York University Journal of International Law and Politics* 290.

Crawford, J, 'Democracy and international law' (1993) 64 *British Yearbook of International Law* 119–23.

Crawford, J and Marks, S, 'The global democracy deficit: an essay in international law and its limits', in Archibugi, D, Held, D and Köhler, M (eds), *Re-imagining Political Community – Studies in Cosmopolitan Democracy* (Cambridge: Polity, 1998).

D'Aspermont, J, 'Legitimacy of Governments in the Age of Democracy' (2006) 38 *New York University Journal of International Law and Politics* 880.

Dicke, K, 'The Founding Function of Human Dignity in the Universal Declaration of Human Rights', in Kretzmer, D and Klein, E, *The Concept of Human Dignity in Human Rights Discourse* (Kluwer Law International, 2002).

Donnelly, J, 'Human rights, democracy and development' (1999) 21 *Human Rights Quarterly* 608.

Eide, A and Alfresdsson, G, 'Introduction' in Eide A, *et al* (eds) *The Universal Declaration of Human Rights – A Commentary* (Oslo: Scandinavan University Press, 1192).

Franck, T, 'The Emerging Right to Democratic Governance' (1992) 86 *American Journal of International Law* 46.

Fox, G and Roth, B, 'Introduction: the spread of liberal democracy and its implications for international law', in Fox, G and Roth, B (eds), *Democratic Governance and International Law* (Cambridge: Cambridge University Press, 2000).

Glendon, M A, *A World Made New: Eleanor Roosevelt and the Universal Declaration of Human Rights* (New York, NY: Random House, 2001).

Goodhart, M, *Democracy as Human Rights: Freedom and Equality in the Age of Globalization* (London: Routledge, 2005).

Held, D, 'Democracy and Globalization', in Archibugi, D, Held, D and Köhler, M (eds), *Re-imagining Political Community – Studies in Cosmopolitan Democracy* (Cambridge: Polity, 1998).

——, *Models of Democracy* (3rd edn, Cambridge: Polity, 2006).

Higgins, R, *Problems and Processes: International Law and How We Use It* (Oxford: Oxford University Press, 1994).

Huntington, S, *The Third Wave: Democratization in the Late Twentieth Century* (Norman OK: Oklahoma University Press, 1991).

James, A, *Sovereign Statehood: The Basis of International Society* (London: Allen and Unwin, 1986).

Kortteinen, J, Myntti, K and Hannikainen, L, 'Article 19', in Alfredsson, G and Eide, A, *The Universal Declaration of Human Rights: A Common Standard of Achievement* (The Hague/London: Kluwer, 1999).

Lindholm, T, 'Article 1', in Eide A, *et al* (eds) *The Universal Declaration of Human Rights – A Commentary* (Oslo: Scandinavian University Press, 1992).

Macey, J and Miller, G, 'The end of history and the new world order: the triumph of capitalism and the competition between liberalism and democracy' (1992) 25 *Cornell International Law Journal* 277.

Macpherson, C B, *Democratic Theory: Essays in Retrieval* (Oxford: Oxford University Press, 1973).

Macpherson, C B, *The Life and Times of Liberal Democracy (*Oxford: Oxford University Press, 1977).
Marks, S, 'Guarding the gates with two faces: international law and political reconstruction' (1999) 6 *Indiana Journal of Global Legal Studies* 457.
——, 'The "Emerging Norm": Conceptualizing "Democratic Governance"' (1997) 91 *ASIL Proceedings* 376.
——, *The Riddle of All Constitutions: International Law, Democracy and the Critique of Ideology* (Oxford: Oxford University Press, 2000).
Morsink, J, 'The Philosophy of the Universal Declaration' (1984) 6 *Human Rights Quarterly* 324–2.
——, *The Universal Declaration of Human Rights: Origins, Drafting and Intent* (Philadelphia, PA: University of Pennsylvania Press, 2000).
Newman, E and Rich, R (eds), *The UN Role in Promoting Democracy: Between Ideals and Reality* (Tokyo: United Nations University Press, 2004).
Nyamu, C, 'Human Rights, Democracy and Free Markets: Is it a Package?' (1999) *ASIL Proceedings* 121–3.
Opsahl, T, 'Articles 29 and 30', in Eide A, *et al* (eds) *The Universal Declaration of Human Rights – A Commentary* (Oslo: Scandinavian University Press, 1992).
Rosas, A, 'Article 21', in Eide A, *et al* (eds), *The Universal Declaration of Human Rights – A Commentary* (Oslo: Scandinavian University Press, 1992).
Roth, B, *Governmental Illegitimacy in International Law* (Oxford: Oxford University Press, 1999).
Sen, A, *Development as Freedom* (Oxford: Oxford University Press, 1999).
Scheinin, M, 'Article 20', in Alfredsson, G and Eide, A, *The Universal Declaration of Human Rights: A Common Standard of Achievement* (The Hague/London: Kluwer, 1999).
——, 'The Right to Self-determination under the Covenant on Civil and Political Rights', in Aikio, P and Scheinin, M (eds), *Operationalizing the Right of Indigenous Peoples to Self-Determination* (Turku/Abo: Institute for Human Rights, Abo Akademi University, 2000).
Simpson, G, *Great Powers and Outlaw States: Unequal Sovereigns in the International Law Order* (Cambridge: Cambridge University Press, 2004).
Stein, E, 'International integration and democracy: no love at first sight' (2001) 95 *American Journal of International Law* 493.
Tawney, R H, *Equality* (London: Allen & Unwin Publishers, 1964).

4 Human rights dimensions of contemporary environmental protection

Engobo Emeseh

4.1 Introduction

Perhaps understandable for the times, the environment is not specifically mentioned under the United Nations Declaration of Human Rights (UDHR) 1948.[1] International attention regarding the need for proper management and protection of the environment did not gain momentum until the 1960s, only crystallising itself at the United Nations Conference on the Human Environment (UNCHE) held at Stockholm in 1972. Since that Conference, however, and in particular, Principle 1 of the Stockholm Declaration[2] which specifically recognised the right to a healthy environment for the first time, human rights approaches have permeated various aspects of the discourse on the environment. Interestingly, despite its recent origins, the link between the environment and human rights has ultimately been traced back to the UDHR and the subsequent International Covenant on Political and Civil Rights (ICPCR)[3] and the International Covenant on Economic, Social and Cultural Rights (ICESCR),[4] both of which opened for signature on 16 December 1966.

This chapter maps these developments, focusing in particular on the three main issues which have dominated the discourse. These are the right to a healthy environment,[5] environmental justice issues dealing with equitable distribution of the causes and impacts of pollution at national and international levels, and the liability of non-state entities such as multinational corporations for human rights abuses related to the environment. These discussions demonstrate the huge steps that have been made in appropriating rights-based approaches to environmental protection. Nevertheless, this chapter questions whether the current focus of environment and human rights discourse on the implications of environmental pollution and degradation on enjoyment of traditional or first generation human rights, presents a full picture of the human rights dimensions of contemporary environmental protection. While environmental pollution has implications for the enjoyment of human rights, do environmental protection laws not also have the potential of encroaching on and even eroding aspects of first generation rights protected under the UDHR? To the extent that this is the case, what, if any, are the implications of the current threat of climate change on further erosion of human rights under the UDHR?

The first part of this chapter explores developments on the recognition of a separate right to a healthy environment. Although acknowledgement is made of the ongoing debate about the existence of this right in international law, the focus is on the progress made so far and their link to the UDHR. The next part of this chapter discusses environmental justice and the liability of non-state actors (multinational corporations) for environmental rights abuses. This is followed by an exploration of the implications of environmental protection on human rights, and finally, the conclusion.

4.2 The right to a healthy environment

It is far from settled amongst academic writers whether, theoretically, there is a separate recognisable right to healthy environment in international law and the nature and scope of this right. Even the utility and desirability of such a right is not agreed. Very broadly, the argument hinges on whether environmental concerns fit traditional frameworks for rights protection; the implications of using human rights approaches to address what some consider essentially social problems, thereby diluting and devaluing the existing human rights framework; and whether there is a binding international law instrument evidencing such a right.[6] In spite of this, human rights approaches to environmental issues have flourished both in legal instruments and the jurisprudence of various courts. Although, the majority of legal instruments on the subject are soft law, there are some binding regional instruments, provisions in national constitutions and decisions of both national and regional courts which either expressly recognise the right to a healthy environment or utilise a rights-based approach for purposes of environmental protection. Clearly, regardless of a consensus, human rights have been appropriated through various mechanisms to address environmental challenges and concerns.[7]

As noted earlier, Principle 1 of the Stockholm Declaration made the first express link between human rights and the environment when it declared that, 'man has a fundamental right to freedom, equality and adequate conditions of life, in an environment of a quality that permits a life of dignity and well-being'. Principle 4 further announces the responsibility to protect and improve the environment for present and future generations. This introduces the added dimension of intergenerational equity and the idea that human rights inheres not only on present, but also in unborn generations. In 1986, the Experts Group of the World Commission on Environment and Development suggested the recognition of this right. Principle 1 of the draft principles states that, 'all human beings have the fundamental right to an environment adequate for their health and well-being'. Similarly, the Right to Development provides for equality of access to basic resources and food,[8] while the Hague Declaration recognises the right of people to 'live in dignity in a viable global environment'.[9] Further, in 1990, the UN General Assembly adopted by consensus a resolution recognising that 'all individuals are entitled to live in an environment adequate for their health and well-being'.[10] This bold approach adopted by the Stockholm Declaration and these subsequent instruments were, however, somewhat reined back in the Rio Conference, with Principle 1 of the Rio Declaration merely providing that 'human beings are the centre of concerns for sustainable development. They are entitled to a healthy and productive life in harmony with nature'.[11]

Despite this, more recent activities by international, regional and domestic bodies demonstrate that the right to a clean and healthy environment, whether as an independent substantive right or through the interpretation and application of other human rights or environmental instruments, is emerging as an important component of international law.[12] Actions and statements from international bodies in the form of international court decisions, treaties, resolutions and reports from commissions, committees, secretariats, specialised agencies and similar entities continue to shape this emerging right. For instance, the Report on Human Rights and the Environment of the Human Rights Sub-commission on the Prevention of Discrimination and Protection of Minorities (Ktsentini Report) concluded that 'all persons have the right to a secure, healthy and ecologically sound environment'.[13] The Draft Declaration of Principles on Human Rights and the Environment (which were incorporated into the sub-commission's final report) sets out the content of the right to a secure, healthy and ecologically sound environment.[14] It also sets out substantive and procedural environmental rights and the corresponding duties of individuals, states, international organisations and trans-national corporations to respect this right.[15] Other international instruments linking the enjoyment of human rights and environmental protection include the UN Declaration of the Rights of Indigenous Peoples,[16] which recognises the distinctive and profound relationship which indigenous peoples have with their land and provides for 'prevention from and redress for dispossession of their lands, territories or resources'.[17] Recent work by other UN organs and agencies, such as the United Nations Economic and Social Council (ECOSOC),[18] UN Human Rights Council (Formerly UN Commission on Human Rights (UNCHR)),[19] UN Environment Programme (UNEP),[20] among others,[21] establish the link between environmental protection and human rights and recognise directly or indirectly the right to a clean and healthy environment, urging Member States to strengthen the mechanisms for actualising this right.

Arguably, the above being soft law instruments lack the binding legal force evidencing a recognisable right to a healthy environment. However, such soft law may harden through state practice.[22] There is already some evidence of general acceptability by states. Two regional human rights instruments – Article 24 of the African Charter on Human and Peoples' Rights[23] and Article 11 of the Additional Protocol to the American Convention on Human Rights in the Area of Economic, Social and Cultural Rights (Protocol of San Salvador)[24] both recognise the right to a healthy environment. Also, a 2007 report by Earth Justice showed 118 countries with constitutional provisions on the right to an environment of a particular quality.[25] Although the US Constitution has no express provisions on environmental rights, some state constitutions such as Article III of the Constitution of Montana provide for such a right.[26] Principle 10 of the Rio Declaration, which articulates the procedural aspect of this right, laying down the framework for public participation in environmental decision-making is now enshrined in the binding Aarhus Convention[27] implemented across various nations. International bodies such as the World Bank in its 2006 World Development Report also recognised the importance of procedural rights under the Aarhus Convention, in helping to address the environmental effect of projects funded by the Bank and the impact they have on the rights of the local communities.[28]

Decisions from regional human rights institutions,[29] national courts in South America,[30] Asia,[31] and Africa,[32] as well as in the US[33] lend further credence to the increasing general acceptability of the emerging environmental rights. Courts have recognised the existence of this right even where there are no express provisions in the Constitutions[34] or such constitutional provisions are not self-executing,[35] through reinterpreting of first generation rights such as the right to life. Although the right to a healthy environment is not specifically recognised under the European Convention on Human Rights, existing rights have been used by the courts to address environmental concerns.[36]

4.3 Environmental justice

The environmental justice movement had its origins in the US after the civil rights movements, and is concerned about the equitable distribution of environmental burdens.[37] The US Environmental Protection Agency defines environmental justice as the 'fair treatment and meaningful involvement of all people regardless of race, colour, national origin, or income with respect to the development, implementation, and enforcement of environmental laws, regulations and policies … where everyone enjoys the same degree of protection from environmental and health hazards and equal access to the decision-making process to have a healthy environment in which to live, learn and work'.[38] The Environmental Justice movement follows from recognition of the right of everyone to a healthy environment, juxtaposed against the unequal skewing of environmental hazards and impacts against the poorer and the weaker sections (or groups) in society at both international and national levels. Although both the rich and poor, from developed or developing countries alike are or will be affected by the collapse of our ecosystems, certain groups – minorities and residents of economically disadvantaged areas and developing countries – bear an unequal burden in environmental impacts and yet receive the least benefits from the processes that give rise to these impacts. It is argued that this inequality arises from the institutionalisation and commodification of land, water and air and the unresponsive government policies and regulations which may adversely affect the less powerful and less privileged members of the society who do not have the resources to influence decision making processes or redress any injuries suffered as a result.[39]

According to one writer, 'human environmental rights abuse occurs because it is socially, culturally, and legally acceptable to protect the health of some people while knowingly placing other humans at risk'.[40] This is evident from the World

Bank's infamous memo on toxic industries,[41] the dumping of hazardous wastes,[42] the location of polluting industries in minority and economically disadvantaged neighbourhoods,[43] or in developing countries. This is by no means a recent development. In the old case of *Sturges v Bridgman*, Lord Justice Thesiger famously held that 'what would be a nuisance in Belgrave Square would not necessarily be so in Bermondsey'.[44] Instances abound of the siting of 'dirty' industries in places populated or inhabited by minorities and the less privileged such as the disproportionate location of petrochemical products manufacturing facilities in the notorious 'Cancer Alley' in Louisiana, uranium mining in New Mexico which contaminated the Navajo water supply with uranium, the exposure of illegal Latinos farm workers to pesticides who could not protest against regular exposure to these chemicals, and the continuing environmental pollution of the Niger Delta areas of Nigeria by multinational oil companies operating in that country in ways inconceivable in the developed countries in which they operate. Even within Nigeria, the people of the Niger Delta are one of the minority ethnic groups with very little political influence and power.[45] In the UK, a study by Friends of the Earth found that factories located in the most deprived 20% of local authority wards accounted for 82% of carcinogenic chemicals emitted to the air from large factories in England in 1999.[46]

Climate change further demonstrates aptly the unequal burdens borne by the rich and poor both within and between nations with respect to environmental concerns. Although the poorer developing countries have contributed the least to climate change occurring, they are more likely to suffer from the impacts of climate change and least able to put in place adaptation strategies to mitigate these impacts.[47] Research further suggests that levels of vulnerability to climate change even within countries are significantly influenced by pre-existing social, political and economic inequities[48] and poorer sections are most likely to be impacted by strategies to combat climate change.[49]

A rights-based approach predicated on redistributive justice and equity has therefore been a fundamental feature of measures adopted to address the current imbalance either directly through a human rights framework or in environmental laws. According to David Miliband who at the time was the UK Secretary of State for the Environment, 'socially, climate change raises profound questions of justice and equity: between generations, between the developing and developed worlds; between rich and poor within each country. The challenge is to find an equitable distribution of responsibilities and rights'.[50] This informs the common but differentiated responsibilities principle which underlies climate change regulation under the UN Framework Convention on Climate Change[51] and the Kyoto Protocol.[52] It has been suggested that the inclusion of the right to a healthy environment in the post apartheid South African Constitution stems in part from a recognition of the unfair and unequal environmental and health burdens borne by thousands of black South Africans.[53] Procedural rights, including participation in decision making processes and access to information as enshrined in the Aarhus Convention are also important tools for addressing environmental justice concerns.

4.4 Actions of non-state actors – multinational corporations

The responsibility of multinational corporations (MNCs) for human rights abuses is another area where the human rights approach to address environmental concerns is evolving. Traditionally, the human rights system is aimed at nation states and was designed to protect individuals from the excesses of the state and its organs.[54] Also, under international law, it is states which have the obligation to regulate activities within their jurisdiction and to protect their citizens against human rights abuses committed by non-state actors. States are primarily responsible where they participate directly or indirectly, or tacitly support or condone any acts of non-state entities which give rise to abuse of the human rights of their citizens; or if they fail to act with due diligence to prevent such abuse or provide adequate remedies where it occurs.[55] This is the reason for instance that the Maastricht Guidelines on Violations of Economic, Social and Cultural Rights, adopted in 1997 stated that:

> The obligation to protect includes the States responsibility to ensure that private entities or individuals, including trans-national corporations over which they exercise jurisdiction, do not deprive individuals of their economic, social and cultural rights.[56]

In the same vein the Human Rights Committee stressed the positive obligations of States Parties that covenant rights will only be fully discharged if individuals are protected not just against violations of its agents, but also against acts committed by private persons or entities which may impair the enjoyment of their rights.[57] In *SERAC v Nigeria*, the African Human Rights Commission was of the opinion that:

> Governments have a duty to protect their citizens, not only through appropriate legislation but also by protecting them from damaging acts that may be perpetrated by private parties. This duty calls for positive action on the part of governments in fulfilling their obligations under human rights instruments.[58]

However, the rigid dichotomy in the law's treatment of state and non-state actors, especially MNCs, is increasingly being blunted in today's globalised world. The reasons for this are not far-fetched. MNCs are the main drivers of the global economy, with the capacity to exert significant influence over the countries in which they operate, and their activities have serious impacts on the peoples and the environments.[59] This is particularly so in developing countries with lower GDPs and weaker legislative and enforcement regimes.[60] There is a huge body of evidence of the serious environmental, social, health and economic impacts that MNC operations in various industries have had in developing countries.[61] Usually, protests against such actions by the locals have been met with repression and intimidation by their own government, sometimes with tacit support of the MNCs.[62]

Since the 1970s, there have been developments at the international level seeking to impose obligations directly on MNCs and to hold them accountable for the impacts of their operations. Starting with the International Labour Organization's (ILO) 1977 Tripartite Declaration of Principles Concerning Multinational Enterprises and Social Policy,[63] various United Nations institutions[64] and the Organisation for Economic Cooperation and Development (OECD) have also sponsored and developed various instruments to curtail MNC excesses.[65] The human rights approach is a common denominator in all of these, as exemplified in the UN Norms on the Responsibilities of Transnational Corporations and Other Business Enterprises with Regard to Human Rights for Business 2003.[66] Corporations themselves appear to have bought into this trend with various voluntary codes espousing a commitment to ethical behaviour including respect for human rights. Still, the law on MNCs' responsibility for human rights violations is far from settled,[67] and a common criticism of these developments has been their non-binding and voluntary nature. In 2005, following recommendation from the United Nations High Commissioner for Human Rights,[68] the then Secretary General of the UN appointed a Special Representative on business and human rights with a mandate amongst others to 'identify and clarify standards of ... corporations and other business enterprises with regard to human rights'.[69] According to the Special Representative in his 2006 report, '[A]ll existing instruments specifically aimed at holding corporations to international human rights standards ... are of a voluntary nature. Relevant instruments that do have international legal force, including some ILO labour standards, the Convention on the Elimination of All Forms of Discrimination Against Women (CEDAW), the OECD and the UN anti-bribery Conventions, impose obligations on states, not companies, including the obligation that states prevent private actors from violating human rights'.[70] Nevertheless, the prominence that this issue has had at such high levels and the various initiatives by the UN in recent times underlies the centrality of human rights discourse with regards to MNCs.

Another mechanism by which human rights law is being utilised to curtail MNCs' excesses is through transnational reach of domestic laws, in particular the US Alien Torts Claim Act (ATCA) 1789. In *Doe v Unocal*, a landmark decision was delivered 'recognising that corporations that aid and abet egregious human rights abuses can be held accountable' and that 'U.S. Corporations cannot violate international human rights with impunity'.[71] In June 2009, following over 13 years of litigation, the *Wiwa v Shell*[72] case filed in the federal district court in New York, over human right abuses by Shell in Ogoni in the Niger Delta, was settled by the company for $15.5 million.[73] While this does not develop the jurisprudence in this subject matter, at an existential level, it provides some practical relief to the plaintiffs. However, as once again demonstrated in the recent decision in *Bowoto v Chevron Texaco*,[74] there are very serious limitations and difficulties inherent in actions under the ATCA.[75] Another possible area in the future, albeit quite remote at the present time, is that the work of the International Criminal Court set up under the Rome Statute in 1998 with universal jurisdiction for serious human rights violations such as crimes against humanity and genocide, would provide a window of opportunity to prosecute senior employees of corporations implicated for serious human rights violations which may be equated to crimes against humanity and genocide.[76]

4.5 Human rights approaches to environmental protection and the UDHR

Although, environmental rights are not specifically recognised under the UDHR, yet the origins and rationale of each of the main strands of the human rights discourse on environment above has been linked to this document. This is because at the root of the emergence of human rights approach to environmental issues is the recognition that a certain quality of environment is essential for the realisation and enjoyment of a number of other substantive human rights, and that a human rights-based approach to environmental protection, both substantive and procedural can provide an effective framework for addressing these issues.[77] This sentiment is well captured in the *Gabcíkovo-Nagymaros Project* case, where Judge Weeramantry of the International Court of Justice emphasised that the protection of the environment is a vital part of contemporary human rights doctrine, as it is a *sine qua non* to the enjoyment of other human rights such as the right to health and the right to life itself. He further stated that it is dawning upon the judicial conscience of mankind that damage to the environment anywhere can impair and undermine all human rights spoken of in the UDHR and other human rights instruments.[78] Although Judge Weeramantry did not proclaim the recognition or enforceability of a separate and express right to a healthy environment, he emphasised its importance particularly with reference to other recognised human rights.

Elements of this right could be inferred from the provisions of the UDHR itself as well as the subsequent Covenants (ICCPR and the ICESCR).[79] The link between an environment of a certain quality and achievement of fundamental human rights was clearly made in Article 12(2)(b) of the ICESCR 1966 which recognises 'improvement in all aspects of environmental and industrial hygiene' as a condition for achievement of the right to health.[80] This is ultimately traceable to core provisions of the UDHR such as the right to life which cannot be realised without a healthy environment. Similarly, none of the rights under Article 25 of the UDHR[81] are realisable without an environment of a certain quality. As stated by the African Commission, 'the right to life is the fulcrum of all other rights. It is the fountain through which other rights flow ... '.[82] Similar sentiments were expressed in *Surya Dhungel v Godavary Marble Industry*,[83] where the court stated that a clean and healthy environment is a part of the entirety of life and therefore, a polluted environment is a threat to life. According to the Supreme Court of Bangladesh:

> the right to life ... encompasses within its ambit, the protection and preservation of the environment, ecological balance free from pollution of air and water and sanitation without which life can hardly be enjoyed. Any act or omission contrary thereto will be violative of the said right to life.[84]

Thus ecological abuse or environmental degradation appear to be as serious (if not more serious in certain respects) than physical abuse such as violence, torture or inhuman and degrading treatment. Ecological abuse and environmental degradation takes a different turn when it is sustained and carried out with impunity or state-sponsored as it is usually coupled with indiscriminate exploitation of natural resources and oftentimes inequitable distribution of associated environmental hazards by MNCs and/or their powerful local collaborators.[85] Since human rights are also intended to protect people's means of livelihood and well-being, threat to the environment on which a peoples' means of livelihood depends entails violation of their most fundamental human rights.[86] Despoliation of land and river for farming and fishing communities or the pollution of fresh water courses will inevitably threaten life as there would be no food to eat or water to drink, directly impinging on their right to life, right to food[87] and right to water.[88] Indeed, the rights to life and to health are directly violated by environmental degradation, the right to equality before the law is affected by the disproportionate distribution of environmental burden-environmental discrimination, while the right to property is affected by environmental degradation and pollution.

The idea that the obligation to protect the human rights of its citizens may not be limited to states can arguably also be supported by the UDHR when it provides in its Preamble that:

> ... every individual and every organ of society, keeping this Declaration constantly in mind, shall strive by teaching and education to promote respect for these rights and freedoms and by progressive measures, national and international, to secure their universal and effective recognition and observance. ... [89]

The obligation imposed on 'every individual and every organ of society' extends to 'individuals' including corporations and to all categories of rights, whether civil, political or economic, social and cultural rights.[90] According to Henkin:

> Every individual includes juridical persons. Every individual and every organ of society excludes no one, no company, no market, no cyberspace. The Universal Declaration applies to them all.[91]

In the same vein, when the UDHR recognises that, 'Everyone is entitled to a social and international order in which the rights and freedoms set forth in this Declaration can be fully realised', arguably, this 'order' includes the environmental concerns of this day and age.[92]

4.6 Potential implications of environmental regulation on human rights

The above discussions would appear to suggest that the only rights dimensions of current environmental challenges are the human rights implications of pollution and environmental degradation and the consequent need to appropriate rights-based approaches to address these concerns. This is, however, not the case as it is not only environmental pollution and degradation but also environmental laws and regulations geared towards proper use and management of the environment and its resources that may curtail, encroach upon or even erode existing rights under the UDHR.

One area where this has been most evident is the curtailment of property rights by placing regulatory burdens which limit full enjoyment of the benefits of their property.[93] Waste management and conservation laws for example typify how environmental protection may curtail one's use of property by placing restrictions on what one can bring onto or deposit on their land, or otherwise deal with their land in terms of ploughing, felling of trees, and repair of private fences. On the whole, this is perfectly reasonable and not problematic to most individuals. This is because, understandably, as with most human rights, the right to property is not absolute and could be derogated from, usually for the overriding public interest. This is clearly stated for instance in Article 1 of Protocol No 1 to the European Convention on Human Rights.[94] The question though is what limits, if any, are there on the constraints or burdens that environmental law may place on individual's enjoyment of their right to property, and indeed other human rights? Aren't there issues of equitable distribution of the burdens of environmental goals when they are borne by individuals or certain groups within society over and above those of others? In the US case of *Armstrong v United States*,[95] the Supreme Court stated that the constitutional prohibition on uncompensated takings was designed to bar government from forcing some people alone to bear public burdens for the public good. However, under certain environmental law regimes, there has been increasing encroachment on the rights of certain individuals and groups.

One area where such burdens can be seen is in the contaminated land regime in the UK where liability for clean-up of historically contaminated land may be borne by the current occupier even where he was not actually responsible for the pollution.[96]Another area is the nature conservation laws in the UK,[97] which place increasing burdens and restrictions to conserve either under the Sites of Special Scientific Interest (SSSI) regime or other countryside protection laws, on landowners for overriding public interest. Arguably, without adequate compensation, these individuals could be said to bear an undue environmental burden over and above that of the general population. Roger Pilon, in his testimony to the US Congress Committee on Environment and Public Works, on 27 June 1999 recognised the current dilemma when he said that, 'As federal, state and local regulations have increased in number and scope, property owners have frequently found themselves unable to use their property and unable to recover their losses … One result, unfortunately, is an understandable backlash against legitimate environmental protection'.[98]

Such use of conservation laws has a long history with several examples in developing countries both during colonial times and current governments, where entire groups have been displaced from their lands to make way for games reserves, parks and other forms of conservation, usually without any compensation.[99] This raises even further issues. As Crispin once wrote, albeit in another context, 'sustainability and conservation should complement each other. In reality, they represent convoys of ideas which sometimes sail together but can all too easily diverge'.[100] Conservation measures in developing countries can have a direct impact on production and consumption patterns, thereby jeopardising the rights to subsistence, if it is not effectively built into the socio-cultural and economic patterns. The human rights aspect of such practices was recently recognised in a landmark decision by the African Commission on Human and Peoples' Rights in May 2009 where it decided in favour of an indigenous group in Kenya who were evicted from their ancestral homes in the 1970s to make way for game reserves.[101]

Exploring the human rights dimensions of environmental regulation is particularly pertinent under the current threat of climate change, which is increasingly being presented as a security issue and appears to be taking on 'emergency' status. For instance, in the words of the UN Deputy High Commissioner for Human Rights, '[G]lobal warming and extreme weather conditions may have calamitous consequences for the human rights of millions of people … [countries] have an obligation to prevent and address some of the direst consequences'.[102] It is not so much that such predictions may be incorrect, but the reality that in times of emergency, existing human rights are sacrificed.

Recent history with the war on terror and the practices of leading democratic countries such as the UK and US[103] comes readily to mind. It is therefore not farfetched that environmental laws may become even more draconian as the threat of climate change appears more apparent. With the current mild encroachment of laws geared towards addressing climate change in local council waste disposal laws[104] and discussions about carbon footprints,[105] it is not too early for conversations about the kind of environmental framework that is acceptable and compatible with existing rights under the UDHR.

4.7 Conclusion

In a very short space of time, very significant progress has been made in developing a human rights approach to addressing the challenge of environmental pollution and degradation. The centrality of environment to enjoyment of existing rights has helped drive this process. Environmental degradation creates or heightens poverty when exhaustible natural resources are depleted, thereby raising humanitarian issues, such as the case of environmental refugees. In addition, resource constraints related to environmental degradation, like lack of water, food shortages, and disruption of access to means of livelihood may lead to intercommunity tensions, violence and even wars. Situations such as these bring to the fore the relationship between human rights and the environment and the need to address discriminatory standards, the need for social participation and protection of vulnerable groups in formulating environment policies or in undertaking economic activities which may have impact on the environment. At the same time, the human rights system would be strengthened by the incorporation of environmental concerns, which would expand the scope of human rights protection and provide concrete solutions in cases of abuses.[106] By so doing, victims of environmental degradation would have access to justice and other mechanisms provided by human rights law.

Despite this, battle rages on in the theatre of theoretical and academic discourse about the legitimacy or utility of such an approach. The main attention so far has been overcoming doctrinal or theoretical constraints towards mobilising human right approaches in the protection of the environment. Far less attention has been paid to the possible encroachment of environmental regulations on existing individual human rights. However, this is a very real concern, especially in light of global focus on the impacts of climate change. Eroding some of our existing rights may perhaps be the only solution to reversing the possibly cataclysmic impacts of climate change, and therefore acceptable to all. However, this ought to be done within the framework of informed debate and consensus.

Notes

1 Universal Declaration of Human Rights, UNGA Res 217A (12 December 1948), UN Doc A/810.

2 UN Conference on the Human Environment, Stockholm, Sweden (5–16 June 1972), Declaration of the United Nations Conference on the Human Environment, UN Doc A/CONF.48/14 (hereinafter Stockholm Declaration).

3 International Covenant on Civil and Political Rights, UNGA Res 2200A (XXI) (16 December 1966), UN Doc A/6316 999 UNTS 171.

4 International Covenant on Economic, Social and Cultural Rights, UNGA Res 2200A (XXI) (16 December 1966), UN Doc A/6316 993 UNTS 3.

5 The right to a healthy environment is used generically to represent the various terms used in legal instruments and the literature to refer to an environment of a certain quality.

6 See for instance, P Alston, 'Conjuring Up New Human Rights: A Proposal for Quality Control' (1984) 78 *American Journal of International Law* 607; P M Pevato, 'A Right to Environment in International Law: Current Status and Future Outlook' (1999) 8(3) *Review of European Community and International Environmental Law* 309–21; J G Merrills, 'Environmental Protection and Human Rights: Conceptual Aspects', in Alan E Boyle and Michael R Anderson (eds), *Human Rights Approaches to Environmental Protection* (Oxford: Oxford University Press, 1996), pp 25–42; C D Stone, 'Should Trees have Standing? Towards Legal Rights for Natural Objects' (1972) 45 *Southern Carolina Law Review* 450–501; P E Taylor, 'From Environmental to Ecological Human Right: A New Dynamic in International Law?' (1990) 10 *Georgia International Environmental Law Review* 309–97; J Hancock, *Power Ethics and the Law* (Aldershot: Ashgate, 2003).

7 See generally, D Shelton, 'Human Rights and Environment Issues in Multilateral Treaties Adopted between 1991 and 2001', Joint UNEP-OHCHR Expert Seminar on Human Rights and the Environment (14–16 January 2002) Geneva, Background Paper No 1, <www2.ohchr.org/english/issues/environment/environ/bp1.htm> (accessed 15 February 2010).

8 Declaration of the Right to Development, UNGA Res 41/128, 186 (4 December 1986), UN Doc A/41/53.

9 Hague Declaration on the Environment (11 March 1989) reprinted in 20 *ILM* 1308, reprinted in 'Selected International Legal Materials for Global Warming' (1990) 5 *American University Journal of International Law and Policy* 513.

10 UNGA Res 45/94 (14 December 1990), UN Doc A/45/749.

11 UN Conference on Environment and Development, Rio de Janeiro, Brazil (3–14 June 1992), UN Doc A/CONF.151/26 (12 August 1992).

12 See EarthJustice, *Environmental Rights Report 2007: Human Rights and the Environment*, <www.earthjustice.org/library/references/2007-environmental-rights-report.pdf> (accessed 20 January 2010). International legal norms typically arise from international conventions, international custom, or as general principles of law recognised by civilised nations. See the Statute of the International Court of Justice (ICJ Statute) (26 June 1945), 59 Stat 1055, TS No 993, 3 Bevans 1179, art 38(1).

13 The Draft Declaration of Principles on Human Rights and the Environment (Ksentini Report), UN Doc 3/CN.4/Sub.2/1994/9, reproduced in (1994) 3 *Review of European Community and International Environmental Law* 79–80, Annex I, Principle 2.

14 Draft Declaration of Principles on Human Rights and the Environment, UN Doc 3/CN.4/Sub.2/1994/9, reproduced in (1994) 3 *RECEIL* 259–61.

15 A F Aguilar, and A F Popovic, 'Lawmaking in the United Nations: The UN Study on Human Rights and the Environment' (1994) 3 *Review of European Community and International Environmental Law* 197–205, 201.

16 Adopted by the UN General Assembly on 13 September 2007, UN Doc A/61/L.67 and Add.1.

17 UN Economic and Social Council (ECOSOC), Commission on Human Rights, Sub-Commission on Prevention of Discrimination and Protection of Minorities, *Draft Declaration on the Rights of Indigenous Peoples* (20 April 1994), UN Doc E/CN.4/Sub.2/1994/2/Add.1.

18 United Nations Economic and Social Council (ECOSOC), UN Communication on Sustainable Development, Report on the Thirteenth Session (22 April 2005), UN Doc E/CN.17/2005/12, <www.un.org/esa/sustdev/documents/docs_csd13.htm> (accessed 20 January 2010).

19 Human Rights Council, Resolutions Adopted at the 61st Session, <http://ap.ohchr.org/documents/sdpage_e.aspx> (accessed 24 January 2008).

20 United Nations Environment Programme, *President's Summary of twenty-third session of Governing Council/Global Ministerial Environmental Forum* (24 February 2005), UN Doc UNEP/GC.23/L.3/Rev.1.

21 Others include the Global Environment Facility, which is the financial mechanism for implementing international conventions on biodiversity, climate change and persistent organic pollutants as well as for Convention to Combat Desertification (see Global Environment Facility, *2005 Annual Report, Fertile Ground: Seeding National Actions for the Global Environment*, <www.gefweb.org/Outreach/outreach-publications/documents/2005_Annual_Report.pdf.> (accessed 27 April 2007); World Health Organization (WHO), whose recent resolution in December 2005 acknowledged how environmental circumstances affect disease transmission, the intensity of natural disasters, drinking water supplies, fuel supply and human nutrition, among others (see WHO, 'Ecosystems and Human Health: Some findings from the Millennium Ecosystem Assessment', <www.millenniumassessment.org/en/index.aspx> (accessed 8 April 2007)); International Labour Organization (ILO), whose mission is to promote social justice, human rights and labour rights (see ILO, *About ILO*, <www.ilo.org/public/english/about/index.htm> (accessed 12 February 2010)).

22 Soft law can thus harden if generally adopted in practice by states and become norms of customary international law which are binding and legally enforceable. See M N Shaw, *International Law* (4th end, Cambridge: Cambridge University Press, 1997), p 69.

23 African Charter on Human and Peoples' Rights (Banjul Charter) (27 June 1981), 21 *ILM* 58.

24 Organization of American States, Additional Protocol to the American Convention on Human Rights in the Area of Economic, Social and Cultural Rights (17 November 1988), OAS Treaty Series No 69, 28 *ILM* 161.

25 Op. cit., Earthjustice, fn 12.

26 It provides, *inter alia*, 'All persons are born free and have certain inalienable rights. They include the right to a clean and healthful environment … '. Other states with similar provisions include Hawaii, Massachusetts and Rhodes Island. See further B Adams, A Garner, B Gunson, A Hansen and M Holje, 'Environmental and Natural Resources Provisions in State Constitutions' (2002) 22 *Journal of Land Resources & Environmental Law* 73 which shows that 46 states of the US have constitutional provisions referring to national resources and environment.

27 Convention on Access to Information, Public Participation in Decision-making and Access to Justice in Environmental Matters (Aarhus: UNECE, 1998), 38 *ILM* 517 (1999).

28 World Bank, *World Development Report 2006: Equity and Development* (Washington DC: World Bank, September 2006), <http://siteresources.worldbank.org/INTWDR2007/Resources/1489782-1158107976655/overview.pdf> (accessed 15 February 2010).

29 Such as the African Human Rights Commission in *Social and Economic Rights Action Centre and the Centre for Economic and Social Rights & the Centre for Economic and Social Rights v Nigeria*, Communication 155/96 (*SERAC v Nigeria*), <www.serac.org/African%20Commn%20Communication%20and%20Decision.doc> (accessed 15 February 2010).

30 See *Kattan v National Govt* (1983); *Irazu Margarita v Copetro SA* (1993) – Argentina; *Fundepublico v Mayor of Bulgalagrande* – Columbia; *Antonio Mauricio Monroy Cespeded* I (1993) – Columbia; *Carlos Roberto Garcia Chacon* (1993) – (Costa Rica); *Consesiones otorgadas por el Ministerio de Energia y minas a Empress Petroleras* (1999) – Guatemala. These cases are discussed in A Fabra and E Arnal, *Review of Jurisprudence on Human Rights and the Environment in Latin America* (2002), Joint UNEP-OHCHR Expert Seminar on Human Rights and the Environment, 14–16 January 2002, Geneva, Background Paper No 6, <www2.ohchr.org/english/issues/environment/environ/bp6.htm> (accessed 15 February 2010).

31 *Oposa v Secretary of State for the Environment* (33 *ILM* 173 (1994)) – Philippines; *Farooque v Bangladesh*; *Subash Kumar v State of Bihar* (AIR 1991 SC 420/ 1991, (1) SCC 598) – India; *M C Mehta v Union of India* ([1998] 9 SCC 589); *Shehla Zia v WAPDA* (PLD 1994 SC 693) – Pakistan.

32 *Gbemre & ors v Shell Petroleum Development Company Ltd & ors* – Nigeria, Suit FHC/CS/B/153/2005, Federal High Court, Benin City, judgment of 14 November 2005 (unreported), <www.climatelaw.org/media/gas.flaring.suit.nov_2005> (accessed 8 August 2009).

33 *Save Ourselves Inc v Louisiana Environmental Control Commission and the Louisiana Department of Natural Resources* 452 So 2d 1153 (La 1984); *Montana Environmental Information Center v Department of Environmental Quality* 988 P 2d 1236 (Mont 1999).

34 An example is the case of Bangladesh.

35 As in Nigeria where the right to a healthy environment provision is contained in the fundamental objectives of state policy section and not under fundamental human rights. See Federal Constitution of Nigeria 1999, section 20.

36 For instance, the Right to life (Art 2), respect for one's private life (Art 8), peaceful enjoyment of one's possessions (First Protocol to Convention) have all been used to protect environment concerns. See further the cases of *Powell & Rayner v UK* 172 Eur Ct HR (1990); *Lopez Ostra v Spain* [1995] 20 EHRR 277; *Guerra (and Others) v Italy* [1998] 26 EHRR 357; *Hatton v UK* [2002] 34 EHRR 1; *Giacomelli v Italy* [2006] (Application no 59909/00) (Strasbourg judgment, 2 November 2006).

37 See C Stephens, S Bullock and A Scott, 'Environmental Justice: Rights and means to a healthy environment for all', ESRC/FOE Special Briefing No 7 (2001), <www.foe.co.uk/resource/reports/environmental_justice.pdf> (accessed 15 February 2010).

38 US EPA website, <www.epa.gov/environmentaljustice/> (accessed on 18 April 2010).

39 See generally, M Matsuoka, 'Building Healthy Communities from the Ground Up: Environmental Justice in California' (September 2003), <www.cbecal.org/pdf/healthy-communities.pdf> (accessed 18 April 2010).

40 B R Johnson, 'Human Environmental Rights', in Barbara Rose Johnson (ed), *Who Pays the Price? The Socio-cultural Context of Environmental Crisis* (Washington DC: Island Press, 1994), p 101. Johnson contributed to the work of the Special Rapporteur on Human Rights and the Environment.

41 Internal memo titled 'Dirty Industries' from Larry Summers to the staff of the World Bank (dated 12 December 1991) in which he reportedly said: 'Just between you and me, shouldn't the World Bank be encouraging more migration of the dirty industries to the LDCs (Less Developed Countries)?', <www.globalpolicy.org/component/content/article/212/45462.html> (accessed 15 February 2010).

42 G Capdevila, 'Dumping of Toxic Waste is a Human Rights Issue' (IPS) (18 April 1998), <www.users.westnet.gr/-cgian/toxwaste.htm> (accessed 10 November 2004).

43 A Ali, 'A Conceptual Framework for Environmental Justice Based on Shared but Differentiated Responsibilities' (2001), p 14, <www.uea.ac.uk/env/cserge/publications/wp/edm/edm 01_02. pdf> (accessed 12 January 2010).

44 [1879] LR 11 Ch D 852.

45 See generally, E Emeseh, 'Limitations of Law in Promoting Synergy between Environment and Development Policies in Developing Countries: A Case Study of the Petroleum Industry in Nigeria' (2006) 24 *Journal of Energy & Natural Resources Law* 574–606, 582.

46 Friends of the Earth, *Pollution and Poverty – Breaking the Link* (London: Friends of the Earth, 2001).

47 This is aptly demonstrated in the impacts of climate change on small island states, and countries such as Bangladesh. See Alliance of Small Island States/The United Nations Foundation, Global Climate Change And Small Island Developing States: Financing Adaptation, Green Paper Draft of February 2008, <www.un.int/wcm/webdav/site/suriname/shared/documents/papers/CLIMATECHANGEAOSIS_GreenPaper_Feb52008_.pdf> (accessed 15 February 2010).

48 See K O'Brien and R Leichenko, 'Climate Change, Equity and Human Security', paper presented at Human Security and Climate Change, an International Workshop, Holmen Fjord Hotel, Asker, near Oslo (21–23 June 2005), <www.gechs.org/downloads/holmen/OBrien_Leichenko.pdf> (accessed 12 February 2010).

49 G Owen, 'Towards an Equitable Climate Change Policy for the UK: The Costs and Benefits for Low Income Households of UK Climate Change Policy' (2008), <www.eaga.com/downloads/pdf/3867%20eaga%20Equity%20&%20Climate%2036ppg%20PROOF.pdf> (accessed 15 February 2010).

50 D Miliband MP, 'Building an Environmental Union', speech delivered in Berlin (19 October 2006), <www.defra.gov.uk/corporate/ministers/speeches/david-miliband/dm061019.htm> (accessed 27 December 2006).

51 See Article 3(1) of the United Nations Framework Convention on Climate Change, opened for signature on 4 June 1992, 31 *ILM* 849 (1992).

52 See Article 5 of the Kyoto Protocol to the United Nations Framework Convention on Climate Change, <http://unfccc.int/kyoto_protocol/items/2830.php> (accessed 15 February 2010).

53 See D McDonald, *Environmental Justice in South Africa* (Cape Town: Ohio University Press, 2002).

54 J K Minkah-Premo, 'The Role of Judicial Enforcement of ECOSOC Rights in National Development: The Case of Ghana' (1999) 11 *African Society of International & Comparative Law, ASICL Proc* 71.

55 *Ibid.* See also, OECD, 'Due Diligence in the International Law of Liability', in OECD, *Legal Aspects of Transfrontier Pollution* (Paris: OECD, 1977), p 369. In the case of Velasquez Rodriguez where Manfredo Velasquez Rodriguez was kidnapped, forcibly disappeared and probably killed by the Honduran Army, the Inter-American Human Rights Court, stated that 'An illegal act which violates human rights and which is not directly imputable to a State can lead to international responsibility of the State, not

because of the act itself, but because of the lack of due diligence to prevent the violation or to respond to it as required by the State Convention'.

56 See para 18. A similar declaration was also made by the African Commission in *SERAC v Nigeria*, above, fn 29.

57 Quoted in 'Nigeria: Are Human Rights in the Pipeline?' (9 November 2004) *Amnesty International* 19.

58 See above, fn 29; see also, *Yanomami v Brazil* Resolution No 12/85, Case 7615, reported in *Annual Report of the Inter-American Commission on Human Rights* (Washington, DC: IACHR, 1985).

59 World Bank, *Striking a better balance: the World Bank Group and extractive industries. The Final Report of the Extractive Industries Review, Volume I (December 2003)* (Washington, DC: World Bank, 2003); H J Steiner, P Alston and R Goodman, *International Human Rights in Context: Law, Politics, Moral. Text and Materials* (3rd edn, Oxford: Oxford University Press, 2008), p 1385; D Szablowski, *Transnational Law And Local Struggles: Mining, Communities and the World Bank* (Oxford: Hart, 2007).

60 See for instance, Report of the Special Representative of the Secretary-General on the issue of human rights and transnational corporations and other business enterprises, *Corporations and human rights: a survey of the scope and patterns of alleged corporate-related human rights abuse* (23 May 2008), A/HRC/8/5/Add.2, p 10, which showed that while human rights abuses by MNCs occurred in all regions of the world, 68% of allegations comes from Africa, Asia and Latin America.

61 See generally, B Manby, *The Price of Oil: Corporate Responsibility and Human Rights Violations in Nigeria's Oil Producing Communities* (New York, NY: Human Rights Watch, 1998); E Emeseh, R Ako, P Okonmah and L O Obokoh, 'Corporations, CSR and Self Regulation: What Lessons from the Global Financial Crisis' (2010) *German Law Journal* 230–59.

62 M Lyons, 'A Case Study in Multinational Corporate Accountability: Ecuador's Indigenous Peoples Struggle for Redress' (2004) 32 *Denver Journal of International Law and Policy* 701–32; W Godnick, D Klein, C González-Posso, I Mendoza and S Meneses (2008) *Conflict, Economy, International Co-operation and Non-Renewable Natural Resources* (IfP/International Alert/INDEPAZ/PLASA/Socios Peru), <www.initiativeforpeacebuilding.eu/pdf/Conflict_Economy_International_Cooperation_and_Non_RenewableNatural_Resources.pdf> (accessed 11 January 2009); *SERAC v Nigeria*, above, fn 29.

63 International Labour Organization (ILO), Tripartite Declaration of Principles Concerning Multinational Enterprises and Social Policy, Geneva, International Labour Office, (2001), <www.ilo.org/public/english/employment/multi/download/english.pdf> (accessed 27 May 2005).

64 Such as the United Nations Commission on Transnational Corporations and its successor, United Nations Conference on Trade and Development.

65 For an overview of these developments, see op. cit., Emeseh *et al*, fn 61, pp 238–46.

66 The UN Norms on the Responsibilities of Transnational Corporations and Other Business Enterprises with Regard to Human Rights for business (26 August 2003), UN Doc E/CN.4/Sub.2/2003/12/Rev.2.

67 See generally, P Alston, *Non-state actors and human rights* (Oxford: Oxford University Press, 2005).

68 United Nations High Commissioner for Human Rights on the responsibilities of transnational corporations and related business enterprises with regard to human rights (15 February 2005), UN Doc E/CN.4/2005/91.

69 UN Commission on Human Rights, Resolution 2005/69, Human Rights and Transnational Corporations and Other Business Enterprises (20 April 2005), XVII, UN Doc E/CN.4/2005/L.10/Add.17.

70 Interim Report of the Special Representative of the Secretary-General on the Issue of Human Rights and Transnational Corporations and Other Business Enterprises (22 February 2006), UN Doc E/CN.4/2006/97, 15, para 61.

71 248 F 3d 915 (9th Cir 2001). For full court documents on this case and a general discussion, see <www.earthrights.org/legal/doe-v-unocal> (accessed 15 February 2010). See further, R L Herz, 'Unocal Can be Held Liable for Human Rights Crimes in Burma, Says Appeals Court', <www.earthrights.org/legal/unocal-can-be-held-liable-human-rights-crimes-burma-says-appeals-court> (accessed 15 February 2010).

72 Complaint, *Wiwa et al v Royal Dutch Petroleum et al* (SDNY) (No 96 Civ 8386), <http://ccrjustice.org/files/3.16.09%205th%20Amended%20Complaint.pdf> (accessed 15 February 2010).

73 Settlement Agreement Between Wiwa Plaintiffs and Energy Equity Resources Limited RE *Wiwa v Shell Settlement, Wiwa v Shell Petroleum Development Co*, No 04 Civ 2665 (SDNY) (7 June 2009), <http://wiwavshell.org/documents/Wiwa_v_Shell_SETTLEMENT_AGREEMENT.Signed.pdf> (accessed 15 February 2010).

74 *Bowoto v Chevron Texaco*, <www.earthrights.org/chevron/index.shtml> (accessed 15 February 2010); see Caroline Kaeb, 'Emerging Issues of Human Rights Responsibility in the Extractive and Manufacturing Industries: Patterns and Liability Risks' (2008) 6(2) *Northwestern Journal of International Human Rights* 335–6.

75 The length of time it takes to bring these actions, the expense and inconvenience of litigating in a foreign land, and the narrow ambiguity of the principles make these actions incredibly difficult to venture. *Wiwa v Royal Dutch Petroleum* for instance was settled without an admission of any form of liability by Shell.

76 International Council on Human Rights, 'Beyond Voluntarism: Human Rights and the Developing International Legal Obligations of Companies' (2002) *International Council on Human Rights Policy* 63, <www.ichrp.org/files/reports/7/107_report_en.pdf> (accessed November 2009).

77 Op. cit., Earthjustice, fn 12, p 6.

78 *Gabcí'kovo-Nagymaros Project case* (judgment of 25 September 1997), Individual opinion of Judge Weeramantry, [1997] *ICJ Reports* 91–2.

79 Op. cit., Taylor, fn 6, p 315; A Kiss and D Shelton, *International Environmental Law* (2nd edn, Ardsley, NY: Transnational Publishers, 2000), p 27; V Vukasovic, *Human Rights and Environmental Issues*, <www.unu.edu.unupress/unupbooks/uu06he/uu06he0i.htm> (accessed 1 May 2004).

80 Article 24 of the Convention on the Rights of the Child also expressly links environmental quality to the right to health. Convention on the Rights of the Child, UNGA Res 44/25 (20 November 1989), UN Doc A/RES/44/25.

81 'Everyone has the right to a standard of living adequate for the health and well-being of himself and of his family, including food, clothing, housing and medical care and necessary social services, and the right to security in the event of unemployment, sickness, disability, widowhood, old age or other lack of livelihood in circumstances beyond his control'.

82 African Commission in Communication 223/98-*Forum of Conscience v Sierra Leone* (2000), para 19.

83 (1995) Special Issue 2052 *Nepal Kanoon Patrika* (*Nepal Law Reports*) 169.

84 See similar cases such as *Awas Tingni Mayagna (Sumo) Indigenous Community v Nicaragua*, quoted in D Shelton, 'Human Rights and the Environment: Jurisprudence of Human Rights Bodies', Background Paper No 2, Joint UNEP-OHCHR Expert Seminar on Human Rights and the Environment (14–16 January 2002), Geneva; *Yanomami v Brazil*, Case 7615 (Brazil), INTER-AM CH R, *1984–1985 Annual Report*, p 24, OEA/Ser L/V/II.66, doc.10, rev.1 (1985).

85 F O Adeola, 'Environmental Injustice and Human Rights Abuse: The State, MNC and Repression of Minority Groups in the World' (2001) 8(1) *Human Ecology Review* 39–59.

86 Articles 3, 17 and 25 of the Universal Declaration of Human Rights are germane to this. In Article 3, everyone has the right to life, liberty, and security; Article 17 stipulates that everyone has the right to own property and no one shall be arbitrarily

deprived of his/her property, and in Article 25, everyone has the right to a standard of living adequate for the health and well-being of him/herself and his/her family, including food, clothing, housing, and medical care and necessary social services, and the right to security. A draft of the UN Declaration on Human Rights and the Environment stipulates that: (i) All persons have the right to a secure healthy, and ecologically sound environment; (ii) All persons are entitled to be free from discrimination regarding actions and decisions that affect the environment; (iii) All persons have the right to an environment adequate to meet equitably the needs of present generations without impairing the similar right of future generations; (iv) All persons have the right to freedom from pollution and environmental degradation that threaten life, health, livelihood, and well-being within, across, or outside national boundaries; (v) All persons have the right to information concerning the environment; and (vi) All persons have the right to participate in planning and decision-making activities that impact the environment. See *ibid.*

87 Article 25 of the UDHR; Article 11 of the ICESCR.

88 Articles 11 and 12 of the ICESCR.

89 Similar provisions can be found in other international instruments, including the United Nations Declaration on the Elimination of All Forms of Racial Discrimination, (adopted on 20 November 1963), UNGA Res 1904 (XVIII), Art 2; the Rio Declaration on the Environment and Development, Adopted by the UN Conference on Environment and Development, Rio de Janeiro (13 June 1992), UN Doc A/CONF 151/26 (Vol 1) (1992); the Copenhagen Declaration on Social Development and Programme of Action, Adopted by the World Summit for Social Development in Copenhagen (12 March 1995), UN Doc A /CONF 166/9 (1995). Paragraph 12 of this Declaration states that economic growth and market forces conducive to social development require the encouragement of 'national and transnational corporations to operate in a framework of respect for the environment … with proper consideration for the social and cultural impact of their activities … '.

90 It has been argued that, 'while companies may not be in the habit of referring to themselves as "organs of society", they are a fundamental part of society' (Amnesty International and Prince of Wales Business Leaders Forum 2000: 23), quoted in Danwood Mzikenge Chirwa, 'Obligations of Non-State Actors in Relation to Economic, Social and Cultural Rights under the South African Constitution' (2002) *Social-Economic Rights Project Community Law Centre, University of Western Cape,* <http://community-lawcentre.org.za> (accessed 22 November 2007).

91 Op. cit., ICHR, fn 76, p 58.

92 *Human Rights and the Environment,* Final report prepared by Mrs Fatma Zohra Ksentini, Special Rapporteur (6 July 1994), E/CN.4/Sub.2/1994/9, Section B, 34. (hereafter referred to as the Ksentini Report).

93 This right is enshrined in Article 17 of the UDHR, regional instruments, and national constitutions.

94 Protocol to the Convention for the Protection of Human Rights and Fundamental Freedoms as amended by Protocol No 11, Paris, 20.III.1952 (ETS No 155). See further, A Grgiae, Z Mataga, M Longar and A Vilfan, 'The right to property under the European Convention on Human Rights: A guide to the implementation of the European Convention on Human Rights and its protocols' (Strasbourg: Council of Europe, 2007), <http://echr.coe.int/NR/rdonlyres/97564258-437D-4FFD-A54D-2766DE255CCA/0/DG2ENHRHAND102007.pdf> (accessed 15 February 2010).

95 Cited by Jonathan H Adler, *Property Rights, Regulatory Takings and Environmental Protection,* (31 March 1996), <http://cei.org/gencon/025,01452.cfm> (accessed 18 April 2010).

96 Section 38F (2–4), Part IIA of the Environmental Protection Act 1990.

97 See for instance the Wildlife and Countryside Act 1981 – see especially section 28; and the Conservation (Natural Habitats, &c.) Regulations 1994 (SI 1994/2716).

98 See R Pilon, Senior Fellow and Director Centre for Constitutional Studies, Cato Institute, Washington DC, testimony (27 June 1995), <www.cato.org/testimony/ct-pe627.html> (accessed 15 February 2010); see also Louis Rose, 'Property Rights and Environmental Public Policy', *Florida Student Philosophy Blog* (3 March 2010), <http://unfspb.wordpress.com/2010/03/03/property-rights-and-environmental-public-policy/> (accessed 18 April 2010); C Rodgers, 'Property rights, land use and the rural environment: A case for reform, Land Use Policy' (2009) 26S S134–S14.

99 J C Murombedzi, 'Pre-Colonial and Colonial Conservation Practices in Southern Africa and their Legacy Today' (February 2003), <http://dss.ucsd.edu/~ccgibson/docs/Murombedzi%20-%20Pre-colonial%20and%20Colonial%20Origins.pdf> (accessed 15 February 2010); M Rangarajan and G Shahabuddin, 'Displacement and Relocation from Protected Areas: Towards a Biological and Historical Synthesis' (2006) 4(3) *Conservation and Society* 359–78.

100 T Crispin, 'Sustainability and Conservation: Prospects for Johannesburg, Society for Conservation Biology, Conference at the University of Kent at Canterbury (15 July 2002), <www.crispintickell.com/page20.html> (accessed 15 February 2010).

101 *Centre for Minority Rights Development (Kenya) and Minority Rights Group International on behalf of Endorois Welfare Council v Kenya*, 276/2003, African Commission on Human and Peoples' Rights (4 February 2010), <www.unhcr.org/refworld/docid/4b8275a12.html> (accessed 25 April 2010). The Commission ordered the government to restore their land and pay compensation. This decision was adopted by the African Union on 4 February 2010.

102 L MacInnis, 'Climate change threatens human rights of millions: UN' (2008) *Reuters* (19 February 2008), <www.reuters.com/article/idUSL1912377820080219> (accessed 15 February 2010).

103 For the leader of the free world, the war on terror has taken a heavy toll on its human rights credentials. With such allegations as torture, kidnappings, extra-ordinary renditions, detention without trial, all perhaps symbolised in the Guantanamo Bay detention centre, human rights have been sacrificed at the altar of security. Indeed, both the US (USA Patriotic Act of October 2001) and the UK (Terrorism Act 2000; the Anti-Terrorism, Crime and Security Act 2001; the Prevention of Terrorism Act 2005; the Terrorism Act 2006; and the Counter-Terrorism Act 2008) enacted laws broadening definitions of terrorism, enhancing policing powers, and restricting existing rights. See further J Fitzpatrick, 'Speaking Law to Power: The War against Terrorism and Human Rights' (2003) 14(2) *European Journal of International Law* 241–64; D Cassel, 'Washington's War Against Terrorism and Human Rights: The View from Abroad' (2006) 33(1) *Human Rights* 11–14, 22, <www.abanet.org/irr/hr/winter06/cassel.html> (accessed 15 February 2010).

104 Arguably on the right to privacy.

105 Possible encroachment on freedom of movement.

106 M R Anderson, 'Human Rights Approaches to Environmental Protection: An Overview', in A E Boyle and M R Anderson (eds), *Human Rights Approaches to Environmental Protection* (New York: Oxford University Press, 1996), pp 1–4, 21–3.

Bibliography

Adams, B, Garner, A, Gunson, B, Hansen, A and Holje, M, 'Environmental and Natural Resources Provisions in State Constitutions' (2002) 22 *Journal of Land Resources Environmental Injustice and Human Rights Abuse: The State, MNC and Repression of Minority Groups in the World' (2001) 8(1)* Human Ecology Review *39–59.*

Aguilar, A F and Popovic, A F, 'Lawmaking in the United Nations: The UN Study on Human Rights and the Environment' (1994) 3 *Review of European Community and International Environmental Law* 197–205.

Alston, P, 'Conjuring Up New Human Rights: A Proposal for Quality Control' (1984) 78 *American Journal of International Law* 607.

——, *Non-state actors and human rights* (Oxford: Oxford University Press, 2005).

Anderson, M R, 'Human Rights Approaches to Environmental Protection: An Overview', in Boyle, A.E and Anderson, M R (eds), *Human Rights Approaches to Environmental Protection* (New York, NY: Oxford University Press, 1996), pp 1–4, 21–23.

Cassel, D, 'Washington's War Against Terrorism and Human Rights: The View from Abroad' (2006) 33(1) *Human Rights* 11–14.

Emeseh, E, 'Limitations of Law in Promoting Synergy between Environment and Development Policies in Developing Countries: A Case Study of the Petroleum Industry in Nigeria' (2006) 24 *Journal of Energy 606*.

Emeseh, E, Ako, R, Okonmah, P and Obokoh, L O, 'Corporations, CSR and Self Regulation: What Lessons from the Global Financial Crisis' (2010) *German Law Journal* 230–59.

Fitzpatrick, J, 'Speaking Law to Power: The War against Terrorism and Human Rights' (2003) 14/2 *European Journal of International Law* 241–64.

Friends of the Earth, *Pollution and Poverty – Breaking the Link* (London: Friends of the Earth, 2001).

Hague Declaration on the Environment (1989) *American University Journal of International Law and Policy* 513.

Hancock, J, *Power Ethics and the Law* (Aldershot: Ashgate, 2003).

Johnson, B R, 'Human Environmental Rights', in Johnson, B R (ed), *Who Pays the Price? The Socio-cultural Context of Environmental Crisis* (Washington DC: Island Press, 1994), p 101.

Kaeb, C, 'Emerging Issues of Human Rights Responsibility in the Extractive and Manufacturing Industries: Patterns and Liability Risks' (2008) 6(2) *Northwestern Journal of International Human Rights* 335–3.

Kiss, A and Shelton, D, *International Environmental Law* (2nd edn, Ardsley, NY: Transnational Publishers, 2000), p 27.

Lyons, M, 'A Case Study in Multinational Corporate Accountability: Ecuador's Indigenous Peoples Struggle for Redress' (2004) 32 *Denver Journal of International Law and Policy* 701–32.

Manby, B, *The Price of Oil: Corporate Responsibility and Human Rights Violations in Nigeria's Oil Producing Communities* (New York, NY: Human Rights Watch, 1998).

McDonald, D, *Environmental Justice in South Africa* (Cape Town: Ohio University Press, 2002).

Merrills, J G, 'Environmental Protection and Human Rights: Conceptual Aspects', in Boyle, A E and Anderson, M R (eds), *Human Rights Approaches to Environmental Protection* (Oxford: Oxford University Press, 1996), pp 25–42.

Minkah-Premo, J K, 'The Role of Judicial Enforcement of ECOSOC Rights in National Development: The Case of Ghana' (1999) 11 *African Society of International & Comparative Law, ASICL Proc* 71.

OECD, 'Due Diligence in the International Law of Liability', in OECD, *Legal Aspects of Transfrontier Pollution* (Paris: OECD, 1977), p. 369.

Pevato, P M, 'A Right to Environment in International Law: Current Status and Future Outlook' (1999) 8(3) *Review of European Community and International Environmental Law* 309–21.

Rangarajan, M and Shahabuddin, G, 'Displacement and Relocation from Protected Areas: Towards a Biological and Historical Synthesis' (2006) 4(3) *Conservation and Society* 359–78.

Rodgers, C, 'Property rights, land use and the rural environment: A case for reform, Land Use Policy' (2009) 26S S134–S14.

Shaw, M N, *International Law* (4th edn, Cambridge: Cambridge University Press, 1997), p 69.

Steiner, H J, Alston, P and Goodman, R, *International Human Rights in Context: Law, Politics, Moral. Text and Materials* (3rd edn, Oxford: Oxford University Press, 2008).

Stone, C D, 'Should Trees have Standing? Towards Legal Rights for Natural Objects' (1972) 45 *Southern Carolina Law Review* 450–501.

Szablowski, D, *Transnational Law And Local Struggles: Mining, Communities and the World Bank* (Oxford: Hart, 2007).

Taylor, P E, 'From Environmental to Ecological Human Right: A New Dynamic in International Law?' (1990) 10 *Georgia International Environmental Law Review* 309–97.

World Bank, *Striking a better balance: the World Bank Group and extractive industries. The Final Report of the Extractive Industries Review, Volume I* (December 2003) (Washington DC: World Bank, 2003).

——, *World Development Report 2006: Equity and Development* (Washington DC: World Bank, September 2006).

Zohra Ksentini, F, *Human Rights and the Environment,* Final report prepared by Mrs. Fatma Zohra Ksentini, Special Rapporteur (6 July 1994), E/CN.4/Sub.2/1994/9, Section B, 34.

5 Offenders, deviants or patients? Human rights and the incarcerated offender

Gareth Norris

5.1 Introduction

The first part of the title of this chapter is borrowed from the work of Herschel Prins, who published his initial account of the problematic interface between mental health and the criminal justice system nearly three decades ago.[1] The question skilfully captures the complicated nature of mental health in general, and its somewhat more problematical relationship to the criminal justice system. It is now over two centuries since the first formal piece of legislation was established to deal with the 'criminally insane'; the Criminal Lunatics Act 1800 – alongside the opening of the secure Bethlam hospital in 1816 – was the beginning of the move to promote diversions from prison for those with mental health problems.[2] With a relatively long history it could be easily assumed that the knowledge and processes for dealing with such individuals would be well established, fair and humane. In reality, the complicated nature of the issues, resources, and even prejudice resulting from simple misunderstandings, frequently and consistently mean that these basic principles – many synonymous with human rights – are seldom realised in practice.

Somewhat erroneously, the issue that is most often at the forefront of concerns with regards to mental health and the criminal justice system centres on the matter of culpability and, in particular, the notion of 'not guilty by reason of insanity' (NGI) – the benchmark with which many judge the mental state of the offender(s) (including also, for similar reasons, unfitness to plead and diminished responsibility). However, this is only a very small element with regards to understanding the link between mental health and criminal behaviour. In 1843, the decision by the House of Lords in the *McNaughton*[3] case laid the foundations for the Trial of Lunatics Act 1883, the court ruling that:

> It must be clearly proved that, at the time of committing the act, the accused was labouring under such a defect of reason from disease of the mind that he did not know the nature and quality of the act, or so as not to know that what he was doing was wrong.

Although Mackay, Mitchell and Howe[4] report on some significant changes to the insanity plea that has modernised the *McNaughton* ruling, the definitions and wording from the original verdict are still judged, to a degree, as a benchmark for establishing NGI. This abnormality of mind that can result in 'a defect of reasoning' can be of an organic nature, for example, arrested development in the form of a learning disability, or any other cause resulting from, for example, disease or a head injury. Even personality disorders (which will be discussed later in this chapter) have been successfully argued as grounds for diminished responsibility in court (see *R v Byrne*[5]). The recent case of teenager Brian Blackwell[6] who, following the calculating murder of his parents, received a lesser manslaughter charge on the grounds of diminished responsibility as he was deemed to be suffering from Narcissistic Personality Disorder, provides a more contemporary example. The House of Lords recently commented upon the manner in which professionals attempted to quantify culpability for specific acts, suggesting that, 'psychiatrists do not feel qualified to pontificate on degrees of responsibility, though they may be qualified to pontificate on abnormality of mind. So often it comes down to making a judgement on a sliding scale of moral quality'.[7] Hence, difficulties emerge when there is a need to establish the 'true' nature of a person's actions. In the most serious cases, the moral and public backlash involving such pleas, often results in the – arguably unfair – trial of those with serious mental problems. The case of Peter Sutcliffe, detained in a secure mental institution and receiving treatment for paranoid schizophrenia (although found sufficiently sane to stand trial), highlights another of the problems with regards to the 'public interest' surrounding such cases.[8]

To elaborate on the main points for discussion in this chapter, the first key issue to arise concerns the nature of the 'act' and its relationship with the individual, i.e. do the people in question suffer with mental health issues and have they subsequently offended? Or are they offenders who also happen to have mental health problems? More specifically, the questions surround establishing what is the impact, influence or relationship between their mental state and their offending behaviour. This is important for a number of reasons and, in particular, with regards to the type of treatment and/or sentence they may receive. It has been estimated that 37% of offenders have an identifiable mental disorder.[9] The corresponding figures for personality disorders and those on remand are substantially higher.[10] Peay has argued that the types of crime that are committed by mentally disordered offenders are largely similar to those of 'normal' offenders;[11] however, the results of a Swedish study suggested that the chances of males having a criminal record by age 30 were 50% and 32% respectively.[12] This therefore suggests that there is an overlap or 'blurring of the boundaries' with regards to the definitions of both mental disorder and criminal behaviour. In extreme cases, such as psychopathy and 'dangerous and severe personality disorder' (DSPD), prior criminal behaviour may even be used as a diagnostic characteristic, actually confirming the presence of that mental disorder within the individual.[13]

The second important point relevant to the current discussion centres on the notion of public protection and the recent preoccupation with 'risk', both in society generally, but particularly within the criminal justice system. The stereotypical 'mentally disordered offender' at the forefront of the general public's imagination is most probably analogous to the 'knife-wielding paranoid-schizophrenic' who commits random acts of extreme violence against innocent strangers.[14] Such a scenario is thankfully rare: in the US, where the debate is further complicated by access to firearms, it is estimated that only 3% of violent crimes are committed by people with mental health issues – being male, drug and alcohol use, and social class appear to be consistently the most prominent causes.[15] Nevertheless, the potential danger posed by mentally ill individuals for engaging in all types of criminal behaviour is real, although far outweighed by sensational media reporting and a preoccupation with violence.[16] Cases such as that of Michael Stone, who murdered a young mother and her daughter upon his release for a prior murder charge, only serve to complicate the issues and create a climate of fear amongst the public and a corresponding reaction from policy makers.[17]

Thankfully, amongst these concerns some glimmers of hope have emerged for the incarcerated offender with mental health problems, and human rights legislation has been at the forefront of this movement. Indeed, some of the earliest cases brought before the European Court of Human Rights (ECtHR) from the UK (and elsewhere) were in relation to the confinement and access to treatment of those suffering with mental health difficulties.[18] Mostly the court has acted objectively in such instances and has ordered that either liberty be restored or treatment for an illness begins or continues. However, complications arise when criminal sanctions are imposed on any decision and it is here that the court has appeared reluctant to interfere with domestic decisions and policies. Fortunately, there seems to be some recognition amongst policy makers of the scale and gravity of the problem. For example, in 2003 funding for prison health care was awarded to the Department of Health with the longer-term aim of placing the responsibility ultimately on the NHS as outlined in the *Future Organisation* paper.[19] Although these 'progressive' movements are to be applauded, it should be recalled that a collection of papers published back in 1985 by The Prison Reform Trust also made similar recommendations.[20]

5.2 Historical attitudes to mental health

One of the major barriers to securing adequate mental health provisions for patients incarcerated in prison is the general lack of acceptance of the 'equivalence of care' for those convicted of criminal offences.[21] Despite recent changes in attitude from the public and policy makers, there is still a wide gap between those who receive care in the community and those who are languishing in non-medical secure units. Historically, mental health has been associated with 'madness' and the labels used to describe certain behaviours have reflected these assumptions, e.g. the 'Lunacy Act' of 1845. Although our understanding of mental illness and mental health has advanced considerably since the nineteenth century, there is still a general lack of appreciation of the complex issues surrounding the diagnosis and treatment of the increasing range of disorders. Such a misunderstanding can fuel a certain level of stigma for people suffering with mental health issues, although this is despite the fact that as many as one in four people will suffer with clinical depression at some point in their lives.[22] Increasing understanding, allaying misconceptions, and avoiding making these issues 'taboo' is as important for furthering the human rights of these individuals as formal legislation.

Generally, mental disorders are not *caused* by neuro-chemical or hormonal imbalances. The majority of research in this area has failed to discover one simple biological explanation (although there may be some physiological changes or degeneration in some specific types of mental disorders). Mental disorders are also not specifically a 'disease' that you can either catch or cause through your own behaviour. However, some groups of people, who may be genetically predisposed to mental health problems, can exasperate their chances of developing a disorder by some of their lifestyle choices. The example which is often cited is the link between cannabis consumption and schizophrenia.[23] Generally speaking, most mental disorders have three independent – yet inter-related – elements, which contribute disproportionately, according to the individual *and* the disorder, to the chances of developing a mental health problem:[24]

Biological – genetic and other physiological factors, such as drug use, brain injury, etc.

Psychological – a person's individual make-up, including personality factors, developmental history, etc.

Social – includes environmental factors (for example, the effect of pollution or poor diet), social networks, socio-economic status, etc.

In order to alleviate and/or control a mental disorder, successful treatment will usually seek to address a combination of these factors. For example, it is frequently the case that both a psychiatrist and a psychologist will deal with an individual patient – the former to prescribe medication and the latter to conduct therapy.

The recognition of mental illness as a legitimate health problem has not been as swift as many probably realise or expect. Utilitarian ethics dominated English philosophy for the majority of the nineteenth century and the rule-based assumptions and reliance upon 'science' and 'order' would dictate any social reforms. Problems and their potential solutions would require an evaluation of the dictum 'maximising the happiness for the greatest number of people'. Prominent philosophers of the time, such as Jeremy Bentham, would debate the policies and the punishments for non-compliance. Common law would then become a driving force behind social change; examples include the abolishment of slavery, poverty, prison conditions and also the curtailment of the death penalty for the insane. The reign of Queen Victoria (1837–1901) saw the British Empire's wealth and power provide state intervention in mental health care on an unprecedented scale, with the first public asylums created to house the mentally unwell.[25] These continued, controversially, for many years until the 'care in the community' model became predominant in the later part of the twentieth century.

In 1949, the World Health Organization (WHO) released the sixth edition of the *International Classification of Diseases* (ICD). For the first time there were sections relating to mental health specifically as a 'disease' and classification and treatment guidelines were incorporated into the manual. In 1952, the American Psychiatric Association (APA) published the first edition of its *Diagnostic and Statistical Manual* (DSM).[26] Both of these diagnostic systems are closely related, and possibly represent the two most accepted standards for identifying mental health problems. Indeed, the eighth edition of the ICD was heavily informed by the same medical professionals who had jointly created the initial DSM. Despite the obvious and deliberate overlap, the two are now in the 10th (ICD) and 4th (DSM) editions. The main emphasis in both of these manuals has been in the development and standardisation of disorders, their symptoms, and developmental pathways. Naturally, the ICD covers a wider range of diseases, not just mental health issues; hence, the DSM is often seen as more comprehensive and specific in psychiatric contexts. Many mental health problems are separated from 'normal' functioning only by a degree of deviation from the general 'norm', which is itself prone to fluctuation according to culture and time. For example, pre-menstrual dysphonic disorder was removed during the revision of the DSM-III, and homosexuality likewise from the DSM-II. Intended to clarify the statistical population deviation issue, clinical significance requires that symptoms cause 'significant distress or impairment in social, occupational, or other important areas of functioning'.[27] Consequently, the presence of symptoms representative of a mental disorder do not necessarily give cause for concern if they do not impact unduly upon the individual.

5.3 The European Convention on Human Rights in relation to mental health

The adoption of the Universal Declaration of Human Rights (UDHR) in 1948 was a landmark for establishing a range of 'standards' that all people throughout the world could expect, regardless of their race, gender or any other difficulty characteristic. Whilst there are obvious problems with implementing these declarations in their entirety and in all jurisdictions, human rights law has been a powerful motivator of change and a useful standard with which to judge the treatment of many groups of individuals, including those with mental health issues. However, the rights and freedoms of those with mental health problems have, in many instances, not advanced considerably in the five decades since its inception. Gostin identifies three of the most prominent and problematic relationships between mental health and human rights:

> Mental health policies, programs, and practices can actually violate human rights themselves – although modern mental health policy and practice encourages non-coercion, consent and humane treatment, mental health law is essentially the use of government control. It legitimises the use of restraints, the compulsion to treat, and in some cases, can deny many basic rights of the 'free' citizen (e.g. the right to vote). Despite these powers being exercised for the benefit of the individual and/or society, it affects a range of taken for granted notions, e.g. privacy, integrity, liberty, etc. In many instances, these can give powerful indications of human rights violations.

Human rights issues can themselves feed into mental health problems – serious violations of human rights, for example, rape, torture, genocide, can lead to a range of mental health issues. The suffering can be long and intense for the individuals involved, but also have effects on families, communities, and wider society for generations to come. These violations are designed to break up communities and resistance to wider forces. On a less destructive scale, other human rights violations, for example, discrimination, denial of legal rights and invasion of privacy, can undermine dignity and result in the deterioration of mental health.

On a more philosophical level, human rights and mental health are both concerned with the betterment of human beings. Good mental health is important for those participating in social and political life and human rights are necessary to allow the security to express opinions and beliefs, and the freedom from harm and restraint. One example is race. Without good mental health, people from minority groups, for example, cannot function in the family or workplace, and even less so in the political sphere. And without human rights, there will be instances where they may suffer discrimination and unfair treatment, resulting in poor mental health. Hence, both pieces of legislation are of equal importance in the improvement of human experience.[28]

As well as the UDHR, in 1966, two-thirds of the original Member States also adopted the International Covenant on Civil and Political Rights (ICCPR) and the International Covenant on Economic, Social and Cultural Rights (ICESCR). Despite the inclusion of various non-specific health rights in the original UDHR (see Article 25), there were now more specific mentions of mental health in Article 12 of the ICESCR, e.g. 'the right of everyone to the highest attainable standard of physical and mental health'. However, these rights could be limited in situations of national security, for example, and also for the protection of 'public order, public health, or morals or the rights and freedoms of others' (Article 12.3 of the ICCPR). It is in these contexts that mental health law and human rights often find themselves in conflict.

Following the United Nations 'Decade for the Disabled' (1983–92), the General Assembly of the UN adopted the Principles for the Protection of Persons with Mental Illness and for the Improvement of Mental Health Care. Following a lengthy consultation, what was to become widely referred to as the MI [mental illness] Principles became the first real statement on the rights of those with mental health problems.[29] However, these resolutions are not explicitly legally binding on Member States, and can subsequently lead to instances whereby governments can reject the points on the grounds that they are not legally required to conform. Gostin argues that, despite their limited legal adherence, these are vitally important because they both establish a 'baseline' for the fair treatment of those with mental health issues, and additionally allow the monitoring of abuse of these rights by forwarding an 'acceptable minimum' standard.[30]

Most importantly, the MI Principles established minimum legal standards and procedures for when the mentally ill are admitted to hospital involuntarily:

They must be suffering from a mental illness that has been diagnosed according to internationally recognised criteria and standards;
Only in instances where there is a possibility of serious harm to themselves or others;
If the individual in question is suffering from a critical mental illness and that their judgement is impaired sufficiently that a deterioration in their condition will result.

In addition to these safeguards from Principle 16, Principles 17 and 18 also offered some procedural guarantees that those detained would be eligible for fair hearings before an impartial judiciary and entitled to independent representation. There were limitations to these recommended standards, however, and in particular the often uncomfortable issue of compulsory treatment.[31] Similarly, Article 5 of the European Convention on Human Rights (ECHR) is primarily concerned with security of the person and the right to liberty. It is here that the 'legal' grounds for depriving people of their freedom are detailed. Various subparagraphs address issues surrounding 'psychiatric arrest', the review of cases by independent tribunals, and rights to compensation, etc. Most importantly, the issue of whether someone has been legally 'detained' or not is pertinent to their rights under Article 5. In instances where detention cannot be readily certified, the safeguards provided do not generally become enforceable. Many of the 'grey' areas surrounding this principle of legal detention in regards to mental health result from the conflict over the terms 'liberty' vs 'security of the person' (which stem from Article 5). Specifically, the definition of detention has been questioned from the standpoint of degree/intensity rather than *absolute* restriction of movement.[32] The confusion and relative flexibility of the definition of detention can result in many instances of human rights neglect for people admitted to hospital or other institutions for mental health problems.

In cases involving the detention of individuals with mental health issues, there is an obvious requirement by the state to conform to existing laws on holding people in secure conditions. These procedures are usually covered by the current domestic Mental Health Act, and for the detention to be considered lawful, it must therefore be consistent with the reasons with which the person was admitted in the first instance. In the case of *Van der Leer v the Netherlands*,[33] the ruling established that the detention of the patient had been somewhat arbitrary in nature, resulting in a violation of Article 5(1). In another case emanating from the Netherlands (*DSE v the Netherlands*),[34] the Court also reiterated the failure to comply with established domestic law in the detention of a person with mental health issues. In this instance, the initial confinement was not judged to have been beyond normal procedural safeguards, but instead the informal *extension* of the patient's stay in hospital was contrary to Article 5(1). Due to an apparent 'procedural oversight', the patient had remained in a secure unit long after the 'reasons' for doing so had since expired. Article 5(1) has been the most referred to article under the ECHR with regards to mental health and, in particular, the issue of treatment and appropriate facilities has been challenged many times using this legislation.

In another leading case involving mental health care, this time with reference to Article 3 (*Aerts v Belguim*),[35] it was conceded that the general conditions of the psychiatric unit in question had fallen well below the minimum expected. However, the Court was unwilling to find the case to be explicitly in violation of Article 3, due to the inability to prove that the care itself was actually degrading or inhuman. There appears to be reluctance from the Court to address potential Article 3 violations, seemingly due to the complex relationship between treatment and coercion for those who, in many instances, are often unable to consent or appreciate the benefits of their proposed treatment.[36] One of the only cases to enact a successful verdict was in the case of *A* v *the United Kingdom*,[37] whereby practice of a particular form of seclusion was deemed to be inhumane and the court awarded a 'friendly' settlement in acknowledgement of this. The majority of the UK cases have applied to the Mental Health Act 1983, although the 2007 Act has now superseded this, and, alongside addressing many of the failings highlighted on human rights grounds, has subsequently introduced a whole range of new issues for debate.

5.4 The Mental Health Act 2007

The main piece of legislation that governs mental health in the UK is the Mental Health Act 2007 (MHA 2007). It was introduced in November 2008 and, as with many new pieces of law, there is a transitional stage whereby old policies and procedures are phased out and replaced with new ones. The existing legislation prior to the introduction of the new Act was the Mental Health Act 1983 (MHA 1983). Clearly, the 24 years separating the two statutes was considerable in length and the overhaul was well overdue. It is also important to note, however, that there have been interim Bills introduced, for example, the Mental Capacity Act 2005 (MCA 2005), which updated and amended specific points. Nevertheless, change in mental health law is a gradual process and the new act aims to simplify and clarify many of the old systems and definitions.

Significant changes to any Act are considerably lengthy and often complicated by the terminology used. The Department of Health has summarised the changes to the MHA 1983 by the 2007 legislation as follows:

Definition of mental disorder: it changes the way the 1983 Act defines mental disorder, so that a single definition applies throughout the Act, and abolishes references to categories of disorder;

Criteria for detention: it introduces a new 'appropriate medical treatment' test which will apply to all the longer-term powers of detention. As a result, it will not be possible for patients to be compulsorily detained or their detention continued unless medical treatment which is appropriate to the patient's mental disorder and all other circumstances of the case is available to that patient. At the same time, the so-called 'treatability test' will be abolished;

Professional roles: it is broadening the group of practitioners who can take on the functions currently performed by the approved social worker (ASW) and responsible medical officer (RMO);

Nearest relative (1): it gives to patients the right to make an application to the county court to displace their nearest relative and enables county courts to displace a nearest relative who it thinks is not suitable to act as such;

Nearest relative (2): the provisions for determining the nearest relative were amended to include civil partners amongst the list of relatives;

Supervised community treatment (SCT): it introduces SCT for patients following a period of detention in hospital. It is expected that this will allow a small number of patients with a mental disorder to be discharged from detention subject to the possibility of recall to hospital if necessary. Currently some patients leave hospital and do not continue with their treatment, their health deteriorates and they require detention again – the so called 'revolving door';

Electro-convulsive therapy: it introduces new safeguards for patients;

Tribunal: it reduces the periods after which hospital managers must refer certain patients' cases to the Tribunal if they do not apply themselves and introduces an order-making power to make further reductions in due course;

Advocacy: it will place a duty on the appropriate national authority to make arrangements for help to be provided by independent mental health advocates;

Age-appropriate services: it will require hospital managers to ensure that patients aged under 18 admitted to hospital for mental disorder are accommodated in an environment that is suitable for their age (subject to their needs).[38]

The continued pressure on the UK government to modernise the MHA 1983 was given increased momentum by various lobby groups and Europe to introduce laws and policy that would comply with the ECHR. Despite the ECHR being ratified in the 1950s, there was still a necessity to bring domestic laws in line with the requirements of the Convention. The changing knowledge and definitions of mental health make these often incongruent with 'fixed' statutes and only ever really represent the current knowledge and prevailing opinions of that time.

In the UK, the MHA 2007 has also changed its definitions of mental disorder from those adhered to under the 1983 Act:

Removal of categories of mental disorder:

(1) Section 1(2) of the 1983 Act (key definitions) is amended as set out in subsections (2) and (3).

(2) For the definitions of 'mental disorder' and 'mentally disordered'
Substitute—'mental disorder' means any disorder or disability of the mind; and 'mentally disordered' shall be construed accordingly;

(3) The following definitions are omitted:
  (a) those of 'severe mental impairment' and 'severely mentally impaired',
  (b) those of 'mental impairment' and 'mentally impaired', and
  (c) that of 'psychopathic disorder'.

(4) Schedule 1 (which contains further amendments to the 1983 Act and amendments to other Acts) has effect.

In order to adequately define mental health, there are increasingly more elaborate definitions which result, in many instances, in confusion and poor understanding. In addition, the interpretation can be a major force in allowing human rights to be circumvented to varying degrees. Where definitions are not specific, the courts are open to clarify as to the precise meanings of these terms and the manner in which they have been acted upon. One such area has been in the realms of treatability and, specifically, whether there should be an onus on the mental health system to provide treatment to individuals ascribed with a mental illness.[39] To further complicate matters, there then needs to be a discussion on what form should that treatment take.

Commentators looking at the recent MHA 2007 have voiced concerns in a number of key areas. In particular, the 'treatability test' has been one of the most prominent to result in breaches of human rights. Specifically, the new Act not only removed the different categories for mental disorder, replacing it with the blanket term 'mental disorder', but also amended section 3 so that the consequence or aims of treatment were less specific. Previously, where the MHA 1983 stated that people could only be detained when treatment can 'improve, alleviate, or prevent', the MHA 2007 simply states that they can be held where there is 'appropriate treatment for them' and does not elaborate on what form that should take. This has raised specific concerns with regards to people diagnosed with personality disorders and public safety. However, the need to protect the public has been reiterated by the government in a response to the Parliamentary Joint Committee:

> We consider that the Committee's concerns about the balance of public safety and patient autonomy miss the point that our concern is about the balance between patient and public safety and patient autonomy. The great majority of people with a serious mental disorder are more likely to harm themselves than others, and it is wrong to paint a picture of a government or society obsessed with public safety. The Government's and society's concern is to protect very vulnerable people from harming themselves or, much more occasionally, others. And the concern to ensure that people can get the treatment they need to protect them from harming themselves or others is balanced by a concern to respect patients' rights to make decisions for themselves. We must stress that we see no conflict between protection from harm and ensuring that patient rights are fully and appropriately promoted. The Bill does both.[40]

The shift in penal policy from the 1980s to the infamous 'Prison Works' speech from then Home Secretary Michael Howard, marked 1993 out as a pivotal moment in the incarceration of mentally ill offenders. Despite the more humanitarian proposals outlined in the Woolf and Reed reports at the beginning of this decade, the bleak economy coupled with some high profile cases, for example, the unprovoked murder of Jonathon Zito by the mentally ill Christopher Clunis,[41] signalled the end for many of the long standing Conservative government's policies, including the 'care in the community' model. When power was relinquished to the 'New Labour' government in 1997, there had already been significant shifts toward 'risk management' as a fundamental principle in 'penal populism'.[42] Commenting upon these changes in the early 1990s, Stern suggests that with regards to the human rights of offenders:

> Even those who did not ally themselves with better treatment of prisoners, and did not see themselves as protectors of human rights, were persuaded by a completely different set of arguments, springing from a completely different set of values – efficiency, value for money, good management.[43]

This shift in penal policy from punishment (for punishments sake) to containment and management was exemplified by the proposals for dealing with the DSPD population. Previously deemed 'untreatable', the shift in emphasis to management is perhaps the most contentious programme for dealing with offenders with mental health issues in recent years.

5.5 Personality disordered offenders

In 1999, the government published a Green Paper entitled *Managing People with Severe Personality Disorders*,[44] which was in partial reaction/consideration to the Michael Stone case. Stone had been released from prison in 1987 for robbery and possession of a firearm, but was again convicted with burglary and unlawful possession of a gun in 1994, for which he was placed on probation. Later that year he was committed to a psychiatric unit for a short period of compulsory detention. He was in contact with various criminal justice and health agency workers and made repeated assertions that he intended to harm people, culminating in the threat to murder his probation officer shortly before the murder of Lin and Megan Russell in July 1997. It would be nearly a year before Stone's psychiatrist would contact the BBC's *Crimewatch* programme suspecting that his patient was quite possibly responsible for the attacks. There was little evidence linking Stone to the crime, with the exception of confessions to two of his cell mates whilst on remand, and he maintained his innocence throughout the original trial, retrial and rejection of his grounds to appeal.

The murders of a young mother and her child (and the attempted murder of Megan's sister Josie who was left for dead at the scene) are a tragic incident and understandably caused national outrage and fearful reaction. Contrary to common assumptions about the case, Stone had not been allowed to 'roam free' and had been in almost monthly contact with each of his probation officer, forensic psychiatric worker, and drug counsellor over the year leading up to the murders.[45] A statement released after the initial conviction concluded that Stone was not mentally ill, but suffering from a personality disorder. However, the then Home Secretary, Jack Straw, placed much of the responsibility for the events upon the psychiatric profession for not detaining Stone under the existing provisions laid out in the MHA 1983. It had been the practice of many doctors not to detain people under the MHA where it was deemed that there was no likelihood that the patient would respond to treatment. Such is the pervasive nature of personality disorders, so deeply ingrained are they in the individuals psyche, that in most instances treatment is largely unsuccessful.[46] Giving evidence to the Home Affairs Committee on the DSPD programme in 2000, a consultant to the project, Nigel Eastman, stated in reference to the comparability of personality disorders to general illness (including mental health), that:

> A personality disorder is very different from that [an illness that moves people away from their normal functioning] because it is essentially a developmental disorder, it is the person and it is not, so to speak, treatable in the same way as an illness.[47]

The issue of treatability is, for most, central to mental health law. Critics of the MHA 2007 have envisaged that many doctors and health professionals will inevitably be required to serve as 'jailors', as, if there is no need for specific treatment or explicit therapeutic benefit, then technically the Act would extend to cover an increasingly wide range of behaviours.[48] This argument is particularly relevant for people diagnosed with DSPD. Individuals falling into the DSPD criteria are problematic as there is no general consensus on whether there even is a suitable or successful treatment(s) for this category of patients. The ECHR, acting under Article 5(e) in the case of *Hutchinson Read v UK*,[49] held that it was permissible to detain a mentally disordered patient for the purposes of protecting others and that therefore no explicit treatment was necessary. The MHA 2007 makes provisions for 'care' under the rubric of a therapeutic environment, which are deemed acceptable.

There are, however, a number of problems with these definitions. First, there is basic disagreement as to what exactly constitutes a DSPD, and there are indeed, separate legal and clinical definitions. Second, DSPD is seldom diagnosed by itself; there are issues of co-morbidity (dual- or multiple-diagnoses) and this is true of many personality disorders. Coid reported an average of three personality disorders for males also classified as psychopaths, as the classification systems allow a range of behaviours to overlap.[50] Finally, there is also some controversy around the definition of 'severe' in relation to these disorders. Although not all personality disorders are inherently dangerous or lead to risky behaviours, by the virtue of human differences they will vary in intensity. Tyrer developed a range of classification systems for judging the severity of a personality disorder, ranging from 1 (meets sub-threshold criteria for one or more personality disorders) through to 5 (two or more personality disorders from different clusters (including cluster B) plus gross societal disturbance).[51] The inclusion of a person with a 'B' cluster (anti-social, histrionic, borderline, etc) in combination with 'gross societal disturbance' in this manner, virtually guarantees that psychopathic individuals are diagnosed as having a severe personality disorder. Coupled with the fact that, by virtue of also being an offender, then this further implies this severe personality disorder is therefore dangerous. The concern raised by human rights groups is that this arbitrary diagnosis allows the government to detain DSPD offenders in special treatment centres for the primary purpose of public protection.

Treatment of offenders in general is a contentious issue, and when combined with issues of mental illness, particularly personality disorders, there are a number of complications which occur. The WHO has identified a number of issues that should be attended to post-sentencing:

> The law must provide for transfer of prisoners with severe mental disorders to a mental health facility for treatment if they cannot be adequately treated within the prison […] One of the difficulties in keeping mentally ill offenders out of prison is that many countries do not have appropriate facilities to house people regarded as 'criminal and dangerous' […] In summary, mental health legislation can and should provide a framework for treatment and support rather than punishment.[52]

Whilst the legislature has a duty of care to its citizens with regards to protecting them from dangerous offenders, it is difficult to envisage how the DSPD programme can realistically deliver this safeguard whilst not seriously infringing upon these (DSPD offenders) individuals human rights. Many will argue that the nature of their offending negates their rights to some degree. Regardless of the moral arguments surrounding these issues, it should also be remembered that many of these detentions are ordered upon the basis of risk assessments and predictions of future dangerousness. The ability to accurately measure this has been the subject of significant debate.[53] The practice of risk assessment is not scientifically robust enough to be used as a criterion in order to detain people (potentially indefinitely) to within even a modicum of accuracy. To put this into context, Buchanan and Leese estimate that six people would need to be detained under the DSPD plans each year in order to prevent just one person acting violently upon release; for every 10 who would be violent, only five would be identified and a similar number overlooked.[54]

In order to sum up the debate on the issue of DSPD, the following quote by Lord Carlile of Berriew attempts to address the wider issue and place into perspective the actual risk posed by such individuals:

> We know the Government intend to introduce a new Bill […] I plead with them that we should not find ourselves getting bogged down in the Michael Stone question all over again. Mental health is not about a small number of people who unfortunately are not cured, are released from hospital, possibly by mistake or maybe by negligence, and commit terrible acts […] those kinds of accidents happen from time to time. We must talk about the real questions in mental health and not the headline questions, such as Michael Stone.[55]

The MHA 2007 has now been introduced and, alongside the longstanding tradition of treatment being a – if not *the* – primary focus of mental health, the definition of medical treatment has now been expanded to include 'care' within this remit. Specifically, this is intended to allow those who might not recover from their mental illness to be detained in a medical institution indefinitely. Such care does not exclusively apply to DSPD, but can also be relevant for patients with degenerative disorders, such as Alzheimer's, where there is as yet no cure but only the ability to minimise the rate of decline. However, for the 'untreatable' DSPD 'patients' this may also mean prolonged or even indefinite detention.

5.6 Conclusion

Following the humanitarian disasters experienced during the Second World War, there was an emergence of human rights legislation and the recognition of the – often differential – treatment of certain groups of people, including those with a mental illness. The policies which bind the UK are determined centrally by the ECHR, and do not allow significant deviation from their standards and procedures. However, mental health law is one such area where there are a number of potential deviations from these standards, for example, treatment without consent. It is in these cases that the state is afforded rights over and above those of the individual, including those set out by the ECHR, and, hence, potentials for abuse are often alleged. Many cases which have been brought before the ECHR have been in relation to mental health. For example, in the case of *Soering v United Kingdom*,[56] the court ruled:

> Inherent in the Convention is a search for a fair balance between the demands of the general interest of the community and the requirements of the protection of the individual's fundamental rights.

Similarly, in another European jurisdiction (*Kjeldsen v Denmark*[57]), the court interpreted the ECHR as:

> An instrument designed to maintain and promote ideals and value of a democratic society.

These cases and others of a similar nature (e.g. *Tyrer v United Kingdom*[58]) have established a benchmark for the 'testing' of whether a violation of the ECHR has been potentially reached. In particular, the interference must be:

Lawful;
Intended to pursue a legitimate aim;
Necessary in a democratic society;
Not discriminatory.

The above points raise some doubt as to the ability for states to strictly adhere to the ECHR in all cases. The problems for mental health are the fluid nature of its definitions and continually developing treatments, and, equally as important, the overall cultural significance of mental illness. In particular, the 'danger' posed by individuals with poor mental health, coupled with the relatively poor ability to accurately and reliably evaluate these risks, will undoubtedly inflict – often unintentionally – human rights abuses. Similarly, in response to the MHA 1983, Lord Phillips asserted:

> First, it is an extremely complex piece of legislation. It is not easy to interpret the effect of some of its important provisions. Secondly, it does not make adequate provisions for these patients for whom ongoing treatment is essential, if those who could provide the necessary facilities and treatment in the community refuse to do so, perhaps because they consider that the treatment should be administered in a hospital. There is no obvious way of compelling them to do so. Nor is there any power to compel the patient to submit to treatment in the community, although the threat of being recalled to hospital will in some cases be an effective sanction. If an impasse develops so that discharge of a patient is indefinitely deferred, the patient may not have sufficiently speedy access to the Tribunal to satisfy the requirements of Article 5 (4) [of the ECHR]. Finally, the requirement that those suffering from psychopathic disorder or mental impairment can only be detained in hospital if they are susceptible to treatment means that some patients have to be discharged albeit that they pose a danger to the public.[59]

Nevertheless, the ECHR and the ECtHR bind Member States to standards of care and increased effort has been made to comply. In *R* v *Mental Health Tribunal*, it was reported:

> The United Kingdom has of course been a signatory to the European Convention since its outset in 1951. Since 1966 it has granted the right to individual access, and there have been a considerable number of cases against the United Kingdom before the court. We now have incorporated the Convention into our law by the Human Rights Act of 1998. But, it seems to me, the view that makes a sea-change is an erroneous one. We have had, over the years since 1951, to comply with the terms of the Convention. Sometimes, as decisions of the court have made plain, we have not succeeded in doing so. But for the most part, the practices and procedures carried out in this country do comply with the terms of the Convention, and it is wrong to approach the matter with a view that there may be a breach. Rather, as it seems to me, the approach should be that the court will not accept a breach unless persuaded and satisfied that there is one.[60]

It seems that, although far from perfect, in the context of mental health care in the UK, practitioners and policy makers are reasonably satisfied that the provisions for mental health care and treatment meet the standards laid out by the ECHR. In cases where this falls short, the processes that are open to address these shortcomings are also accessible and work to an acceptable degree. The highly complex interaction between mental health and human rights, two very evolving and, at times, subjective pieces of legal doctrine, are slowly guiding each other through a process of change and acceptance, showing a delicate balance between ideals and aspirations on the one hand, and practicality and reality on the other.

Notes

1 H Prins, *Offenders, Deviants or Patients?* (London: Routledge, 1980).
2 T Seddon, *Punishment and Madness: Governing Prisoners with Mental Health Problems* (Abingdon: Routledge-Cavendish, 2007).
3 *R v McNaughton*, 10 Cl and F 200, 8 Eng Rep 718, 1843.
4 R Mackay, B J Mitchell and L Howe, 'More facts about the insanity defence' (2006) *Criminal Law Review* 399–411.
5 *R v Byrne* [1960] 2 QB 396.
6 See <http://news.bbc.co.uk/1/hi/england/merseyside/4633339.stm> (accessed 24 August 2010).
7 Baroness Murphy, *Hansard*, HL Deb (1 March 2007), cols 1700–01.
8 S Fazel, J McMillan and I O'Donnell, 'Dementia in prison: ethical and legal implications' (2002) 28 *Journal of Medical Ethics* 156–9.
9 J Gunn, A Maden and M Swinton, 'Treatment needs of prisoners with psychiatric disorders' (1991) 303 *British Medical Journal* 338–41.
10 L Birmingham, D Mason and D Grubin, 'Prevalence of mental disorders in remand prisoners: a consecutive study' (1996) 313 *British Medical Journal* 1521–4.
11 J Peay, 'Mentally disorder offenders, mental health and crime', in M Maguire, R Morgan and R Reiner (eds), *The Oxford Handbook of Criminology* (4th edn, Oxford: Oxford University Press, 2007), pp 496–527. See also P Lindqvist and P Allebeck, 'Schizophrenia and crime. A longitudinal follow-up of 644 schizophrenics in Stockholm' (1990) 157 *The British Journal of Psychiatry* 345–50.
12 S Hodgins and R Muller-Isberner (eds), *Violence, Crime and Mentally Disordered Offenders: Concepts and Methods for Effective Treatment* (Cullompton: Wiley, 2000).
13 N Eastman, 'Psychopathic disorder and therapeutic jurisprudence', in H Van Marle (ed), *Challenges in Forensic Psychotherapy* (London: Jessica Kingsley, 1997).
14 P J Taylor and J Gunn 'Homicides by people with mental illness: myth and reality' (1999) 174 *British Journal of Psychiatry* 9–14.
15 J Monahan, H Steadman, E Silver, P Appelbaum, P Robbins, E Mulvey, L Roth, T Grisso and S Banks, *Rethinking Risk Assessment: the MacArthur Study of Mental Disorder and Violence* (New York, NY: Oxford University Press, 2001).
16 D Howitt, *Crime, the Media, and the Law* (Chichester: Wiley, 1998).
17 For example, B Paterson, 'Newspaper representations of mental illness and the impact of the reporting of "events" on social policy: the "framing" of Isabel Schwarz and Jonathan Zito' (2006) 13 Journal of Psychiatric Mental Health Nursing 294–300.
18 C Heginbotham and M Kinton, 'Developing a capacity test for compulsion in mental health law' (2007) *Journal of Mental Health Law*, May, 72–84.
19 Prison Service/National Health Service, *The Future Organisation of Prison Health Care* (London: HMSO, 1999).
20 Prison Reform Trust, *Troubled Inside: Responding to the Mental Health Needs of Men in Prison* (London: Prison Reform Trust, 2005).
21 Op. cit., Peay, fn 11.
22 L D Rosenstein, 'Differential diagnosis of the major progressive dementias and depression in middle and late adulthood: a summary of the literature of the early 1990s' (1998) 8 *Neuropsychology Review* 109–67.
23 C J Laker, 'A literature review to assess the reliability and validity of measures appropriate for use in research to evaluate the efficacy of a brief harm reduction

strategy in reducing cannabis use among people with schizophrenia in acute inpatient settings' (2008) 15 *Journal of Psychiatric and Mental Health Nursing* 777–83.

24 E Munro and J Rumgay, 'Role of risk assessment in reducing homicides by people with mental illness' (2001) 176 *British Journal of Psychiatry* 176, 116–20; Royal College of Psychiatrists, *Offenders with Personality Disorder*. Council Report CR71 (London: Royal College of Psychiatrists, 1999).

25 Op. cit., Seddon, fn 2.

26 American Psychiatric Association, *Diagnostic and statistical manual of mental disorders* (Washington, DC: APA, 1952).

27 American Psychiatric Association, *Diagnostic and statistical manual of mental disorders* (4th edn, Washington, DC: APA 1994), p 72.

28 L O Gostin, 'Human rights of persons with mental disabilities: The European Convention of Human Rights' (2000) 23 *International Journal of Law and Psychiatry* 125–59, 28.

29 Principles for the Protection of Persons With Mental Illness and the Improvement of Mental Health Care (MI Principles), UNGA Res 46/119 (17 December 1991).

30 Op. cit., Gostin, fn 28, pp 23, 125–59.

31 Op. cit., Heginbotham and Kinton, fn 18, pp 72–84.

32 R Jones, 'Deprivations of liberty: Mental Health Act or Mental Capacity Act?' (2007) *Journal of Mental Health Law* 170–3.

33 *Van der Leer v the Netherlands* – 170-A (21 February 1990).

34 See [1998] 1 *European Human Rights Law Review* 99–101.

35 *Aerts v Belgium* [1998] Rep V, fasc 83 (30 July 1998).

36 Op. cit., Heginbotham and Kinton, fn 18, pp 72–84.

37 *A v the United Kingdom* [2002] no 35373/97 (Sect 2), ECHR – X – (17 December 2002).

38 Department of Health, *Dangerous and Severe Personality Disorder (DSPD): High Secure Services: Planning and Delivery Guide* (London: Home Office, 2005).

39 D Chiswick, 'Dangerous severe personality disorder: from notion to law' (2001) 25 *Psychiatric Bulletin* 282–3.

40 Op. cit., Department of Health, fn 38, p 3.

41 J Coid, 'The Christopher Clunis Enquiry' (1994) 18 Psychiatric Bulletin 449–52.

42 R Sparks, 'Degrees of estrangement: The cultural theory of risk and comparative penology' (2001) 5 *Theoretical Criminology* 159–76.

43 V Stern, *Bricks of Shame: Britain's Prisons* (2nd edn, Harmondsworth: Penguin, 1993, p 268.

44 Department of Health/Home Office, *Managing Dangerous People with Severe Personality Disorder: Proposals for Policy Development* (London: Department of Health, 1999).

45 C Dyer, 'Better care for Michael Stone might still not have prevented the killings' (2006) 333 British Medical Journal 670.

46 P Tyrer, 'Practice guideline for the treatment of personality disorders: a bridge too far' (2002) 16 *Journal of Personality Disorders* 113–18.

47 Home Affairs Committee, *First Report: Managing Dangerous People with Severe Personality Disorder* (London: The Stationery Office, 2000), para 176.

48 Op. cit., Chiswick, fn 39, pp 25, 282–3.

49 *Hutchison Reid v the United Kingdom* [2003] no 50272/99 (Sect 3), ECHR-IV – (20 February 2003).

50 J W Coid, 'DSM-III diagnosis in criminal psychopaths: a way forward' (1992) 2 *Criminal Behaviour and Mental Health* 78–89.

51 P Tyrer, 'Deconstructing personality disorder' (2006) 1 *Quarterly Journal of Mental Health* 20–4.

52 World Health Organization, *WHO Resource Book on Mental Health, Human Rights and Legislation: Dare to Care* (Geneva: WHO, 2005).

53 F Farnham and D James, 'Dangerousness and dangerous law' (2001) 358 *The Lancet* 1926; L Smith, 'Dangerous and severe personality disorder: difficulties in assessment' (2003) 51 *Criminal Justice Matters* 16–17.

54 A Buchanan and M Leese, 'Detention of people with dangerous severe personality disorders: a systematic review' (2001) 358 *The Lancet* 1955–9.
55 *Hansard*, HL Deb (60612–22) (12 June 2006), col 95.
56 *Soering v the United Kingdom* – 161 (7 July 1989) EHRR 439.
57 *Kjeldsen, Busk Madsen and Pedersen v Denmark* – 23 (7 December 1976) EHRR 711.
58 *Tyrer v the United Kingdom* (25 April 1978) EHRR 1.
59 *R (B) v Ashworth Hospital Authority* [2005] UKHL 20.
60 *R v MHRT London South, ex parte C* [2001] *Lloyds Rep Med* 340.

Bibliography

American Psychiatric Association, *Diagnostic and statistical manual of mental disorders* (Washington, DC: APA, 1952).

American Psychiatric Association, *Diagnostic and statistical manual of mental disorders* (4th edn, Washington, DC: APA, 1994).

Birmingham, L, Mason, D and Grubin, D, 'Prevalence of mental disorders in remand prisoners: a consecutive study' (1996) 313 *British Medical Journal* 1521–4.

Buchanan, A and Leese, M, 'Detention of people with dangerous severe personality disorders: a systematic review' (2001) 358 *The Lancet* 1955–9.

Chiswick, D, 'Dangerous severe personality disorder: from notion to law' (2001) 25 *Psychiatric Bulletin* 282–3.

Coid, J W, 'DSM-III diagnosis in criminal psychopaths: a way forward' (1992) 2 *Criminal Behaviour and Mental Health* 78–89.

Coid J, 'The Christopher Clunis Enquiry' (1994) 18 *Psychiatric Bulletin* 449–52.

Department of Health/Home Office, *Managing Dangerous People with Severe Personality Disorder: Proposals for Policy Development* (London: Department of Health, 1999).

Department of Health, *Dangerous and Severe Personality Disorder (DSPD): High Secure Services: Planning and Delivery Guide* (London: Home Office, 2005).

Dyer, C, 'Better care for Michael Stone might still not have prevented the killings' (2006) 333 *British Medical Journal* 670.

Eastman, N, 'Psychopathic disorder and therapeutic jurisprudence', in Van Marle, H (ed), *Challenges in Forensic Psychotherapy* (London: Jessica Kingsley, 1997).

Farnham, F and James, D, 'Dangerousness and dangerous law' (2001) 358 *The Lancet* 1926.

Fazel, S, McMillan, J and O'Donnell, I, 'Dementia in prison: ethical and legal implications' (2002) 28 *Journal of Medical Ethics* 156–9.

Gostin, L O, 'Human rights of persons with mental disabilities: The European Convention of Human Rights' (2000) 23 *International Journal of Law and Psychiatry* 125–59.

Gunn, J, Maden, A and Swinton, M, 'Treatment needs of prisoners with psychiatric disorders' (1991) 303 *British Medical Journal* 338–41.

Heginbotham, C and Kinton, M, 'Developing a capacity test for compulsion in mental health law' (2007) *Journal of Mental Health Law*, May, 72–84.

Hodgins, S and Muller-Isberner, R (eds), *Violence, Crime and Mentally Disordered Offenders: Concepts and Methods for Effective Treatment* (Cullompton: Wiley, 2000).

Home Affairs Committee, *First Report: Managing Dangerous People with Severe Personality Disorder* (London: The Stationery Office, 2000).

Howitt, D, *Crime, the Media, and the Law* (Chichester: Wiley, 1998).

Jones, R, 'Deprivations of liberty: Mental Health Act or Mental Capacity Act?' (2007) *Journal of Mental Health Law* 170–3.

Laker, C J, 'A literature review to assess the reliability and validity of measures appropriate for use in research to evaluate the efficacy of a brief harm reduction strategy in reducing cannabis use among people with schizophrenia in acute inpatient settings' (2008) 15 *Journal of Psychiatric and Mental Health Nursing* 777–83.

Lindqvist, P and Allebeck, P, 'Schizophrenia and crime. A longitudinal follow-up of 644 schizophrenics in Stockholm' (1990) 157 *The British Journal of Psychiatry* 345–50.

Mackay, R, Mitchell, B J and Howe, L, 'More facts about the insanity defence' (2006) *Criminal Law Review* 399–411.

Monahan, J, Steadman, H, Silver, E, Appelbaum, P, Robbins, P, Mulvey, E, Roth, L, Grisso, T and Banks, S, *Rethinking Risk Assessment: the MacArthur Study of Mental Disorder and Violence* (New York: Oxford University Press, 2001).

Munro, E and Rumgay, J, 'Role of risk assessment in reducing homicides by people with mental illness' (2001) 176 *British Journal of Psychiatry* 116–20.

Murphy, Baroness (2007) *Hansard*, HL Deb (1 March 2007) cols 1700–01.

Paterson, B, 'Newspaper representations of mental illness and the impact of the reporting of "events" on social policy: the "framing" of Isabel Schwarz and Jonathan Zito' (2006) 13 *Journal of Psychiatric Mental Health Nursing* 294–300.

Peay, J, 'Mentally disorder offenders, mental health and crime', in Maguire, M, Morgan, R and Reiner, R (eds), *The Oxford Handbook of Criminology* (4th edn, Oxford: Oxford University Press, 2007), pp 496–527.

Prins, H, *Offenders, Deviants or Patients?* (London: Routledge, 1980).

Prison Reform Trust, *Troubled Inside: Responding to the Mental Health Needs of Men in Prison* (London: Prison Reform Trust, 2005).

Prison Service/National Health Service, *The Future Organisation of Prison Health Care* (London: HMSO, 1999).

Rosenstein, L D, 'Differential diagnosis of the major progressive dementias and depression in middle and late adulthood: a summary of the literature of the early 1990s' (1998) 8 *Neuropsychology Review* 109–67.

Royal College of Psychiatrists, *Offenders with Personality Disorder.* Council Report CR71 (London: Royal College of Psychiatrists, London, 1999).

Seddon, T, *Punishment and Madness: Governing Prisoners with Mental Health Problems* (Abingdon: Routledge-Cavendish, 2007).

Smith, L, 'Dangerous and severe personality disorder: difficulties in assessment' (2003) 51 *Criminal Justice Matters* 16–17.

Sparks, R, 'Degrees of estrangement: The cultural theory of risk and comparative penology' (2001) 5 *Theoretical Criminology* 159–76.

Stern, V, *Bricks of Shame: Britain's Prisons* (2nd edn, Harmondsworth: Penguin, 1993).

Taylor, P J and Gunn, J, 'Homicides by people with mental illness: myth and reality' (1999) 174 *British Journal of Psychiatry* 9–14.

Tyrer, P, 'Practice guideline for the treatment of personality disorders: a bridge too far' (2002) 16 *Journal of Personality Disorders* 113–18.

Tyrer, P, 'Deconstructing personality disorder' (2006) 1 *Quarterly Journal of Mental Health* 20–24.

World Health Organization, *International classification of diseases* (Geneva: WHO, 1949).

——, *International classification of diseases. Classification of mental and behavioural disorders: clinical descriptions and diagnostic guidelines* (10th edn, Geneva: WHO, 1992).

——, *WHO Resource Book on Mental Health, Human Rights and Legislation: Dare to Care* (Geneva: WHO, 2005).

6 Indigenous rights in the constitutional state

Marco Odello

6.1 Introduction

This chapter deals with several legal problems related to the recognition and protection of indigenous rights in contemporary democratic states. The presence of different groups with different identities within the contemporary state is a central element of this debate. In the democratic state, based on the rule of law, democratic institutions, separation of powers and protection of fundamental rights, the recognition of different rights defined at international level and incorporated often in constitutional law represents an important chance for groups within the state to obtain certain specific rights. The recently adopted United Nations Declaration on Indigenous Peoples[1] (UNDIP) provides an interesting basis for the analysis of the legal significance of the rights of indigenous peoples in contemporary democratic states. Furthermore, this issue leads to the not easy recognition of indigenous peoples in modern constitutional states, with special attention to their rights of social and political organisation, including the use of legal traditions, use of lands and forms of traditional government. Such a complex system of rights has been sometimes related to the idea of a right to cultural identity[2] which would represent a set of rights for certain identified groups within the state. The Universal Declaration of Human Rights (UDHR) and the role of international human rights will be considered to clarify the critical points of the rights of indigenous peoples. The chapter is based on international and comparative legal perspectives that can provide an outline of the difficult issues concerning the recognition and application of indigenous rights within and by states.

As is well known, international law usually provides a general and abstract set of rules, the fruit of lengthy and complex negotiations and compromises. In addition, it would be a serious lack of pragmatism to forget that individuals and communities, both domestic and foreign, are today under the jurisdiction of states. Therefore, the responsible entities for ensuring their protection are the state's authorities at their different levels, from national to local government. This protection is given through national legal norms, the system of courts and other mechanisms for the protection of human rights, such as ombudsmen and national human rights commissions.

A relevant area for an analysis towards a definition of the concept of rights of indigenous peoples has to deal with national implementation, in particular in constitutional law. From a comparative perspective, the degree of recognition, protection and definition of human rights within national legislation provides interesting examples. If the international context seems to open remarkable spaces towards the definition of cultural rights to raise new perspectives for collective rights, national legal norms seem to lack a full acceptance of this category of fundamental rights.

The state is a typical contemporary social organisational expression. It is the result of a long doctrinal and political development which has been inherited from the 1648 Peace of Westphalia, and which has been consolidated through centuries in Europe and which has been exported and transplanted in all the continents. This model is based on certain criteria, one of which is the national identity of the population. This is an issue which becomes particularly relevant when dealing with the rights of indigenous populations, which pre-existed the formation of modern states' structures. This chapter will look at some issues that should be considered when dealing with the recognition of indigenous cultural rights in the constitutional democratic state. The first part of the chapter deals briefly with the definition of indigenous rights. In particular, it will look at how indigenous rights are part of emerging human rights based on the international human rights documents. The second part will look at specific examples that show how rights have been recognised and incorporated into the national legal systems. Finally, some considerations will be based on several problems that concern the protection of indigenous rights within the democratic state. The chapter shall take into consideration examples of Latin American countries, which are usually less analysed in English literature.

6.2 Defining indigenous rights

Indigenous rights are a relatively new area of development in the international human rights system. Originally identified and included in the protection of minorities, they have acquired a more independent and defined dimension due to the evolution of the international debate within the United Nations (UN). In this chapter it is impossible to deal with all issues linked to the protection of indigenous rights.[3] The scope is to look at the general features of the protection under international law, and then focus on some examples that show the relevance of indigenous rights within the state. In particular, this chapter will look at an aspect of indigenous peoples in the context of their recognition of their cultural identity as an important element for the definition of specific rights that indigenous peoples claim both at international and national level.

Neither the UDHR nor the 1966 International Covenants on Civil and Political Rights (ICCPR) and on Economic, Social and Cultural Rights (ICESCR) make reference to indigenous rights. Universal human rights defined in the UDHR, and in subsequent international legal documents, have provided the background for better forms of protection of their rights. The most recent document adopted by the UN General Assembly is the 2008 UNDIP that defines quite specific rights. The Declaration is a non-legally binding document but represents the advanced set of rights that should be recognised to indigenous peoples also on the basis of general human rights law and principles. Indigenous peoples have specific cultural rights that become particularly relevant in the definition and in the recognition of their characteristics. This is an issue that raises interesting questions for the practical application of human rights within the state.

Only in the 1980s, with the 1986 study of the UN Special Rapporteur on the Problem of Discrimination against Indigenous Populations[4] and the adoption of the 1989 International Labour Organisation Convention 169 on Indigenous and Tribal Peoples,[5] did the international human rights movement take more into consideration the rights of indigenous peoples. Part of the problem was linked to the issue of the right of self-determination of peoples, and the anxieties of states about possible forms of secession and independence that could be claimed by certain indigenous peoples. A Working Group on Indigenous Populations was established within the UN in 1982. It contributed to the development of the debate on indigenous peoples at international level, and in 1985 it started the drafting of the UNDIP. It took more than 20 years to negotiate the final document of the Declaration. This shows that the process was not easy and difficulties emerged in the negotiations among states. Other relevant UN bodies were established to support the recognition of indigenous rights: the Permanent Forum on Indigenous Issues in 2000[6] and the Special Rapporteur on human rights and fundamental freedoms of indigenous peoples in 2001.[7] Their action contributes to the international recognition and awareness of indigenous rights in the context of the international human rights movement. They also provide an important means of expression of indigenous groups in the context of international institutions, and a way to support the international recognition of their fundamental rights.

6.3 Indigenous identity and human rights

Part of the debate on indigenous rights can be focused on the specificity of the indigenous peoples, compared to the category of minority populations. Even the most recent 2008 UNDIP does not provide a definition, due to the different positions among states on this matter. An internationally recognised definition is provided in the Study of the UN Special Rapporteur Martínez Cobo also used in the ILO Convention 169. The definition states that:

> Indigenous communities, peoples and nations are those which, having a historical continuity with pre-invasion and pre-colonial societies that developed on their territories, consider themselves distinct from other sectors of the societies now prevailing in those territories, or parts of them. They form at present non-dominant sectors of society and are determined to preserve, develop and transmit to future generations their ancestral territories, and their ethnic identity, as the basis of their continued existence as peoples, in accordance with their own cultural patterns, social institutions and legal systems.[8]

It is clear that cultural issues are central to this definition. Cultural rights have been considered to be underestimated compared to other international human rights, such as civil and political rights. The developments provided in the UNDIP present cultural elements which become essential in the protection of indigenous rights. Article 1 of the Declaration affirms that, 'Indigenous peoples have the right to the full enjoyment, as a collective or as individuals, of all human rights and fundamental freedoms as recognized in the Charter of the United Nations, the Universal Declaration of Human Rights and international human rights law'. Therefore, there is a clear link to the generally accepted human rights provisions which derive from the UDHR. It also refers to collective rights, which are not usually clearly defined and recognised at an international level. The UNDIP refers to several cultural issues that are particularly relevant for indigenous peoples. For instance, the term 'identity' is mentioned in Article 2 of the UNDIP with reference to non-discrimination based on identity or 'indigenous origin'. Indigenous culture is also mentioned in Article 8, with reference to peoples and individuals 'not to be subjected to forced assimilation or destruction of their culture'. Article 11(1) mentions 'the right to practise and revitalise their cultural traditions and customs'. More specifically, indigenous rights include the right to maintain, protect and develop the past, present and future manifestations of their cultures, such as archaeological and historical sites, artefacts, designs, ceremonies, technologies and visual and performing arts and literature. Other cultural rights are mentioned taking into account an anthropological concept of culture, which include 'the right to manifest, practise, develop and teach their spiritual and religious traditions, customs and ceremonies; the right to maintain, protect, and have access in privacy to their religious and cultural sites; the right to the use and control of their ceremonial objects; and the right to the repatriation of their human remains' (Article 12). Also included is the right to maintain and transfer to future generations 'histories, languages, oral traditions, philosophies, writing systems and literatures, and to designate and retain their own names for communities, places and persons' (Article 13). Other manifestations of culture include the right of indigenous peoples 'to their traditional medicines and to maintain their health practices, including the conservation of their vital medicinal plants, animals and minerals' (Article 24). The preservation of the cultural identity of indigenous peoples can be based on existing fundamental rights which are recognised in relation to minorities, such as the right to use local indigenous languages and the right of children 'to have access, when possible, to an education in their own culture and provided in their own language' (Article 14(3)).

The above mentioned rights become therefore an essential element for the protection of the right to the cultural survival of indigenous populations. Many of the mentioned rights are already based on the existing set of international human rights. For instance, the right to use languages and to receive education in the local language are already internationally recognised.[9] The issue of cultural rights has also been clarified in the 2001 UNESCO Declaration on Cultural Diversity,[10] which in Article 2 stresses the importance of 'harmonious interaction among people and groups with plural, varied and dynamic cultural identities'. The issue of cultural identity is not fully developed but the importance of cultural rights as an integral part of human rights is clearly stated,[11] also in line with the principle of interdependence and interrelation of all human rights affirmed in the 1993 Vienna Declaration.

6.4 State, constitution, human rights and culture

In the debate on the recognition and definition of indigenous rights it is relevant to understand where these rights fit, and the context which should provide specific protection of indigenous populations. The contemporary constitutional state, based on the recognition and protection of fundamental rights may face uncomfortable situations. This is not only in the case of indigenous rights, but in general when dealing with minority rights and the rights related to cultural groups within the state. This issue derives from the foundation of the modern state, and in a way is a relevant test to understand the limits and boundaries of the protection of human rights within the states' borders. National states have been created under certain historical, political and theoretical conditions, including the settling of a national people on a certain territory. Centuries of internal and international wars have been the basis for the consolidation of international borders and homogenisation of the national population, speaking the same language, under the same flag and possibly with a single (official) religion. The affirmation of human rights and their incorporation in democratic states provides a not very easy test for the recognition of diversity and different identities, which should be accommodated within the borders of the state. The case of indigenous rights represents a very challenging example of how human rights have to be balanced to protect individuals, but also communities, within the wider context of the national borders. For this reason it is interesting to address some of the issues that are now relevant when dealing with the protection of indigenous rights.

6.4.1 Purpose of the state

For the contractualist political theories of the seventeenth and eighteenth centuries, associated with Thomas Hobbes, John Locke and Jean-Jacques Rousseau,[12] the main purpose of the state is to ensure the legitimacy of power, and to guarantee the respect of the rights of human beings and of their fundamental freedoms.[13] In this regard, Article 16 of the French Declaration of Rights of the Man stated that 'every society in which the guarantee of the rights is not assured has no Constitution'. Since then, most constitutional documents include a set of standards and principles for the recognition and protection of fundamental rights.[14]

This trend was further strengthened thanks to developments and international action since the adoption of the UDHR and the international codification of human rights. This has led to interesting forms of relationship between international law and domestic law, as exemplified in Article 10(2) of the Spanish Constitution, which makes explicit reference to the UDHR for the interpretation of the fundamental rights contained in the same Constitution.[15] This principle was confirmed by the Spanish Constitutional Court in the judgment of 15 June of 1981, which affirmed that 'fundamental rights respond to a system of values and principles of universal scope that [...] must shape all our legal order'.[16]

According to Walzer, a function of the state is to ensure the cultural conservation of its citizens, apart from their physical survival.[17] The state, in its traditional definition under international law, is a group of people settled on a territory, and under an independent government which exercises sovereignty over it.[18] The state, as a political entity, also has the principal function to maintain and protect the community of people under its control. If we think how modern states have emerged, after international wars and revolutions, we can see that one of the characteristics of many states has been the consolidation of nominally uniform cultural entities, integrated under the same religion, language, law, etc.

The national cultural unity has been used in different ways and with different purposes to facilitate and justify the unification of states (i.e. Italy and Germany in the nineteenth century), to create a basis for cohesion of the state and of its citizens against potential foreign threats. Nationalism has also been used to justify territorial expansion (the case of Prussia and Germany in the First and Second World Wars), and to promote unity within the state. Under this view, all forms of cultural differences (linguistic, religious, racial, legal, etc) might represent a potential threat to the security of the state as a political territorial entity.

With the development of international human rights law, not only of citizens but of all persons within the territory of the state, a change of the purposes and justification of the contemporary state is necessary. The principles of non-discrimination and equal rights require a respect for diversities that in the past was subject to repressive and restrictive policies of rights and freedoms.

It is therefore particularly difficult to ensure forms of multicultural expressions in the state, as it affects a well established idea of the state. Examples of minorities that call for more autonomy or independence, and cultural events which contrast with the dominant 'national' culture in a given state, especially in strong immigration areas, show this complex situation and the difficult and often contradictory ways by which democratic states try to deal with the phenomenon of the so-called multiculturalism or cultural pluralism.

6.4.2 The function of law

Among other possible functions, it can be affirmed that the law, and the state, within a centralised law-making system, are the means by which to manage a peaceful society. If looked at in the spirit and purpose of human rights law, the law's primary task is to provide a peaceful tool for the governing of society, not an instrument of repression and inequality, but for the sake of justice.

This purpose consists of trying to avoid conflicts through a system of norms and mechanisms of dispute resolution, which recognise and guarantee substantial rights and procedural rules. The function of the constitution is to establish a state based on the rule of law, and to ensure the peaceful coexistence of the subjects that are under the jurisdiction of that state. With the recognition of fundamental human rights, the peaceful coexistence of its population becomes one of the primary objectives of the state. This is expressed with the transformation of the liberal state into the social and welfare state.[19] The concept is clearly expressed, for instance, in the preamble to the Spanish Constitution of 1978, which affirms that:

> The Spanish Nation, desiring to establish justice, liberty, and security, and to promote the well-being of all its members, in the exercise of its sovereignty, proclaims its will to:
>
> Guarantee democratic coexistence within the Constitution and the laws, in accordance with a fair economic and social order.
> Consolidate a State of Law which ensures the rule of law as the expression of the popular will.
> Protect all Spaniards and peoples of Spain in the exercise of human rights, of their culture and traditions, languages and institutions.

Article 1(1) affirms that 'Spain is hereby established as a social and democratic state, subject to the rule of law, which advocates freedom, justice, equality and political pluralism as highest values of its legal system'.

These higher values define the 'axiological dimension' of the Constitution,[20] which is made explicit in Article 10(1) which refers to the dignity of the person to the inviolable, rights to free development of personality, including respect for the law and the rights of others. This would be a functional aim of human rights, as analysed by Professor Pérez Luño[21] and confirmed by the same case law of the Spanish Constitutional Court.[22]

6.4.3 Democracy and human rights

From the short consideration on the purposes of the state, it is now clear that the democratic system is more suitable to recognise and facilitate the respect of individual rights and of different collective entities which exist within its territory. Yet the democratic system does not represent an absolute guarantee of respect for all differences. For instance, France does not officially recognise the existence of languages or minority groups, such as the ones in Corsica, Brittany and Provence.[23]

The US until the mid-twentieth century did not recognise parity of rights to minority groups, in particular the Afro-Americans and the indigenous populations, the Indians of North America. The problems facing Britain in Northern Ireland, regarding the tensions based on religious and political backgrounds are well known and occur in the homeland of modern parliamentary constitutionalism.

Therefore, democracy if simply understood as a system of political organisation has not always been able to guarantee the recognition and protection of the rights of individuals and groups, in particular their cultural rights. When talking about democracy, reference should be made to an open, democratic system recognising the human rights of individuals and groups within the state. According to Antonio Cassese a general rule of international law whose contents consist of the right to a democratic government for all persons under the jurisdiction of a state could be emerging.[24]

It is interesting in this context to mention the doctrine of Peter Häberle, and his theory concerning the constitution as a cultural science.[25] In this regard, the idea of constitution does not only mean a legal instrument, or a normative regulatory mechanism, but also an expression of a stage of cultural development, as a means of cultural self-representation of the people, their cultural heritage and their hopes.[26] Not an entirely new idea, as Montesquieu already had considered political institutions to relate to the 'spirit' of the people or to the set of values and customs in force therein.[27]

If the constitution is understood as an expression of a people or a given culture, it is important to find ways whereby other cultures within the state, especially in the context of multicultural, multi-ethnic, and/or multinational states can co-exist. Otherwise there is a great risk of promoting forms of homogenisation, forced inclusion or exclusion of other cultures within the state, a phenomenon already experienced in the past that led to violations of fundamental human rights.

6.5 Right to cultural identity and constitutional guarantees

Rights relating to the cultural dimension were the first to be recognised as individual rights, in particular in the form of the production and enjoyment of cultural products. They have been defined and recognised in the form of copyrights or the right to access to cultural events. Contemporary constitutions have included these rights, especially in the context of so-called economic, social and cultural rights. The first two meanings of the rights to culture have already been extensively investigated and clarified by the legal doctrine,[28] and they are of less interest for this analysis.

It is more interesting to consider here, from the point of view of individual and collective rights, the concept and content of a broad concept of culture, including the possible implications of cultural rights. In most cases, the right to culture has been confused with cultural rights. In this regard, Professor Puy Muñoz provides a definition of a right to culture understood as the fundamental right of every human being: (1) to participate fully in the poetic or creative activity as a member of an audience with effective access to any work, object, representation or aesthetic; as an artist, intellectual, creator, composer, actor, performer or researcher of all kinds of creations, in particular, literary, artistic, scientific, technical, etc; and (2) to develop as intellectual or viewer in an atmosphere of recreational and creative freedom characterised by pluralism, encouraging the responsibility of creators and audience together.[29]

Depending on how the term culture is understood, it can be possible to specify its content with the entitlement. We can limit the right to culture to mean free access to museums, or expand it to include the freedom to express and exercise the rights related to the source of each culture, and therefore embrace the right to belief, expression, religion, etc. This topic seems particularly interesting with reference to the rights of persons belonging to minorities or groups existing in the territory of a state, and who want to keep or express their own cultural traditions. Several freedoms are already recognised in most constitutional texts, such as the rights of non-discrimination, freedom of religion, freedom of speech and belief, as well as education, that will essentially define the content of culture in a broad sense.

6.5.1 Ownership of the right to culture

Regarding indigenous peoples, some constitutional texts already provide rights that fit into the broad content of culture. In the case of the Mexican Constitution, the ownership rights of indigenous peoples is not clearly defined. Article 2 of the Mexican Constitution, after the 2001 reform, mentions as rights holders the 'communities that make up an indigenous people' who are 'those forming a social, economic and cultural unit cemented in a territory and recognise their own authorities in accordance with their customs and practices'. According to José Ramón Cossío, the Mexican Constitution recognises individual rights to indigenous peoples but in a 'somewhat hidden' way.[30]

Other Latin American constitutions provide examples of this recognition. Article 124 of the 1999 Venezuelan Constitution guarantees and protects collective intellectual ownership of knowledge, technologies and innovations of indigenous peoples.[31] Other examples concerning ownership of collective rights include, for example, Article 67 of the 1985 Guatemalan Constitution and Article 123 of the 1972 Constitution of Panama with specific reference to collective ownership of the land. However, several constitutions simply acknowledge the existence of groups and indigenous communities, without further definition, and therefore leave fairly vague criteria to determine the group membership, and the individual or collective nature of the rights recognised in the constitutional documents.[32]

It should also be mentioned here that in America there are not only indigenous peoples with specific cultural identities. There are other groups as recognised, for example, by Article 83 of the Constitution of Ecuador which mentions also black peoples or Afro-Ecuadorians as 'part of the Ecuadorian, single and indivisible State'. An interesting case is a 2003 decision of the Constitutional Court of Colombia, which safeguards the right to diversity and cultural identity, to ownership, to participation and to continued existence of the black communities of the *Cacarica* region in Colombia. The judgment recognises the rights of the communities of African origin, based on the Colombian Constitution and on ILO Convention 169, which are generally applicable to indigenous peoples. The Court accepted the right of the communities to act for the protection of their rights, and not necessarily only through their representatives in community councils, clearly affirming their personality in the national legal system and their right to stand in front of judicial bodies.

6.5.2 Constitutional guarantees

With regard to the applicability and the guarantee of the right to culture, we may make reference to Article 9(2) of the Preliminary Title of the Spanish Constitution which states that:

> It is the responsibility of the public authorities to promote conditions ensuring that freedom and equality of individuals and of the groups to which they belong are real and effective, to remove the obstacles preventing or hindering their full enjoyment, and to facilitate the participation of all citizens in political, economic, cultural and social life.

In this passage the equality of individuals and groups is mentioned along with the duty of public authorities to ensure the participation of all citizens in cultural life. Therefore the existence of groups is somehow recognised, but still without a proper definition of this concept in the text of the Constitution. National legislsation has to be adopted and implemented by national courts. In many cases, legislative reforms are needed to repeal and reform existing law, which often does not recognise the rights of groups. In many cases, the state has to provide the proper conditions and the means for the enjoyment of certain rights through positive measures. They may include legal and economic support that would sustain the effective enjoyment of several constitutional rights. The judiciary, in particular Constitutional and Supreme Courts, should play an essential role in defining the content of cultural rights. When the concept of cultural identity is used to clarify certain fundamental rights, judges have to balance the different components of the rights involved to ensure a proper protection of individual and collective rights. What is relevant at this stage is to approach the content of the right to cultural identity with special attention to indigenous peoples.

6.6 Cultural rights and indigenous peoples in America

Only in relatively recent times have most constitutions of Latin American countries recognised cultural rights in general and the rights of indigenous peoples in particular. Definitions of culture and cultural rights mentioned in some American constitutional documents with special reference to indigenous peoples will be exemplified in order to understand this concept.

With the end of the colonial system in America, new independent states made reference to their indigenous populations. Those populations had suffered forms of discrimination and segregation during the colonial regime. Based on the nineteenth-century liberal principle of equality, most American states considered that indigenous peoples had to be treated as citizens of the newly established political entities. Nevertheless, there are several examples that serve as a reminder of the treatment received by indigenous populations, even after the colonial domination. The 1853 Argentinean Constitution committed the state to 'evangelise the Indians'; the 1870 Constitution of Paraguay gave the Congress the power of maintaining peaceful relations with the 'Indians' and to promote their conversion to Christianity and civilisation. The 1890 Act No 89 of Colombia defined 'how to treat the savages in order to reduce them to civilized life': a norm that was declared unconstitutional only in 1996 by the Colombian Constitutional Court.[33]

These problems were common to all the indigenous peoples of America. In this context, the affirmation of rights contained in several international instruments has played a very important role in developing the constitutional rights of many American countries. In particular, the Charter of the Organisation of American States[34] affirmed the importance of democratic institutions and the respect of fundamental human rights in the Continent. Chapter VIII of the Charter deals with cultural rights, and Article 74 explicitly refers to American culture, including the 'culture of indigenous groups of the American countries' (Article 74.d). Indigenous populations have received, until recently, very little consideration in the legal texts of many American countries; therefore they have suffered strong discrimination, due to the lack of formal recognition of their existence as cultural entities. In recent years, several constitutional texts have recognised in many states the existence of, and the need to protect and grant rights to, the existing social and cultural entities including indigenous groups.

It cannot be denied that many of the constitutional changes were due to international pressure linked to the recognition of the rights of indigenous peoples, and in general to the need to affirm the protection of fundamental human rights, together with democratic values, particularly after the experience of Latin American dictatorships in the twentieth century.

In the following analysis, three different areas of indigenous peoples' rights will be considered as significant examples for the definition of cultural rights: (1) the recognition of the existence of indigenous groups in the territory of the state; (2) the right to the territory; and (3) the cultural identity rights, including the collective organisational rights.

6.7 Recognition of indigenous groups

All Latin American countries have indigenous communities and groups. The colonial phenomenon destroyed parts of the aboriginal populations and, along with them, much of the indigenous traditions. However, some usages and customs that are part of the original populations have survived. As mentioned earlier, the recognition of the existence of indigenous groups and of their traditions, languages and cultures is a recent trend in Latin American states. In this context at least eight Latin American states – Bolivia, Colombia, Ecuador, Mexico, Nicaragua, Paraguay, Peru and Venezuela – explicitly recognise in their constitutional documents the multi-ethnic character of their societies and the need to protect indigenous groups.

The Constitution of Argentina, amended in 1994, affirms in Article 75, paragraph 17 that it is the competence of the Congress to 'recognise the ethnic and cultural pre-existence of the indigenous Argentine peoples'. The cultural and ethnic pluralism of the nation is expressly recognised in Article 66 of the 1985

Guatemalan Constitution which recognises that 'Guatemala is constituted by various ethnic groups including indigenous groups of Mayan descent, and the state recognises, respects and promotes their ways of life, customs, traditions, forms of social organisation, the use of indigenous dress in men and women, languages and dialects'. Other countries have special indigenous legislation. For example, Act No 6172 of Costa Rica, 29 November 1977, in Article 1 provides a definition according to which indigenous people are direct descendants of pre-Colombian ethnic groups and 'retain their own identity'. Obviously, it is relevant to define what is 'identity' to include these groups in the context of the definition.

Mexico has included the recognition of indigenous peoples in its territory through the 2001 constitutional reform.[35] After having ratified the ILO Convention 169 on 11 July 1990, and after the *San Andrés Larrainzar* Agreements, negotiated and signed in February 1996 between the Zapatista National Liberation Army and the Mexican Federal Government, the process of reform concluded on 14 August 2001, to bring the content of the agreements in the Federal Constitution of Mexico. The reform essentially included new rights of indigenous peoples with the aim of guaranteeing the safeguard of their cultural identity. The second paragraph of Article 2 defines indigenous peoples as those who descend from the populations which inhabited the country's current territory at the beginning of the colonisation and who retain their own social, economic, cultural and political institutions, or part of them. This definition is based on the conditions established by ILO Convention 169 which defines the two main criteria for the definition of persons belonging to an indigenous population: 'descent' (Article 1) and proper 'customs or traditions' (Article 1.a).

6.8 The right to territory

One of the strongest indigenous claims is the control and possession of ancestral territories. For the contemporary lawyer this would not be a cultural right, it would be a right related to property, therefore placed within the rights defined in private law. When territorial claims of indigenous peoples are considered, it is possible to observe that they include issues related to indigenous people's specific view of the world, understood as a set of spiritual and cultural values in relation to land.

For indigenous cultures, the land of their ancestors is the source of life and therefore an essential part of their identity. We cannot go into the analysis of different forms of conception of land, but two cases will be mentioned by way of example. In the Mayan tradition, the Sun is the father, the Moon is the grandmother, and the Earth is the mother, whilst in South America, the *Mapuche* people of Argentina identify themselves as the people (*che*) of the land (*Mapu*).

Land ownership is a community matter, because land belongs to the group not to individuals. It is not a commodity that can be sold, rented, mortgaged, etc. This concept is incompatible to the Napoleonic legal tradition of civil codes adopted in Latin American countries. In indigenous cultures the land does not belong to an individual person but is the community, the people, that uses the land and somehow it also belongs to the Earth. For this reason the rights related to the land must be considered as an essential part of the identity and cultural survival of indigenous peoples. This principle has been recognised by part II of the ILO Convention 169, and by all the recent constitutions of Latin America that included this principle in their amended texts.

For example, Article 17 of the Argentinean Constitution proclaims that lands traditionally occupied by indigenous peoples will be neither alienated nor susceptible to charges or embargoes. Most constitutions include variations of this principle. An interesting case is the Constitution of Brazil that affirms that the lands traditionally occupied by indigenous peoples are intended for their permanent possession, with the exclusive usufruct of the wealth of soil, rivers and lakes in their possession (Article 231, paragraph 1). Of course, there is the problem of the enjoyment of the mineral wealth and water resources with energy potential, which should be regulated by law, with the approval of the National Congress, having heard the affected communities, and assuring their participation in the economic advantages (Article 231, paragraph 1).

6.9 Rights and cultural identity

Concerning the rights relating to cultural identity, the various constitutions of Latin American states show a variety of formulations and expressions. Sometimes there are general formulations of cultural protection, including indigenous traditions. In other cases the recognition of indigenous groups and their rights is provided in the opening part of the constitution, in the definition of the state and its general principles, as in some of the examples mentioned in the previous section. In other cases, reference is made to indigenous peoples as atypical entities that need special protection within the state, and finally, there are several cases where the rights and protection of indigenous groups are mentioned in the sections relating to cultural rights.

Article 75(17) of the 1994 Constitution of Argentina ensures the respect for their identity and the right to a bilingual and intercultural education, recognises the legal status of their communities, and the possession and ownership of the lands which they traditionally occupy. In the case of Bolivia, the 1995 Constitution[36] says that social and cultural rights of indigenous peoples living in the national territory are recognised, respected and protected within the framework of the law. Within the organisation of the judiciary, the judicial branch is responsible for providing legal defence free to indigent persons, as well as translation services where their mother tongue is not Spanish.[37]

However, the definition and protection of cultural identity is also a difficult legal concept. It has often been mentioned in UNESCO documents ‘as a moral value worth preserving and as a political value’[38] rather than a specific human right. Cultural identity can be part of general policies that preserve and protect cultural values, and more specific rights. It can be relevant to protect not only cultural rights, as defined in international human rights treaties, but also civil and political rights, such as the right to maintain certain political and legal autochthonous structures, which can contribute to the protection of cultural values and traditions.

6.9.1 Collective rights of organisation

Some national constitutions also recognise specific rights concerning the organisation of indigenous people with the intent to maintain forms of social organisation and the protection of the cultural traditions of existing groups. Article 167, paragraph II of the 1995 Bolivian Constitution says that the state recognises legal status of the indigenous and peasant communities and associations and peasant unions, and paragraph III also recognises the natural authorities of indigenous and peasant communities which may exercise administration powers, including the judicial functions, and the application of alternative form of dispute resolution, in accordance with their customs and procedures, provided that they are not contrary to the Constitution and to laws of the country.

The collective agrarian property is recognised in other constitutions, as in Article 67 of the 1985 Guatemalan Constitution, and Article 123 of the Panama Constitution of 1972 (collective or communal agrarian property). An interesting case in this context is represented by the state of Oaxaca, Mexico where, among the existing 570 municipalities, 412 elect their representatives by various customary practices, and not by the universal and secret suffrage adopted by contemporary democratic states. Some states have sought ways to ensure the participation of communities in the national Government as well. In Colombia, Article 171 of the Constitution establishes that Senators elected by indigenous communities must have previously exercised some form of indigenous authority.

6.9.2 Uses, customs and laws of indigenous peoples

A relevant issue in the protection of a people's culture is the maintenance of traditional forms of social and legal organisation. This simple statement contains a series of problems and challenges the structure of contemporary states and the categories of modern law. Here it is worth mentioning that, with the expression 'indigenous law' two different issues, though related, are identified. The first meaning is the set of state rules relating to indigenous issues, including the recognition of their rights, which are defined as 'ethnic rights', understood as the human rights of ethnic groups whose situation is particularly vulnerable, because of the disadvantages and violations faced by minority groups within a dominant society.[39] The second meaning refers to rules and customs practiced by indigenous peoples.[40] Here the focus is on the second concept and on the potential problems that usages, customs and indigenous rights may face in relation to the definition and protection of cultural identity as a human right.

One of the main problems concerning indigenous peoples is to define the limits of the use of traditions and customs in the context of the modern constitutional state's rules.[41] This phenomenon could be described as the 'right to their own right' possessed by indigenous communities.[42] It is a particularly complex issue affecting both international and national protection of human rights as well as contemporary constitutional law provisions.

If culture, and the right to cultural identity, includes the use and preservation of traditional customs and law, how can we perceive, in the contemporary state, the coexistence of different legal sources? What happens to the traditions and customs which are contrary to international human rights standards? Who should apply these rules? These problems can be divided into two interrelated issues: (1) the problem of indigenous law, or rather of indigenous rights vis-à-vis fundamental rights; and (2) the relationship between indigenous traditional institutions and state institutions.[43]

The phenomenon of social organisation of a particular group is strictly related to the identity of that group within the broader society. It can be said that law and various forms laying down rules governing the organisation of a group are an integral part of the identity of the same group. Therefore, the inclusion of a legal system among the components of the right to cultural identity of indigenous peoples cannot be avoided. In addition, the same concept of legal system has an essentially collective component, because it regulates communities and groups. This is a clear case of a collective right that can be part of the definition of cultural identity. The same application of indigenous rights entails interesting relationships with other cultural rights, such as the use of indigenous languages in judicial proceedings, and the possible recognition and application of indigenous law within national courts.

6.9.3 Concept of indigenous law

Indigenous legal systems represent an interesting area of analysis both in theoretical and practical terms. This is a fertile territory for studies of anthropologists, sociologists and jurists. What interests us here is to understand the relationship between law, uses and indigenous customs and culture, and therefore whether the respect and the use of indigenous legal systems fits into the concept of cultural identity. Indigenous legal systems cannot be framed in the Western categories used by the contemporary states of European tradition. Social standards and organisation of indigenous peoples are much more complex and related to specific social and spiritual elements of each group. Indigenous law can be described as a legal cultural system practised in a specific ethno-region with distinctive spiritual symbolic and religious features of everyday life. The law is part of the cultural heritage of the indigenous peoples which, as such, must be respected and internationally recognised. This heritage transcends the material concept based on objects and museums, and fits into the acceptance of the subjective practice of the community.[44]

When referring to the authorities, systems, standards and procedures used by indigenous peoples, reference is made to 'uses and conventions', 'customs', 'traditional forms of conflict resolution', 'customary law' and, ultimately, 'indigenous laws'. Some of these expressions often involve a negative or disapproving valuation of indigenous regulatory systems. They have no value as law in the positivist classification of state-made law, which has been adopted by modern postcolonial states. In legal language 'custom' is an unwritten rule based on social practice repeated and accepted by a certain community. Although recognised as a source of law, its value in national law is marginal with respect to state-enacted legislation.

It may be relevant to address the relationship between indigenous legal systems, state law, including constitutional law and protection of human rights, as this is a complicated matter in the relationship between cultural identity and protection of fundamental rights.

6.9.4 Legal pluralism and indigenous law

The recognition and implementation of indigenous rights has been a progressive trend and is a very recent phenomenon in the American legal context. This recognition is the result of persistent complaints from indigenous peoples, including the recognition of their cultures and customary legal systems in the administration of justice.[45] Here we briefly mention the most significant examples to show forms which have been integrated and recognised rights and indigenous customs in national legal systems, with particular reference to the right to cultural identity.

An interesting example is the Constitution of Peru which recognises the legal pluralism of the state. The Peruvian Constitution of 1993 defies the legal monism and recognises customary law and indigenous special jurisdiction using as a model the Colombian Constitution of 1991. This recognition is defined in Article 89 of the 1993 Peruvian Constitution which says 'The government respects the cultural identity of the Rural and Native Communities'. The Constitution recognises the individual right to a distinct identity and the collective right to cultural differences for ethnic groups. Article 2(19) establishes the right of every individual 'to his ethnic and cultural identity' and that the government 'recognises and protects the ethnic and cultural plurality of the nation'.

The problem in the case of Peru, compared with Colombia, is that the judges have not implemented the constitutional rule consistently. An emblematic case of the Supreme Court of Ancash, which tried events in 1996, considered the action of *rondas campesinas* (peasants' patrols) which arrested a suspected thief of livestock and made him work three days at the base of each peasant patrol as a form of punishment imposed by the same indigenous organisations. In this case the judges identified a violation of the right to personal freedom, therefore a violation of a fundamental right defined in Article 149 of the Peruvian Constitution,[46] with subsequent condemnation of the defendants for offences against individual freedom. The Constitutional Court of Colombia has considered a similar matter in a different perspective when integrating indigenous law and fundamental rights, which shall be discussed in the next section.

6.9.5 Indigenous rights and fundamental rights

Recognition and the possible application of usages, customs and indigenous rights are limited by the fundamental rights recognised by constitutional documents.

The Constitutions of Colombia, Ecuador[47] and Mexico recognise the jurisdictional autonomy of indigenous peoples. Article 246 of the 1991 Colombian Constitution states that:

> The authorities of the indigenous (Indian) peoples may exercise their jurisdictional functions within their territorial jurisdiction in accordance with their own laws and procedures provided these are not contrary to the Constitution and the laws of the Republic. The law will establish the forms of coordination of this special jurisdiction with the national judicial system.

Although the problem seems thus resolved, it is actually a puzzle for the lawyer. It is relevant to define this relationship with regulatory details that clarify the effective implementation and recognition of indigenous rights in this area.

One interesting solution to this problem has been formulated by the Constitutional Court of Colombia when it said, with reference to the constitutional Article 246, that the analysis of the rule shows four core elements of the indigenous jurisdiction in the Colombian constitutional system: the possibility of judicial indigenous authorities, the power of establishing rules and procedures, the subjection of that jurisdiction to the Constitution and to the law, and the competence of the legislative power clarifies the forms of coordination between indigenous jurisdictions and the national judicial system.[48]

In this specific case the problem relates to the compatibility of constitutional norms with the national Criminal Code. The Court considers that the fundamental right to due process is a clear legal limit for the special jurisdiction exercised by indigenous peoples' authorities which can apply it in accordance with 'their own rules and procedures, provided that they are not contrary to the Constitution and the law' (Article 246 of the Constitution). The Court confirmed that whatever the content of the legal provisions of the indigenous communities, they must respect the rights and principles contained in Article 29 of the Constitution defining the right to due process.

In this context, the Constitutional Court of Colombia offers a variety of cases related to criminal sanctions, which support the compatibility between the national legal systems and indigenous uses. However, the punishment established by indigenous authorities is strictly scrutinised, in particular with regard to non-typified forms of punishment that might lead to cases of torture.[49]

Despite the interesting solutions proposed by the Colombian Constitutional Court, which cannot be discussed in detail, it is difficult to provide a general working approach when dealing with these cases. Is not an easy task, but as a general rule we can mention that there is a need for the legislator to define these fundamental rights in national legislation, particularly in conformity with international human rights standards and obligations. The judiciary has the task of defining the boundaries between different rights and values in specific cases.[50]

As Diego Valadés points out, a new vision of the law is necessary in these cases. He affirms that after centuries of pretermission, all of the demands of indigenous peoples do not fit in the national normative order built to protect other interests.

It is indispensable to accept that the renewal of the rule of law is an imperative of reality and justice. Therefore, he considers that there may be a need to put aside some principles that have been considered immutable until now as a necessary step in the process of building a free and dynamic society.[51]

6.10 Conclusion: The human rights impact on indigenous peoples

From this short analysis of some of the relevant issues in the protection of indigenous peoples' rights, the emergence of a set of rights that may be referred to as cultural identity rights is becoming clear. This is a fairly new and disputed concept that has received quite limited attention, and needs further legal analysis to understand the nature and purpose of a possible right to cultural identity.[52] The case of indigenous peoples and their rights is necessarily linked to this concept which needs further clarification under contemporary human rights law. The existing constitutional state, based on the recognition and respect of fundamental rights, should provide a means to protect cultural values that are part of the diversity and cultural identity of indigenous peoples. It is clear that indigenous peoples have received strong support from the human rights movement. As a result, many of their claims have been included in the international human rights protection system. The examples provided show that there is an emerging trend at both national and international level to provide forms of legal recognition of cultural rights of indigenous peoples.

Cultural identities represent complex and essential components of human groupings. They should be respected, as part of the recognition of cultural differences, and as essential elements for the full development of each human being. Nevertheless, differences and cultural values are to be exercised within the limits that are set out in Article 30 of the UDHR affirming that '[n]othing in this Declaration may be interpreted as implying for any state, group or person any right to engage in any activity or to perform any act aimed at the destruction of any of the rights and freedoms set forth herein'. It is up to the state organs, in particular the legislative and the judiciary powers, to define the legal limits of the exercise of all human rights, but still it should be clear, as a general principle underlying this task, that none can expand or abuse the connotation and meaning of certain human rights to the detriment of other human rights in the name of cultural values.

Notes

1 UN Doc A/Res/61/295. See M Odello, 'United Nations Declaration on Indigenous Peoples' (2008) 82 *Australian Law Journal* 306–11.

2 Y M Donders, *Towards a Right to Cultural Identity?* (Antwerpen: Intersentia, 2002).

3 See J Anaya, *Indigenous Peoples in International Law* (2nd edn, Oxford: Oxford University Press, 2004).

4 United Nations, *Study of the Problem of Discrimination against Indigenous Populations*, UN Doc E/CN.4/Sub.2/1986/7 and Add.1–4.

5 Convention concerning Indigenous and Tribal Peoples in Independent Countries (ILO No 169), 72 ILO Official Bull 59, entered into force 5 September 1991. This Convention was a revised version of the 1957 ILO Convention 107 on the same topic.
6 ECOSOC, Res 2000/22, 28 July 2000.
7 United Nations, Human Rights Commission, UNHRC Res 2001/57, 24 April 2001.
8 UN Doc E/CN.4/Sub.2/1986/7/Add.4, 29, para 379.
9 Article 30 of the UN Convention on the Rights of the Child, adopted and opened for signature, ratification and accession by General Assembly Resolution 44/25 of 20 November 1989, entered into force on 2 September 1990.
10 UNESCO Doc 160 EX/Decision 3.1.1, Part II, (2001).
11 Op. cit., Donders, fn 2, pp 134–7.
12 See D Boucher and P Kelly (eds), *The Social Contract from Hobbes to Rawls* (New York, NY: Routledge, 1994).
13 E Fernández, 'Neocontractualismo, legitimidad y derechos humanos' (1984–85) 3 *Anuario de Derechos Humanos* 49–88 (Madrid: Universidad Complutense).
14 See G Zagrebelsky, *Il diritto mite* (Torino: Einaudi, 1992).
15 On the UDHR in the Spanish Constitution, see G Peces-Barba, 'Reflexiones sobre la teoría general de los derechos fundamentales en la Constitución' (1979) 2 *Revista de la Facultad de Derecho de la Universidad Complutense* 39–50.
16 Spain, STC, 21/1981 (15 June 1981) FJ 10 (the translation is mine).
17 M Walzer, 'Response to Veit Bader' (1995) 23(2) *Political Theory* 247.
18 Article 1 of the Montevideo Convention on Rights and Duties of States (26 December 1933).
19 B González Moreno, *El Estado social. Naturaleza jurídica y estructura de los derechos sociales* (Madrid: Universidad de Vigo/Civitas, 2002).
20 P Lucas Verdú, 'Dimensión Axiológica de la Constitución' (1997) 74 *Anales de la Real Academia de Ciencias Morales y Políticas* 85–168.
21 A E Pérez Luño, 'Análisis funcional de los derechos fundamentales' (1988–89) 5 *Anuario de Derechos Humanos* 201 (Madrid: Universidad Complutense).
22 See Spain, STC 25/1981 (14 July 1981).
23 See N Rouland (ed), S Pierré-Caps and J Poumarède, *Derecho de minorías y de pueblos autóctonos* (México: Siglo XXI, 1999), pp 247–77.
24 A Cassese, *International Law* (Oxford: Oxford University Press, 2001), p 371.
25 See P Häberle, *Teoría de la Constitución como ciencia de la cultura* (2nd edn, Madrid: Tecnos, 2002).
26 P Häberle and M Kotzur, *De la soberanía al derecho constitucional común: palabras clave para un dialogo europeo-latinoamericano* (México: UNAM, 2003), p 6.
27 Anne M Cohler, Basia Carolyn Miller and Harold Samuel Stone (eds), *Montesquieu: Spirit of the Laws* (Cambridge: Cambridge University Press, 1989), book XIX.
28 See P L C Torremans (ed), *Copyright and Human Rights* (The Hague: Kluwer Law International, 2004); UN Committee on Economic, Social and Cultural Rights, *General Comment No 17* (2005), adopted on 21 November 2005, UN Doc E/C.12/GC/17 (12 January 2006).
29 F Puy Muñoz, 'Ensayo de definición de los derechos culturales' (1988–89) 5 *Anuario de Derechos Humanos* 212.
30 J R Cossío, 'La reforma constitucional en materia indígena' (2001) 21 *Documento de trabajo* 20 (México: ITAM/Departamento Académico de derecho).
31 See also Article 84(9) of the 1998 Constitution of Ecuador.
32 In this context we can mention Article 75(17) of the 1994 Argentine Constitution, Article 171 of the Constitution of Bolivia, as well as Articles 231 and 232 of the Brazilian Constitution and Article 66 of the Guatemalan Constitution.
33 Colombia, Corte Constitucional/Constitutional Court, Sentencia no C-139/96 (9 April 1996).

34 Signed in Bogotá in 1948 and amended by the Protocol of Buenos Aires in 1967, by the Protocol of Cartagena de Indias in 1985, by the Protocol of Washington in 1992, and by the Protocol of Managua in 1993.
35 Mexico, *Diario Oficial de la Federación* (14 August 2001). On the constitutional reform process and outcomes see M Carbonell and K Pérez Portilla (coords), *Comentarios a la reforma constitucional en materia indígena* (México: UNAM-IIJ, 2002); E Castellanos Hernández, 'Iniciativa, dictamen y minuta de la Reforma Constitucional en materia de Derechos y cultura de los pueblos indígenas' (2001) 3 *Derecho y Cultura* 73–8.
36 Bolivia, Constitución Política del Estado, Ley no 1615 (6 February 1995).
37 *Ibid*, Article 116.
38 Op. cit., Donders, fn 2. p 138.
39 R Stavenhagen, 'Los derechos indígenas: algunos problemas conceptuales' (1995) 3 *Isonomía* 109–28 (Fontamara: ITAM).
40 A González Galván, 'La validez del derecho indígena en el derecho nacional', in M Carbonell and K Pérez Portilla (coords), *Comentarios a la reforma constitucional en materia indígena* (México: UNAM-IIJ, 2002), p 38.
41 See R Stavenhagen, 'Derechos de las minorías y tolerancia', in M Carbonell *et al* (comps), *Derechos sociales y derechos de las minorías* (2nd edn, México: UNAM/Porrúa, 2001).
42 M Aparicio Wilhelmi, *Los pueblos indígenas y el Estado. El reconocimiento constitucional de los derechos indígenas en América Latina* (Barcelona: CEDECS, 2002), p xiii.
43 See M Carbonell, 'La Constitucionalización de los derechos indígenas en América Latina: una aproximación teórica' (2003) 10 *Boletin Mexicano de Derecho Comparado* 839–61.
44 E A Sandoval Forero, *La ley de las costumbres en los indígenas mazahuas* (Universidad Autónoma del Estado de México and Universidad del Cauca, Popayán, Colombia, 2001), p 13.
45 ONU, Consejo Económico y Social, Las Cuestiones Indígenas, *Los derechos humanos y las cuestiones indígenas, Informe del Relator Especial sobre la situación de los derechos humanos y las libertades fundamentales de los indígenas, Rodolfo Stavenhagen* (26 January 2004) UN doc E/CN.4/2004/80, 19, para 54.
46 Perú, Corte Superior de Ancash, Expediente no 110–98, Sentencia del 23 Noviembre 1998.
47 Article 191, para IV of the Constitution of Ecuador.
48 Colombia, Corte Constitucional, Sentencia C-139, 9 April 1996. See also Colombia, Corte Constitucional, Sentencia no T-254/94, 30 May 1994, párrafo 14. Sentencia no T-496/96, 26 September 1996; and la Sentencia no T-523/97, 15 October 1997.
49 Colombia, Corte Constitucional, Sentencia no SU-510, 18 September 1998, para 49.
50 See R Irigoyen Fajardo, *Pautas de Coordinación entre el Derecho Indígena y el Derecho Estatal* (Guatemala: Fundación Myrna Mack, 1999), chapter IV.2.
51 D Valadés, 'Los derechos de los indígenas y la renovación constitucional en México', in J A González Galván (coord), *Constitución y derechos indígenas* (México: UNAM-IIJ, 2002), p 20.
52 See Op. cit., Donders, fn 2.

Bibliography

Anaya, J, *Indigenous Peoples in International Law* (2nd edn, Oxford: Oxford University Press, 2004).

Aparicio Wilhelmi, M, *Los pueblos indígenas y el Estado. El reconocimiento constitucional de los derechos indígenas en América Latina* (Barcelona: CEDECS, 2002).

Boucher, D and Kelly, P (eds), *The Social Contract from Hobbes to Rawls* (New York, NY: Routledge, 1994).

Carbonell, M, 'La Constitucionalización de los derechos indígenas en América Latina: una aproximación teórica' (2003) 10 *Boletín Mexicano de Derecho Comparado* 839–61.

Carbonell, M and Pérez Portilla, K (coords), *Comentarios a la reforma constitucional en materia indígena* (México: UNAM-IIJ, 2002).

Cassese, A, *International Law* (Oxford: Oxford University Press, 2001).

Castellanos Hernández, E, 'Iniciativa, dictamen y minuta de la Reforma Constitucional en materia de Derechos y cultura de los pueblos indígenas' (2001) 3 *Derecho y Cultura* 73–8.

Cohler, A M, Miller, B C and Stone, H S (eds), *Montesquieu: Spirit of the Laws* (Cambridge: Cambridge University Press, 1989).

Cossío, J R, 'La reforma constitucional en materia indígena' (2001) 21 *Documento de trabajo* 20 (México: ITAM/Departamento Académico de derecho, 2001).

Donders, Y M, *Towards a Right to Cultural identity?* (Antwerpen: Intersentia, 2002).

Fernández, E, 'Neocontractualismo, legitimidad y derechos humanos' (1984–85) 3 *Anuario de Derechos Humanos* 49–88 (Madrid: Universidad Complutense).

González Galván, A, 'La validez del derecho indígena en el derecho nacional', in Carbonell, M and Pérez Portilla, K (coords), *Comentarios a la reforma constitucional en materia indígena* (México: UNAM-IIJ, 2002).

González Moreno, B, *El Estado social. Naturaleza jurídica y estructura de los derechos sociales* (Madrid: Universidad de Vigo/Civitas, 2002).

Häberle, P, *Teoría de la Constitución como ciencia de la cultura*, (2nd edn, Madrid: Tecnos, 2002).

Häberle, P and Kotzur, M, *De la soberanía al derecho constitucional común: palabras clave para un dialogo europeo-latinoamericano* (México: UNAM, 2003).

Irigoyen Fajardo, R, *Pautas de Coordinación entre el Derecho Indígena y el Derecho Estatal* (Guatemala: Fundación Myrna Mack, 1999).

Lucas Verdú, P, 'Dimensión Axiológica de la Constitución' (1997) 74 *Anales de la Real Academia de Ciencias Morales y Políticas* 85–168.

Odello, M, 'United Nations Declaration on Indigenous Peoples' (2008) 82 *Australian Law Journal* 306–11.

Peces-Barba, G, 'Reflexiones sobre la teoría general de los derechos fundamentales en la Constitución' (1979) 2 *Revista de la Facultad de Derecho de la Universidad Complutense* 39–50.

Pérez Luño, A E, 'Análisis funcional de los derechos fundamentales' (1988–89) 5 *Anuario de Derechos Humanos* 177–202 (Madrid: Universidad Complutense).

Puy Muñoz, F, 'Ensayo de definición de los derechos culturales' (1988–89) 5 *Anuario de Derechos Humanos* 203–29 (Madrid: Universidad Complutense).

Rouland, N (ed), Pierré-Caps, S and Poumarède, J, *Derecho de minorías y de pueblos autóctonos* (México: Siglo XXI, 1999).

Sandoval Forero, E A, *La ley de las costumbres en los indígenas mazahuas* (Universidad Autónoma del Estado de México and Universidad del Cauca, Popayán, Colombia, 2001).

Stavenhagen, R, 'Los derechos indígenas: algunos problemas conceptuales', (1995) 3 *Isonomía* 109–28 (Fontamara: ITAM).

——, 'Derechos de las minorías y tolerancia', in Carbonell, M *et al* (comps), *Derechos sociales y derechos de las minorías* (2nd edn, México: UNAM/Porrúa, 2001).

Torremans, P L C (ed), *Copyright and Human Rights* (The Hague: Kluwer Law International, 2004).

United Nations, *Study of the Problem of Discrimination against Indigenous Populations*, UN Doc E/CN.4/Sub.2/1986/7 and Add.1–4.

UN Committee on Economic, Social and Cultural Rights, *General Comment No 17* (2005), adopted on 21 November 2005, UN Doc E/C.12/GC/17 (12 January 2006).

UNESCO, *Declaration on Cultural Diversity*, adopted by the General Conference of the United Nations Educational, Scientific and Cultural Organization at its thirty-first session on 2 November 2001 UNESCO Doc 160 EX/Decision 3.1.1, Part II, 2001.
Valadés, D, 'Los derechos de los indígenas y la renovación constitucional en México', in González Galván, J A (coord), *Constitución y derechos indígenas* (México: UNAM-IIJ, 2002).
Walzer, M, 'Response to Veit Bader' (1995) 23(2) *Political Theory* 247–9.
Zagrebelsky, G, *Il diritto mite* (Torino: Einaudi, 1992).

7 An international convention on the rights of older people?

John Williams

7.1 Introduction

We live in an ageing society and the evidence is that this is set to continue into the middle of the current century. Population ageing represents a great success and also presents significant challenges.[1] The World Assembly on Ageing II predicted that the number of people aged 60 years and over will increase from 600 million to almost 2 billion by 2050. The increase will be most rapid in the developing countries where the older population is predicted to quadruple during the next 50 years. By 2050, 79% of the world's population over 60 years will be in developing countries, 4% will be in countries whose economy is in transition and 18% in developed countries.[2] This period will also see some dramatic changes in dependency ratios; these seek to measure the ratio of dependents (children aged 15 years and under and adults aged 65 years or over) to the number of persons in the working age group. Although a useful indicator of the level of social support needed within a country, dependency ratios make assumptions about, in particular, the nature of older age. The main assumption is that older people are dependent. In fact, older people throughout the world contribute directly or indirectly to economic development and to social care, especially the care of grandchildren.[3] Desai and Tye in their study of the Asian perspective on Ageing, state that:

> (T)he economic contribution of older people in developing countries is not well understood. There is no doubt, however, that there are high rates of economic participation by older men and women. Greater still is their contribution made to the informal economy. Older people have naturally assumed roles such as tending to childcare, cooking and other household tasks and taking on many part-time jobs in the informal sector. Younger adults are 'released' for employment purposes and the cumulative effect is beneficial to the whole household unit.[4]

However, dependency ratios provide a measurement with which the changing balance of the population can be assessed. The global total dependency ratio (that is, children and older people as a ratio of the working age group) will remain roughly the same until 2025 at about 50; it will then increase to 56 by 2050.[5] If this global figure is broken down into developed and developing regions, significant differences arise. For the more developed regions, the ratio will rise to 71 in 2050, whereas the least developed regions will actually see a reduction from the high seventies in 2009 to the low fifties in 2050.[6] However, the most significant message from the dependency ratio data is that in all of the major areas in the world there will be a significant increase in the old-age dependency ratio between 2009 and 2050. In Europe it will move from 24 to 40; Northern America 19 to 36; Oceania 16 to 30; Latin America and the Caribbean 10 to 31; Asia 10 to 27; and Africa 6 to 11.[7] Fertility reduction and an increase in longevity account for the changing balance between young and old dependents.

The above data simplifies what is a complex issue that brings with it opportunities as well as challenges. Growing awareness of an ageing population has generated an interest in the human rights of older people at national, regional and global levels.[8] However, there is a lack of disaggregated data on older people. Much of the data that exists is general in nature and assumes that older age is all that needs to be measured rather than the composition of this complex and diverse group. There is little detailed data on employment amongst older people, their saving and debt practices; chronic illnesses amongst older people; and age, gender and socio-cultural and economic factors that may affect older people's ability to access services. HelpAge International has called upon governments, UN agencies and other organisations to collect and publish data that is disaggregated by age and sex including information on population, employment, poverty levels, and access to services, such as health and social security. It recommends that data should be collected separately for men and women in 10-year age brackets (50–59, 60–69, 70–79 and over 80), rather than as one single 60 years and over cohort. Other information (who is head of household, ethnic background and other demographic information, such as health status and land ownership) should also be collected.[9]

7.2 Abuse of older people's human rights – a global perspective

The rights guaranteed to all people by instruments such as the Universal Declaration of Human Rights (UDHR) do not appear to be applied universally across all age groups. A lack of awareness of the needs of older people, and the exclusion of older people from programmes addressing health, poverty and social care demonstrates that ageism transcends national and regional boundaries and is truly global. Practices continue with regard to older people that would attract condemnation if applied to children. Age awareness, in particular older age, needs to be embedded in the implementation of current international human rights instruments as they do not exclude people on the grounds of age. There are many examples of older people as a group being denied basic human rights without any effective remedy. Some specific examples will now be considered.

7.2.1 Elder abuse

The recent study of the prevalence of elder abuse in the UK by Mowlam *et al* identified significant elder abuse within older people's own homes (4% aged 66 years and over – approximately 342,000 people), often perpetrated by close family members. A significant number of victims (30%) did not report the abuse. Only 4% reported the abuse to the police.[10] More widely, the World Health Organization's (WHO's) report on violence and health included abuse of the elderly as one of the contexts within which violence occurs.[11] It pointed to the paucity of data on elder abuse. The report acknowledges that abuse can take many forms, for example:

> Displacing older people as heads of households and depriving them of their autonomy in the name of affection are cultural norms even in countries where the family is the central institution and the sense of filial obligation is strong. Such infantilization and overprotection can leave the older person isolated, depressed and demoralized, and can be considered a form of abuse.[12]

The WHO notes that in some traditional societies older women are abandoned and their property seized.[13] It concludes that elder abuse cannot be eradicated unless the needs of older people for shelter, food, security and access to health care are met. It encourages the international community to create an environment which accepts ageing as being a natural part of life and where older people are given the right to live in dignity and participate fully in society.[14]

7.2.2 AIDS and HIV

Schmid *et al* draw attention to the fact that there is a surprisingly high prevalence and incidence of HIV amongst people aged 50 years and over. HIV is still rarely linked to illness amongst older people. For older people, there is a shorter time from diagnosis to the onset of AIDS. Partly this is because of age-related factors, but also Schmid *et al* conclude because of a failure of doctors to consider HIV as a potential diagnosis.[15] The World Assembly on Ageing II report that in America 10% of all AIDS cases are people over the age of 50 years, with a quarter of those being aged over 60. For Western Europe 10% of all new infections between 1997 and 2002 were among the over 50 age group. Most deaths from AIDS (83%) have occurred in sub-Saharan Africa, although not much is known about the epidemiology among older people.[16] However, a typical scenario in this region is that of the grandparent, who may be HIV-positive, being the main care provider for grandchildren orphaned by AIDS. HelpAge International found that up to half of the world's children orphaned by AIDS are cared for by an older person. Older people may also provide care for adult children who are HIV-positive or have AIDS. The charity states:

> Over the last decade, the HIV and AIDS epidemic has had a devastating impact on older people, yet this impact remains under-reported and has

> not been properly addressed. Older people's needs and concerns are often overlooked by HIV and AIDS programmes because of the erroneous assumption that older people are not affected. This must change urgently if a comprehensive response to the HIV and AIDS epidemic is to be delivered.[17]

Older people are affected directly and indirectly by HIV/AIDS. HIV testing initiatives often exclude older people on the mistaken assumption that they are not sexually active. Older people may also be responsible for the care of two generations as a consequence of HIV/AIDS and many fear being infected by the person they are caring for.[18]

In addition to the physical and mental strain of caring, older people also experience discrimination. The stigma and irrational fear of mixing with anybody who may live in the same household as an HIV/AIDS person may lead to social isolation. There is also a financial loss as they may be unable to earn or to sell their produce. Nhongo draws attention to the financial implications of caring and also to the impact that this may have on the development of children. In a paper based on family development in Namibia, Nhongo concludes:

> Large numbers of older people simply do not have the resources to cover the cost of bringing up several grandchildren and meeting their own needs. The economic burden is not only a cause of concern for older people, but is also a source of dissatisfaction for some of the children in their care.[19]

Research in Tanzania highlights that some orphans feel they are not well supported and that their needs are not met by their grandparents. Older people echo these sentiments, saying that as they care for the sick and later strive to generate sufficient income to meet food and other basic needs, they are unable to care for the grandchildren in the way they would like.[20]

7.2.3 Disaster relief and older people

There is concern that the needs of older people in disasters are neglected and that the provision of relief does not take account of any special needs that they may have. A strategy is required that addresses their particular needs.[21] Duggan *et al* in their study of the perception of older people to disaster relief, found that older people who had experience of disaster relief expressed concern about the protection of their rights and the prevention of loss of independence in responding and preparing for a disaster. There was a mistrust of government. They also had concerns about the ability to access resources. The contribution that older people can make to disaster relief is emphasised by Deeny *et al.* They warn of the danger of automatically assuming that older people are vulnerable and in need; they may be a very rich resource that can be used to assist in the relief programme.[22]

There is a lack of research on the effect of disasters on older people. Evans notes that they may be more vulnerable because of poverty, long standing health conditions and psychological trauma and that 'insightful preparation' may mitigate the impact of a disaster on older people.[23] Older people may also have more difficulty in coping with the aftermath of a disaster. A study of the earthquake in Newcastle, Australia in 1989 found that older people reported higher overall levels of post-traumatic stress symptoms, with even higher levels being reported amongst older women. Older people may also underutilise support services.[24] The study concludes that ' … the elderly should be the focus of extra assistance following disasters, preferably in the form of augmentation of existing services with which they are familiar'.[25] The need for older people to be direct beneficiaries of relief is important. HelpAge International in its report on the effect of the Tsunami on older people in Aceh, Indonesia, stated that:

> [O]lder people should be recognised as direct beneficiaries of relief aid and rehabilitation efforts. To date, a lot of interventions have focused on the household level. This is based on two assumptions: first, that older people are visible, so special efforts to identify them are not necessary; and second, that families and communities are caring for them. However, experience shows that targeting older people as direct beneficiaries is a very effective way to make older people's needs and capacities more visible, promote intergenerational solidarity and empower older people.[26]

In its Aceh report, HelpAge International recognised the important contribution that older people make in many societies, but found that ' … these capabilities often remain unrecognised or under-utilised during emergency situations'.[27]

7.2.4 Poverty and older people

Poverty and older age are regrettably inextricably linked. The loss of employment, the possibility of failing health, and the inability to access financial services conspire to reduce living standards of many older people. Barrientos, Gorman and Heslop make a number of conclusions in their study of older age poverty in developing countries.[28] They confirm that poverty in older age is significant. Many factors must be considered including:

- The ability to access employment for older people is important for older people from the perspectives of poverty and social inclusion. Although there may be a higher rate of labour force participation of older people in low income countries, the type of employment is predominately informal and precarious.
- Restricted access to health care. Health care priorities undervalue older people.
- The lack of household and social networks contributes to poverty amongst older people.

The earnings of older people in employment are invariably much lower than those of younger people. One study in Vietnam found that older people were paid only 27.4% of the national average.[29]

The reason often given for poverty in older age is that older people no longer have the capacity to undertake employment and maintain themselves. Barrientos, Gorman and Heslop argue that:

> … this view is based on the segmentation of lives into young, 'prime age' and old, with correlates of dependence and independence, and on a purely instrumental valuation of lives. … [D]eveloping an appropriate perspective on old age poverty, and relevant policy, requires focusing on whole lives, rather than segments, and adopting a perspective on the value of lives which includes both instrumental and intrinsic considerations. … Reducing poverty and vulnerability in later life requires acknowledging and facilitating older people's contribution to the development process.[30]

HelpAge International makes a number of recommendations for tackling poverty in older age. These include:

Implement age discrimination legislation to protect older workers from discrimination and exploitation in both the formal and informal economies.
Create flexible economic policies that include and utilise older workers' skills and experience.
Implement non-contributory pensions to ensure income security for all older men and women.
Provide free healthcare to all older people by removing barriers such as user fees.
Facilitate inclusive education and training programmes that are open to men and women throughout their life.
Facilitate access to microfinance programmes, especially microcredit schemes, allowing older women and men to have equal access to financial resources available to other age groups.
Remove mandatory retirement legislation, making the age of retirement flexible and voluntary.
Research and disaggregate data on older workers in the formal and informal economies, thereby recognising their contributions and needs.[31]

These and other initiatives require action by national governments, which is most effectively achieved through global and regional collaboration.

7.2.5 'Witch' killings

A specifically gender based form of discrimination against older women are 'witch' killings. For example, in Tanzania 17,220 women were abused between 1998 and 2001 as a result of witchcraft allegations and 10% of these were killed. Across the nine project districts where HelpAge International works, there were 444 'witch' killings between 1999 and 2004. Of these, all except nine were older women.[32] The causes of such killings are complex:

> The context in which accusations of witchcraft are made is complex. Deep seated cultural beliefs, the low status of women, poverty, and the need to apportion blame and seek redress for a negative event, such as a death in the family or crop failure, all contribute to a culture in which these allegations and subsequent violence is tolerated. Older women are often targeted due to their low status, their low levels of literacy, their inability to defend themselves and, in the event of widowhood, family members wishing to take control of property and assets.[33]

Johann Hari in a report of a visit to Kenya and Tanzania provides a graphic description of 'witch' killing. He reports on the killing of Shikalile Msaji, a woman in her eighties, who was looking after her eight-year-old granddaughter. At six in the evening three strangers appeared at her house:

> 'Your days are over, old woman,' they said after smashing in her front door with a rock. Her granddaughter ran into the next room. 'Stay there and shut up, or you will die, too,' they shouted after her. Then they slashed into Shikalile's skull with machetes, and tried to cut off her hands – suggesting this was a witch-killing. Her granddaughter hid until morning, then ran for help. It was too late. Shikalile's blood still stains the walls, and the small wooden chair where she sat in her last moments of life. Her family – huddled here for the funeral – have to sleep in this room. They have nowhere else to stay until they return to their own villages.[34]

This disturbing example demonstrates the extent to which older people are discriminated against and denied basic human rights often within their own communities.

7.3 Current international protection of human rights

References to older people in international human rights conventions and documents are rare. Why should older people be identified as a specific sub-group in need of additional protection from international law? Unlike children, there are no special rights attaching to older people in addition to those bestowed upon all adults. It is arguable that children are worthy of special protection because they are particularly vulnerable to exploitation by adults (for example, abuse) and by states (for example, military service and lack of education and health care). Older people have autonomy and should be allowed to enjoy it. Many older people throughout the world do so. This argument has an initial attraction. Indeed, to argue against it risks accusations of ageism as it promotes an image of older age as necessarily dependent and vulnerable. Analogies with children and instruments such as the Convention on the Rights of the Child (CRC) are inappropriate as they risk infantilising older people. The counter argument is that older people are marginalised and their age means that they are a discrete group who suffer disproportionately, and as a direct consequence of their age, violations of their basic human rights.

The UDHR does not specifically refer to older people. The significance of the UDHR is its inclusive language. The Preamble to the UDHR refers to the 'equal and inalienable rights of *all members* of the human family'. This is indicative of its aspiration that it is truly a universal document. A number of examples from the UDHR illustrate this:

Article 1:
'All human beings are born free and equal in dignity and rights. They are endowed with reason and conscience and should act towards one another in a spirit of brotherhood.'

Article 2:
'Everyone is entitled to all the rights and freedoms set forth in this Declaration, without distinction of any kind, such as race, colour, sex, language, religion, political or other opinion, national or social origin, property, birth or other status.'

Article 3:
'Everyone has the right to life, liberty and security of person.'

Article 7:
'All are equal before the law and are entitled without any discrimination to equal protection of the law. All are entitled to equal protection against any discrimination in violation of this Declaration and against any incitement to such discrimination.'

Article 22:
'Everyone, as a member of society, has the right to social security and is entitled to realization, through national effort and international co-operation and in accordance with the organization and resources of each State, of the economic, social and cultural rights indispensable for his dignity and the free development of his personality.'

Unusually, a reference to 'old age' is found in Article 25(1):

> Everyone has the right to a standard of living adequate for the health and well-being of himself and of his family, including food, clothing, housing and medical care and necessary social services, and the right to security in the event of unemployment, sickness, disability, widowhood, old age or other lack of livelihood in circumstances beyond his control.

The International Covenant on Civil and Political Rights does not refer specifically to older age, but rather adopts 'other status' to cover those not specifically referred to in the Covenant. Article 2(1) states:

> Each State Party to the present Covenant undertakes to respect and to ensure to all individuals within its territory and subject to its jurisdiction the rights recognized in the present Covenant, without distinction of any kind, such as race, colour, sex, language, religion, political or other opinion, national or social origin, property, birth or other status.

Age is mentioned in the context of no death sentence for juveniles (Article 6), special needs of juveniles in criminal trials (Article 14), and the segregation of juveniles and adult prisoners (Article 10). Article 2(2) of the International Covenant on Economic, Social and Cultural Rights adopt the same formulaic list of specific categories and the residual 'other status' category.

One convention that refers to age discrimination is the International Convention on the Protection of the Rights of All Migrant Workers and Members of their Families.[35] Article 1 states that the Convention applies to all migrant workers without distinction on the basis of a number of grounds including 'age'. Age is also mentioned under the obligation in Article 7 to ensure the enjoyment of all rights under the Convention for all migrant workers.

7.4 International developments on ageing

The Vienna International Plan of Action on Ageing was the first international instrument that concentrated solely on older people. It was passed by the General Assembly of the United Nations in 1982 following adoption by the World Assembly on Ageing earlier that year.[36] In its goals and policy recommendations, the Vienna Plan recognises an important limitation on the role of international collaboration to defeat ageism. It states:

> The Plan of Action can only include proposals for broad guidelines and general principles as to the ways in which the international community, Governments, other institutions and society at large can meet the challenge of the progressive ageing of societies and the needs of the elderly all over the world. More specific approaches and policies must, by their nature, be conceived of and phrased in terms of the traditions, cultural values and practices of each country or ethnic community, and programmes of action must be adapted to the priorities and material capacities of each country or community.[37]

The General Assembly considered its role to be setting broad guidelines and general principles, thus enabling governments and others to implement them in the context of their own societies. However, this is not intended to give governments freedom in how they choose to implement the Plan, or whether they choose to implement it at all. The Vienna Plan refers to ' … a number of basic considerations which reflect general and fundamental human values, independent of culture, religion, race or social status'. These recognise the inevitability of ageing. Mention is made of the disparity of ageing throughout the world given the inequalities in the development of medicine and public health, and the fact that developing countries are ageing without the economic infrastructure to ensure balanced and integrated development. The Vienna Plan notes the changing dependency ratios (to some extent offset by shrinking birth rates) and the implications that this may have for societies where traditional care structures, such as the extended family, are undergoing radical change. Rural depopulation presents a particular challenge.[38] A number of areas of concern are identified including health and nutrition, protection of older consumers; social welfare, income, security and employment; and education.

The Vienna Plan considers the respective roles of national governments and the broader international community (global and regional). National governments have a prominent role to play in implementing the Vienna Plan given the wide differences in the nature of ageing in different societies. Countries should be allowed to decide their own national strategies and targets; however, this must be done within the Plan. Governments must recognise that older people are not a homogenous group and attention should be paid to those who are at a severe disadvantage. In order to ensure that older people are involved in this process at a national level, the Plan recommends that the structure for international cooperation should be mirrored at national level.[39] Globally, the Vienna Plan envisages cooperation through the United Nations and its organs. Technical cooperation and the exchange of information and experience are specifically mentioned as areas of collaboration. In addition, it recognises that the challenge is not static and that studies and reviews are necessary to assess the effectiveness of existing guidelines and to learn from experience.[40] At the regional level, the United Nations regional commissions have responsibility for ensuring that regional plans are periodically reviewed.[41]

In 1991 the United Nations adopted the Principles for Older Persons.[42] This resolution lists five basic rights for older people, namely independence, participation, care, self-fulfilment and dignity. In the Preamble to the Principles, the General Assembly recognises the commitments in the United Nations Charter to 'fundamental human rights, in the dignity and worth of the human person, in the equal rights of men and women and of nations large and small and to promote social progress and better standards of life in larger freedom' and the elaboration of those rights in the UDHR, the International Covenant on Economic, Social and Cultural Rights and the International Covenant on Civil and Political Rights.

The text of the Principles is worthy of quotation in full:

Independence

1. Older persons should have access to adequate food, water, shelter, clothing and health care through the provision of income, family and community support and self-help.
2. Older persons should have the opportunity to work or to have access to other income-generating opportunities.
3. Older persons should be able to participate in determining when and at what pace withdrawal from the labour force takes place.
4. Older persons should have access to appropriate educational and training programmes.
5. Older persons should be able to live in environments that are safe and adaptable to personal preferences and changing capacities.
6. Older persons should be able to reside at home for as long as possible.

Participation

7. Older persons should remain integrated in society, participate actively in the formulation and implementation of policies that directly affect their well-being and share their knowledge and skills with younger generations.
8. Older persons should be able to seek and develop opportunities for service to the community and to serve as volunteers in positions appropriate to their interests and capabilities.
9. Older persons should be able to form movements or associations of older persons.

Care

10. Older persons should benefit from family and community care and protection in accordance with each society's system of cultural values.
11. Older persons should have access to health care to help them to maintain or regain the optimum level of physical, mental and emotional well-being and to prevent or delay the onset of illness.
12. Older persons should have access to social and legal services to enhance their autonomy, protection and care.
13. Older persons should be able to utilize appropriate levels of institutional care providing protection, rehabilitation and social and mental stimulation in a humane and secure environment.
14. Older persons should be able to enjoy human rights and fundamental freedoms when residing in any shelter, care or treatment facility, including full respect for their dignity, beliefs, needs and privacy and for the right to make decisions about their care and the quality of their lives.

Self-fulfilment

15. Older persons should be able to pursue opportunities for the full development of their potential.
16. Older persons should have access to the educational, cultural, spiritual and recreational resources of society.

Dignity

17. Older persons should be able to live in dignity and security and be free of exploitation and physical or mental abuse.
18. Older persons should be treated fairly regardless of age, gender, racial or ethnic background, disability or other status, and be valued independently of their economic contribution.

In 1992 the General Assembly passed the Proclamation on Ageing.[43] It decided that 1999 would be designated the International Year of Older Persons. The Proclamation urged the international community to promote the implementation of the Vienna Plan and to disseminate widely the United Nations Principle for Older Persons.[44] It also encourages the support of national initiatives on ageing in the context of national cultures and conditions. Such initiatives should encourage, *inter alia*, national policies and programmes for older people becoming part of overall development strategies and the engagement of entire populations in preparing for later life.[45]

The Madrid International Plan on Ageing in 2002 identified further areas of concern.[46] It stressed the importance of nations incorporating older people within their social and economic strategies. Older people should also be protected in armed conflict and foreign occupation. In addition the Madrid Plan recognises that older people should be provided with universal and equal access to health care and services. Paragraph 13 captures the thinking behind the Madrid Plan. It states:

> The promotion and protection of all human rights and fundamental freedoms, including the right to development, is essential for the creation of an inclusive society for all ages in which older persons participate fully and without discrimination and on the basis of equality. Combating discrimination based on age and promoting the dignity of older persons is fundamental to ensuring the respect that older persons deserve. Promotion and protection of all human rights and fundamental freedoms is important in order to achieve a society for all ages. In this, the reciprocal relationship between and among generations must be nurtured, emphasized and encouraged through a comprehensive and effective dialogue.

Built into the Madrid Plan is a process of review and this was undertaken in 2008 under the auspices of the United Nations Commission for Social Development. At its 41st session in 2003 the Commission agreed to establish a 'bottom up' participatory approach, which aims to incorporate and link local and national activities to UN regional intergovernmental bodies and global processes of review and appraisal.[47] Of particular interest was the participatory approach to the monitoring and implementation of the Madrid Plan. The Commission was critical of what it perceived to be a disappointing level of commitment to this approach. In the resolution from the Commission that followed the review, a call is made to strengthen the work of the regional commissions to enable them to continue their regional implementation activities. Furthermore, it calls upon governments to continue in their efforts to mainstream the concerns of older people into their policy agendas.[48] A second global review is planned for 2012/13.[49]

Both the Principles and the Madrid Plan state basic rights that all older people should enjoy, although they are not legally enforceable. It is, however, open to states to incorporate them into their own domestic law. The United Nations General Council said it 'encourages governments to incorporate the following principles into their national programmes whenever possible'.[50] An example of such incorporation is found in section 25 of the Commissioner for Older People (Wales) Act 2005:

> In considering, for the purposes of this Act, what constitutes the interests of older people in Wales, the Commissioner must have regard to the United Nations Principles for Older Persons. ...

The Commissioner for Older People (Scotland) Bill also anticipates that a Scottish Commissioner should 'have regard' to the United Nations Principles in the performance of his or her duties.

7.5 An international convention on the rights of older people?

It is evident from the limited discussion above that the international community has failed to protect the human rights of older people. Ageism and discrimination are endemic and older people are invisible. How should the international community respond to this? Whereas there may be agreement on the analysis of the problem, the way forward is less clear. One proposal is that work should commence on preparing an international convention concentrating on the rights of older people. This proposal has attracted considerable support.[51] However, it is important to question whether this is the approach that is most likely to achieve early progress in addressing the human rights deficit for older people. What are the arguments and counter arguments for a convention?

7.5.1 Children have their own convention – why not older people?

The evidence is that despite existing international commitments, older people throughout the world are marginalised and discriminated against and that the generic human rights protection, such as the UDHR, has not worked. Furthermore, the specific measures relating to older people outlined above may be criticised as being aspirational rather than normative and measurable. It is tempting to draw analogies with the arguments in support of the CRC. If children have special protection, why not older people? In 1924 the League of Nations adopted a Declaration of the Rights of the Child with the theme that we owe to the child the best that we can give. A second Declaration was adopted by the United Nations in 1948, the same year as the Universal Declaration of Human Rights was adopted by the General Assembly. In 1959 a third Declaration of the Rights of the Child required states to take note of the 10 principles contained within it. The United Nations declared 1979 as the Year of the Child. The Polish Government, as part of its involvement in the Year of the Child, proposed an international convention and submitted a draft to the United Nations based largely on the 10 principles in the 1959 Declaration. Not surprisingly the Polish draft convention was not immediately adopted. The UN General Secretary sought the views of governments on the draft. Although outright objections to the idea of Convention were rare, objections were raised regarding the proposal as presented. The Danish government expressed concern that the language used in the Draft 'lacked the preciseness and clarity which is required in the formulation of legally binding text'.[52] Instead of adopting the Polish proposal, a working group was established in 1979 by the United Nations Commission on Human Rights to consider the Polish draft. The final Convention was unanimously adopted by the

General Assembly ten years later. The Convention is an impressive achievement considering the complexity of achieving international agreement on contentious issues such as the definition of a 'child', the role of the welfare of the child in decision making, and the role and rights of parents. It contains a mixture of rights involving civil, political, economic and social matters.

The emergence of the idea of the CRC is the recognition of children, as a class, as having rights in addition to those of adults. Although the concept of childhood is changing and children in some societies are maturing earlier, their right to develop is something that is worthy of special protection. Child liberationists may argue that it is wrong to exclude children from the adult world and that children have ability for self-determination.[53] However, the CRC is an international recognition that children do not yet possess a right to autonomy, although society has a duty to develop their capacity to exercise that right upon reaching adulthood, at whatever age that may be.

Fortin writes:

> The Convention recognises that children are active and creative and may need to struggle to shape their own lives. As such they must be assisted to develop their independence and ability to take responsibility for their future ... In particular, they require the liberties essential to notions of autonomy if they are to develop their own capacity for autonomy and play an active part in society.[54]

The need for a convention to enable children to *develop* their capacity for autonomy is the critical distinction between children and older people and a reason for a special convention for the former, but not for the latter. Older people are adults and have rights to autonomy – the challenge for the international and national communities is to ensure that those rights are respected in the same way as other adults. As noted above, the UDHR and other instruments purport to guarantee the rights to 'all human beings'. The question and the challenge is to ensure that older people are not marginalised, rendered invisible within those instruments and excluded from the protection of existing international protection. To provide them with a special convention is arguably ageist and risks infantilising older people.

7.5.2 'Strategy of legality' vs 'the chilling consequences of legality'

In making the case for an international convention on older people, Tang and Lee state:

> The canon of rights has been already enshrined within the body of international human rights instruments that have been adopted in regional and global areas. Human rights activists have invested significant resources in a 'strategy of legality', arguing that claims against human rights norm violations become stronger when encapsulated in law ... As far as the rights of the older people

> are concerned, there is a gap in the existing legal provisions. An international convention that recognizes the specific rights of all older persons and is clearly applicable to older people as citizens of signatory states will be important for older people to assert their rights in the national arena.[55]

The strategy of legality argument discloses a touching confidence in the ability of law, and in this context international law, to address global ageism. The misuse of the strategy of legality is well known – the idea that anything can be justified, provided that it is permitted by a specific law. However, in this context the argument is that law provides strength beyond moral and political persuasion. A coalition of non-governmental organisations (NGOs) including Age UK, the International Federation on Ageing, Global Action on Ageing and the International Association of Gerontology and Geriatrics have recently presented the case for a convention.[56] They argue that:

> A UN Convention on the Rights of Older Persons is necessary to ensure that older women and men can realise their rights. With a new UN convention, and the assistance of a Special Rapporteur, governments can have an explicit legal framework, guidance and support that would enable them to ensure that older people's rights are realised in our increasingly ageing societies.[57]

In its analysis of current international human rights law, the NGOs identify an implementation gap, namely the absence of references to older people in the Universal Periodic Review system.[58] This is a system of four yearly review of the human rights record of all 192 members of the United Nations aimed at improving the human rights situation and addressing violations when they occur. Treaty bodies charged with monitoring human rights undertakings rarely ask questions about the rights of older people. The failure to incorporate older people's issues into national laws, policies and practice has led to the continuation of ageism.[59] The examples referred to above, support this analysis. The paper also refers to the 'normative gap' under current international law. It notes that reference to older people in international human rights does not specifically recognise that age discrimination is unacceptable; similarly regional arrangements do not specifically refer to the rights of older people 'systematically or comprehensively'.[60] Particular reference is made to the absence of international standards on rights within community-based and longer-term care settings for both cared for person and the carer; legal planning for older age; and the abolition of mandatory retirement ages.

The counter argument requires us to consider what can be termed the 'chilling consequences of legalism'. Does the incorporation of rights into an international treaty make it more likely that they will be effective in defeating global ageism? Is it possible to draft a normative based treaty that reflects the diversity of ageing throughout the world? If the aim is to introduce a convention that contains normative provisions, would it be possible to agree on the definition of 'older age'? Achieving agreement on international rights on the standards in community care and longer term care settings is a daunting task. Capturing such standards in a way that has sufficient normative value, whilst at the same time accommodating different social structures would be time consuming and, as with the CRC, compromise would be an inevitable part of the process.[61] Furthermore, standards would need to be drafted with sufficient flexibility to permit developments in the way in which care is delivered, for example the use of technology as part of caring. Given the complexity of amending international conventions, future-proofing the wording of a convention on the rights of older people is essential, although unrealistic. The question needs to be posed whether the objective of eliminating global ageism and ensuring equality of respect is better achieved through a less normative and a more facilitatory approach imposing an obligation on states to base their domestic or regional laws on internationally agreed principles.

The CRC took 10 years of lengthy bi- and multi-lateral negotiations. That is a long time and for older people represents a significant distraction cost. The challenge facing the international community cannot be delayed for 10 years; the problems at the end of that period will be infinitely greater unless action is taken now. The challenge for the international community is not to engage in endless machinations trying to accommodate the diversity of older age in a normative treaty, but to make existing provision for human rights protection work. Arguably, a special convention addressing the human rights deficit experienced by older people is in itself ageist and reinforces the view that older people are always destined to be different from others. Existing rights under the UDHR could be used to tackle many of the abuses of human rights of older people. International bodies, regional organisations and states need to be more aware of older people. Older people's invisibility through their absorption into a wider family unit or a failure to recognise the diverse nature of the cohort, must be challenged. An international convention might not be the answer. Instead, the human rights of older people need to be a pervasive theme within all existing human rights instruments. Procedures for monitoring the impact of existing provision on older people must be enhanced. The Universal Periodic Review system noted above provides a useful way of achieving this.

The 48th Session of the Commission for Social Development considered the implementation of the Madrid International Plan of Action for Ageing. A number of measures were agreed in the draft resolution emanating from the discussions.[62] There is a division of responsibility between states and the wider international community. Among the expectations of states are the mainstreaming of ageing into national policy agendas; legislation designed to promote and protect the rights of older people to provide economic and social security and health care; the mainstreaming of a gender perspective along with full participation of older people; and to continue reviewing national capacity for policy development to enhance their national capacity in this area.[63] It also asks states to recognise:

> … the important role of various international and regional organizations that deal with training, capacity-building, policy design and monitoring at the national and regional levels, in promoting and facilitating the implementation of the Madrid Plan of Action.[64]

Monitoring implementation of the Madrid Plan is essential and the adoption of 'name and shame' tactics for countries that are felt to be underperforming can be an effective way of improving compliance.

At the international level, the draft resolution encourages the international community 'to enhance international cooperation, in keeping with internationally agreed goals' to support national efforts to eradicate poverty. The call to cooperate to achieve 'internationally agreed goals' is welcome alongside improved monitoring. As noted above, the original intention of the Polish plan for a convention on the rights of the child was based largely on the ten Principles in the 1959 Declaration. Although rejected as the way forward for developing a children's convention, it might prove to be a more effective approach for developing the rights of older people. The five Principles for Older Persons provide the basis for national, regional and international action to address the abuse of rights of older people. The Principles are in one sense aspirational, but they do provide a basis on which national, regional and international progress can be measured. They are also living principles and can reflect developments and achievement. Andrews and Clark point out that the Principles recognise 'the widely differing status and consequent needs of older people throughout the world'.[65]

7.6 Conclusion

There is a consensus that older people are subjected to abuses of their human rights and that existing international instruments have failed to address this, and indeed in some cases failed to recognise its existence. It is beyond peradventure that something needs to be done. The idea of a convention on the rights of older people is gathering considerable support. This chapter sounds a note of caution. Passing a law is not a panacea, particularly at the level of international law, and it can have a negative impact. Drafting such a law would be a huge distraction at a time when action rather than discussion is necessary. Current and future generations of older people cannot wait until the drafters, diplomats and politicians have achieved an international consensus. Furthermore, as a matter of principle, why should the international community be relieved of the responsibility to make existing provision work for older people? Surely it reinforces ageism to say that older people need special protection. The challenge is to make existing law work and the way forward should be to promote the UN Principles and increase the pressure on states to incorporate them into their domestic law. The Principles also provide a valuable guide to how current international instruments can be made 'age aware'. Effective monitoring and inspection under the auspices of the Universal Periodic Review system, including the rights of older people, will enable progress to be measured and shortcomings identified. The ultimate challenge must be to achieve a world where older people enjoy the protection of instruments such as the UDHR in the same way as other human beings. This, it is submitted, is a more attractive option than subjecting the rights of older people throughout the world to the chilling consequences of legalism.

Notes

1 World Health Organization, *Active Ageing, A Policy Framework* (Geneva: WHO, 2002).

2 See World Assembly on Ageing II, <www.globalaging.org/waa2/about.htm> (accessed 28 April 2010).

3 A Smith Koslowski, 'Grandparents and the Care of their Grandchildren', in D Kneale, E Coast and J Stillwell Springer (eds), *Fertility, Living Arrangements, Care and Mobility Understanding Population Trends and Processes – Volume 1* (Dordrecht: Springer, 2009), pp 171–90.

4 V Desai and M Tye, 'Critically Understanding Asian Perspectives on Ageing' (2009) 30 *Third World Quarterly* 1007–25, 1016.

5 Economic and Social Affairs, *World Population Ageing* (New York, NY: United Nations, 2009), p 18.

6 *Ibid*, p 18.

7 *Ibid*, p 19.

8 See for example, A Mooney Cotter, *Just a Number: An International Legal Analysis on Age Discrimination* (Aldershot: Ashgate, 2008).

9 HelpAge International, *Lack of Data*, <www.helpage.org/Researchandpolicy/Stateoftheworldsolderpeople/Lackofdata> (accessed 28 April 2010).

10 See A Mowlam, R Tennant, J Dixon and C McCreadie, *UK Study of Abuse and Neglect of Older People: Qualitative Findings* (London: Department of Health and Comic Relief, 2007).

11 E Krug, L Dahlberg, A James, J Mercy, A Zwi and R Lozano, *World report on violence and health* (Geneva: World Health Organisation, 2002), pp 123–47.

12 *Ibid*, p 127.

13 *Ibid*.

14 Op. cit., Krug *et al*, fn 11, p 143.

15 G Schmid, B Williams, J Garcia-Calleja, C Miller, E Segar, M Southworth, D Tonyan, J Wacloff and J Scott, 'The unexplored story of HIV and ageing' (2009) *Bull World Health Organ* 87, 162.

16 World Assembly on Ageing II, *HIV and Older People* (2002), <www.globalaging.org/waa2/articles/hivolder.htm> (accessed 29 April 2010).

17 HelpAge International, *As Heavy as a Mountain Rock: How HIV affects older people* (London: HelpAge International, 2009), p 3.

18 C Munthree, 'Growing Old in the Era of a High Prevalence of HIV/AIDS: The Impact of AIDS on Older Men and Women in KwaZulu-Natal, South Africa' (2010) 32(2) *Research on Aging* 155–74.

19 Tavengwa M Nhongo, 'Impact of HIV/AIDS on Generational roles and intergenerational relationships', Paper Presented at the Workshop on HIV/AIDS and Family Well-being, Namibia (28–30 January 2004), <www.un.org/esa/socdev/unyin/workshops/Windhoek-backgroundpaper2.pdf> (accessed 28 April 2010).

20 T Nhongo, 'The Changing Role of Older People in African Households and the Impact of Ageing on African Family Structures', The Ageing in Africa Conference, Johannesburg (18–20 August 2004), <www.kubatana.net/docs/hivaid/helpage_impact_of_ageing_0408.pdf> (accessed 28 April 2010).

21 L Fernandez, D Byard, C Lin, S Benson and J Barbera, 'Frail Elderly as Disaster Victims: Emergency Management Strategies' (2002) 17(2) Prehospital and Disaster Medicine 67–74, <http://pdm.medicine.wisc.edu> (accessed 27 August 2010).

22 S Duggan, P Deeny, R Spelman and C T Vitale, 'Perceptions of older people on disaster response and preparedness' (2010) *International Journal of Older People Nursing* 71–6.

23 J Evans 'Mapping the vulnerability of older persons to disasters' (2010) *International Journal of Older People Nursing* 63–70.

24 S Ticehurst, R Webster, V Carr and T Lewin, 'The Psychological Impact of an Earthquake on the Elderly' (1996) 11 *International Journal of Geriatric Psychiatry* 943–51.

25 *Ibid*, p 950.
26 HelpAge International, *Older people in Aceh, Indonesia 18 months after the tsunami* (London: HelpAge International, 2006), p 13.
27 *Ibid*, p 4.
28 A Barrientos, M Gorman and A Heslop, 'Old Age Poverty in Developing Countries: Contributions and Dependence in Later Life' (2003) 31(3) *World Development* 555–70.
29 Provincial Department of Labour, *Invalids and Social Affairs: 2008 Data for Quang Binh, Quang Tri and Thua Thien Hue Provinces* (Hanoi: Provincial Department of Labour, 2008).
30 Op. cit., Barrientos *et al*, fn 28, p 568.
31 HelpAge International, *Forgotten workforce: older people and their right to decent work* (London: HelpAge International, 2010), p 44.
32 HelpAge International, *Sukumaland older women's programme* (Phase 2, London: HelpAge International, 2004). See also HelpAge International, *No Place for Old Women*, <www.helpage.org/News/Analysis/rfk3> (accessed 28 April 2010).
33 HelpAge International Tanzania, *NGO Thematic Shadow Report on Older Women's Rights in Tanzania* (London: HelpAge International, 2008), p 7 (submitted to the 41st session of the Committee on the Elimination of All Forms of Discrimination Against Women).
34 Johann Hari, 'Witch hunt: Africa's hidden war on women', *Independent*, 12 March 2009.
35 UNGA Res 45/158 (18 December 1990).
36 UNGA Res 37/51 (3 December 1982).
37 *Ibid*, para III A.
38 *Ibid*, 36 para III A 2.
39 Op. cit., Evans, fn 23.
40 UNGA Res 37/51 (3 December 1982), para IV B 1.
41 *Ibid*, para IV B 2.
42 UNGA Res 46/91 (16 December 1991).
43 UNGA Res 47/5 (16 October 1992).
44 *Ibid*, paras 1(a) and (b).
45 See UNGA Res 47/5 (16 October 1992), para 2(a)–(o).
46 United Nations Programme on Ageing, *Madrid Action Plan on Ageing* (2002), <www.un.org/esa/socdev/ageing/madrid_intlplanaction.html> (accessed 28 April 2010).
47 B Huber, *Implementing the Madrid Plan of Action on Ageing* (New York, NY: United Nations Department of Economic and Social Affairs, 2005), p 8, <www.un.org/esa/population/meetings/EGMPopAge/EGMPopAge_21_RHuber.pdf> (accessed 28 April 2010).
48 UNCSD Res 46/1 (2010).
49 UNCSD Draft Resolution (3–12 February 2010), UN Doc E/CN.5/2010/L.6 (48th Session), <www.un.org/esa/socdev/csd/2010/resolutions/ageing.pdf> (accessed 28 April 2010).
50 UNGA Res 46/91 (16 December 1991).
51 See for example, *Strengthening Older People's Rights: Towards a UN Convention* (INPEA/IFA/ILC-US/IAGG/IAHSA/HelpAge International/GAA/Age UK/AARP, 2010), <www.globalaging.org/agingwatch/convention/humanrights/strengtheningrights.pdf> (accessed 28 April 2010).
52 N Cantwell, 'The Origins, Development and Significance of the United Nations Convention on the Rights of the Child', in S Detrick (ed), *The United Nations Convention on the Rights of the Child: A Guide to the 'Travaux Préparatoires'* (London: Martinus Nijhoff, 1992), pp 19–31, esp 21.
53 See H Foster and D Freed, 'A Bill of Rights for Children' (1972) 6 *Family Law Quarterly* 343; R Farson, *Birthrights* (New York, NY: Collier Macmillan, 1974); and J Holt, *Escape from Childhood: The needs and rights of childhood* (New York, NY: EP Dutton and Co Inc, 1974).
54 J Fortin, *Children's Rights and the Developing Law* (2nd edn, London: Butterworths, 2003), pp 41–1.

55 Kong-Leung Tang and Jik-Joen Lee, 'Global Social Justice for Older People: The Case for an International Convention on the Rights of Older People' (2006) 36 *British Journal of Social Work* 1135–50.
56 Op. cit., *Strengthening Older People's Rights: Towards a UN Convention*, fn 51.
57 Op. cit., *Strengthening Older People's Rights: Towards a UN Convention*, fn 51, p 3.
58 UNGA Res 60/251 (3 April 2006).
59 Op. cit., *Strengthening Older People's Rights: Towards a UN Convention*, fn 51, p 7.
60 Op. cit., *Strengthening Older People's Rights: Towards a UN Convention*, fn 51, p 6.
61 See generally op. cit., Cantwell, fn 52.
62 UNCSD Draft Resolution (3–12 February 2010), UN Doc E/CN.5/2010/L.6 (48th Session), <www.un.org/esa/socdev/csd/2010/resolutions/ageing.pdf> (accessed 28 April 2010).
63 Op. cit., Tang and Lee, fn 55, paras 1–8.
64 Op. cit., Tang and Lee, fn 55, para 11.
65 G Andrews and C Clark, 'The International Year of Older Persons: Putting Aging and Research Onto the Political Agenda' (1999) 54B(1) *Journal of Gerontology* 71–10, 8.

Bibliography

Andrews, G and Clark, C, 'The International Year of Older Persons: Putting Aging and Research Onto the Political Agenda' (1999) 54B(1) *Journal of Gerontology* 71–10, 8.

Barrientos, A, Gorman, M and Heslop, A, 'Old Age Poverty in Developing Countries: Contributions and Dependence in Later Life' (2003) 31(3) *World Development* 555–70.

Cantwell, N, 'The Origins, Development and Significance of the United Nations Convention on the Rights of the Child', in Detrick, S (ed), *The United Nations Convention on the Rights of the Child: A Guide to the 'Travaux Préparatoires'* (London: Martinus Nijhoff, 1992), pp 19–31, esp 21.

Desai, V and Tye, M, 'Critically Understanding Asian Perspectives on Ageing' (2009) 30 *Third World Quarterly* 1007–25, 1016.

Duggan, S, Deeny, P, Spelman, R and Vitale, C T, 'Perceptions of older people on disaster response and preparedness' (2010) *International Journal of Older People Nursing* 71–6.

Economic and Social Affairs, *World Population Ageing* (New York, NY: United Nations, 2009), p 18.

Evans, J, 'Mapping the vulnerability of older persons to disasters' (2010) *International Journal of Older People Nursing* 63–70.

Farson, R, *Birthrights* (New York, NY: Collier Macmillan, 1974).

Fernandez, L, Byard, D, Lin, C, Benson, S and Barbera, J, 'Frail Elderly as Disaster Victims: Emergency Management Strategies' (2002) 17(2) *Prehospital and Disaster Medicine* 67–74, <http://pdm.medicine.wisc.edu>.

Fortin, J, *Children's Rights and the Developing Law* (2nd edn, London: Butterworths, 2003), pp 41–1.

Foster, H and Freed, D, 'A Bill of Rights for Children' (1972) 6 *Family Law Quarterly* 343.

Hari, J, 'Witch hunt: Africa's hidden war on women', *Independent*, 12 March 2009.

HelpAge International, *As Heavy as a Mountain Rock: How HIV affects older people* (London: HelpAge International, 2009), p 3.

——, *Forgotten workforce: older people and their right to decent work* (London: HelpAge International, 2010), p 44.

——, *Older people in Aceh, Indonesia 18 months after the tsunami* (London: HelpAge International, 2006), p 13.

——*Sukumaland older women's programme* (Phase 2, London: HelpAge International, 2004).

HelpAge International Tanzania, *NGO Thematic Shadow Report on Older Women's Rights in Tanzania* (London: HelpAge International, 2008), p 7.

Holt, J, *Escape from Childhood: The needs and rights of childhood* (New York, NY: EP Dutton and Co Inc, 1974).

Huber, B, *Implementing the Madrid Plan of Action on Ageing* (New York, NY: United Nations Department of Economic and Social Affairs, 2005).

Krug, E, Dahlberg, L, James, A, Mercy, J, Zwi, A and Lozano, R, *World report on violence and health* (Geneva: World Health Organization, 2002), pp 123–47.

Mooney Cotter, A, *Just a Number: An International Legal Analysis on Age Discrimination* (Aldershot: Ashgate, 2008).

Mowlam, A, Tennant, R, Dixon, J and McCreadie, C, *UK Study of Abuse and Neglect of Older People: Qualitative Findings* (London: Department of Health and Comic Relief, 2007).

Munthree, C, 'Growing Old in the Era of a High Prevalence of HIV/AIDS: The Impact of AIDS on Older Men and Women in KwaZulu-Natal, South Africa' (2010) 32(2) *Research on Aging* 155–74.

Provincial Department of Labour, *Invalids and Social Affairs: 2008 Data for Quang Binh, Quang Tri and Thua Thien Hue Provinces* (Hanoi: Provincial Department of Labour, 2008).

Schmid, G, Williams, B, Garcia-Calleja, J, Miller, C, Segar, E, Southworth, M, Tonyan, D, Wacloff, J and Scott, J, 'The unexplored story of HIV and ageing' (2009) *Bull World Health Organ* 87, 162.

Smith Koslowski, A, 'Grandparents and the Care of their Grandchildren', in Kneale, D, Coast, E and Stillwell Springer, J (eds), *Fertility, Living Arrangements, Care and Mobility Understanding Population Trends and Processes – Volume 1* (Dordrecht: Springer, 2009), pp 171–90.

Tang, K-L and Lee, J-J, 'Global Social Justice for Older People: The Case for an International Convention on the Rights of Older People' (2006) 36 *British Journal of Social Work* 1135–50.

Ticehurst, S, Webster, R, Carr, V and Lewin, T, 'The Psychological Impact of an Earthquake on the Elderly' (1996) 11 *International Journal of Geriatric Psychiatry* 943–51.

World Health Organization, *Active Ageing, A Policy Framework* (Geneva: WHO, 2002).

8 Humanitarian aid, human rights and corruption

Susan Breau[1] *and Indira Carr*[2]

8.1 Introduction

All human beings are entitled to adequate security in terms of the basic necessities of life, food, shelter, health and well-being. These basic rights are reflected in international instruments, in particular the International Covenant on Economic, Social and Cultural Rights, 1966 (ICESCR) which came into force on 3 January 1976.[3] Whilst the general expectation is that State Parties will protect the fundamental human rights of the inhabitants of that state, governments often are unable or unwilling to protect these fundamental human rights, for instance, at times of natural disasters such as typhoons, earthquakes and tsunamis or man-made disasters such as mismanagement of water resources resulting in drought. In these circumstances international obligations mandate co-operation at the international level in guaranteeing these rights. This obligation is more often than not realised by the provision of financial and humanitarian aid.

Recently, it has become apparent that there are problems with respect to the delivery of humanitarian assistance due to the attendant presence of corruption in emergency situations. Emergency situations and incoming aid offer opportunities for fraud, false accounting, diversion of aid received and exploitation of the needy and the desperate by those in a position of power. The corrupt behaviour of those in a position of power means that the suffering of the vulnerable continues despite humanitarian aid making available food rations and medicines to those affected by the disaster and providing for basic infrastructure in affected areas such as shelter, roads, bridges and sanitation. A case study on Liberia published by the Overseas Development Institute highlights the risks of corruption associated with humanitarian assistance.[4] These include bribery and extortion faced by aid agency staff in dealing with public officials, for instance, in the course of obtaining customs clearance, vehicle registration and visas,[5] inflation of costs and false claims[6] by local contractors and local partners. With the rise of international responsibility as embodied in the development of international human rights law, the notion of human security, the doctrine of the responsibility to protect and the rise of international civil society there is a sense of immediacy in combating the difficulties in humanitarian aid[7] reaching the people who are truly in need.

This chapter addresses the questions set out below and concludes with some recommendations for combating corruption in the context of humanitarian aid:

(1) What does humanitarian aid actually mean? In what circumstances can countries step in to relieve human suffering?
(2) Are there international responsibilities to provide humanitarian aid that are embodied in human rights conventions and international practice?
(3) What are the specific acts of corruption that organisations involved in humanitarian aid face?
(4) What measures are there in place to combat corruption within an international or national law framework?

8.2 Humanitarian aid

The notion of humanitarian aid is closely tied to altruistic (that is, other regarding) emotive notions common to all human beings such as compassion,[8] kindness, protectiveness, sympathy and empathy. The decision to offer assistance to those in need may be motivated by social, political or economic reasons or it could be a combination of these reasons. For instance, a state may offer help to those in need at times of crises in third states as a genuine and dependable global do-gooder at times of crises thus reflecting core values of altruism or it could be for the purposes of spreading its political ideology or for furthering its economic agenda. In common parlance 'humanitarian aid' is understood as going to the assistance of others in extreme circumstances such as natural or man-made disasters regardless of colour, creed, religion or nationality and in the interest of humankind. While it makes some sense in the abstract to talk in these terms in a world that is divided by borders and notions such as state sovereignty, there are a number of core issues that need to be addressed. Among them are, 'In what circumstances would it be reasonable for others to offer assistance?' and 'Who should offer assistance?'. The following illustrations may aid in highlighting some of the issues:[9]

Illustration 1
State X, a least developed country, has faced severe drought for a number of years and there is widespread malnutrition amongst its people, old and young.

Illustration 2
State Y, a developing country, is struck by earthquake and typhoon and thousands of people have died and many have lost their homes. Lack of sanitation means thousands are likely to contract cholera and other water borne diseases thus resulting in a huge loss of human lives.

Illustration 3
There is unrest in state Z which has resulted in a massive ethnic cleansing programme of people belonging to Tribe 1, a minority tribe. The neighbouring state A, a developing country, has seen an influx of members of Tribe 1 into its borders with the result that its infrastructure is under enormous pressure.

Illustration 4
The authoritarian government of State B has mismanaged its economic affairs to such an extent with the result that almost the entire population is reduced to extreme poverty.

In illustrations 1 and 2 it seems only right to say that assistance (technical assistance and assistance in the form of materials) should be provided to alleviate human suffering brought on by natural disasters over which human beings have no control. While in illustration 3 there is a strong argument for providing humanitarian assistance to those who have escaped the atrocities by fleeing into state A, it also raises issues of whether the international community at large has any obligations to protect those who are still within state Z. It depends on the meaning of 'man-made disaster'. Should man-made disasters include civil strife that results in the suffering of the vulnerable or should it be restricted to man-made activities that result in changes in the physical environment, such as drought caused by mismanagement of water? If assistance is to be extended in illustration 3 how should the international community go about doing this and on what grounds? As for illustration 4, it is highly debatable whether there are any grounds for assistance from the international community against the generally accepted notions of sovereignty. However, where the resulting poverty results in widespread hunger, disease and death, an argument on humanitarian grounds could be made for offering assistance, if necessary on a mandatory basis after a finding of a threat to international peace and security.[10]

A universally accepted definition of humanitarian aid that delineates the circumstances in which it would be justifiable for others, be they states, international organisations and non-governmental organisations to provide assistance is however absent, though the national laws of countries may provide some assistance in drafting a definition. The UK in its International Development Act 2002 (IDA) makes a special provision in its section 3 for humanitarian assistance as follows:

> The Secretary of State may provide any person or body with assistance for the purpose of alleviating the effects of a natural or man-made disaster or other emergency on the population of one or more countries outside the United Kingdom.

Assistance is defined in section 5 as any form of assistance including financial or technical assistance and assistance consisting in a supply of materials. It seems the IDA would enable the provision of humanitarian assistance in all of the above examples since section 3 refers to natural or man-made disaster or other emergency. It could be argued that economic mismanagement resulting in widespread abject poverty is an emergency since Article 11(1) of the ICESCR does guarantee an adequate standard of living, that is, the necessary subsistence needs such as housing, nutrition and clothing.[11] The definition of humanitarian assistance seems to be open ended and does not specifically exclude military intervention.

The EU in Council Regulation (EC) No 1257/1996 of 20 June 1996[12] concerning humanitarian aid (EU Regulation) is aimed as a priority at those in developing countries. Article 1 provides:

> The Community's humanitarian aid shall comprise assistance, relief and protection operations on a non-discriminatory basis to help people in third countries, particularly the most vulnerable amongst them, and as a priority those in developing countries, victims of natural disasters, man-made crises, such as wars and outbreaks of fighting, or other exceptional situations or circumstances comparable to natural or man-made disasters. It shall do so for the time needed to meet the humanitarian requirements resulting from these different situations.

The objectives of humanitarian aid are:

(1) saving and preserving life during emergencies and their immediate aftermath and natural disasters that have entailed major loss of life, physical, psychological or social suffering or material damage (Article 2(a));
(2) providing necessary relief and assistance to people affected by longer-lasting crises arising, in particular, from outbreaks of fighting or wars, producing the same effects as described in Article 2(a), especially where their own governments prove unable to help or there is a vacuum of power (Article 2(b));
(3) financing the transportation of aid to ensure that it is accessible to those for whom it is intended and protecting humanitarian goods and personnel, but excluding operations with defence implications (Article 2(c));
(4) carrying out short term rehabilitation and reconstruction work, especially on infrastructure and equipment, in close association with local structures, with a view to facilitating the arrival of relief, preventing the impact of the crisis from worsening and starting to help those affected regain a minimum level of self-sufficiency (Article 2(d));
(5) coping with consequences of population movement (refugees, displaced people and returnees) caused by natural and man-made disasters (Article 2(e));
(6) ensuring preparedness for risks of natural disasters or comparable exceptional circumstances (Article 2(f)); and
(7) supporting civil operations to provide the victims of fighting or comparable emergencies in accordance with international agreements (Article 2(g)).

Unlike the IDA, the EU Regulation defines man-made disasters widely to include crises caused by civil strife or other exceptional circumstances. Applying Article 1 of the Regulation it would be possible to justify humanitarian assistance in the four illustrations given above.

Whilst reflecting on the notion of humanitarian aid above, reference was made to motivations of the provider of assistance. In the absence of an internationally accepted standard meaning of humanitarian aid there is always the danger that such assistance can be conveniently used in disaster struck areas, be it man-made or natural disasters, for other ends, such as political gain. Does the EU Regulation have anything to say about the motivations that guide the giving of humanitarian assistance? While the provisions do not refer to motivations, the Preamble states in part that:

> Whereas humanitarian aid, the sole aim of which is to prevent or relieve human suffering, is accorded to victims without discrimination on the grounds of race, ethnic group, religion, sex, age, nationality or political affiliations *and must not be guided by, or subject to, political considerations*;[13]
>
> Whereas humanitarian aid decisions must be taken impartially and solely according to the victims' needs and interests.

The above taken together establish that the motivations must be solely guided by the need to alleviate human suffering and the victims' needs and interests, in other words it must solely be on compassionate or altruistic grounds and on a non-discriminatory basis.

It would be possible to devise a definition of humanitarian aid or assistance on the basis of these two legal instruments as follows:

> Humanitarian aid is the altruistic providing of assistance to victims in third states or victims from third states for the purposes of relieving suffering caused by natural disasters or man-made disasters without discrimination on the basis of race, ethnicity, gender, sex, age, religion, nationality or political affiliations. Man-made disasters include those brought about by civil strife, wars and circumstances where the consequences are comparable to those of natural disasters.

8.3 Human rights and the human security framework

Although there may be diverse approaches to the parameters within which humanitarian aid is to be provided, the character of the assistance is essentially altruistic and aimed at relieving human suffering resulting from the deprivation of the basic necessities of life. The appropriate delivery of humanitarian assistance can be assessed through two international analytical frameworks, namely through the discourse of human rights and the newer paradigm of human security. Both these frameworks are examined below.

8.3.1 Human rights

The basic necessities for the survival of humankind are embodied in the human rights discourse. As noted in the Introduction, the key human rights convention applicable to humanitarian assistance is the ICESCR which includes rights to food, clothing, housing and health, necessities often missing in natural or man-made disasters.[14] Clearly these rights are essential for survival. Yet the question here is how humanitarian aid might relate to the realisation of these rights. It can be reasonably asserted that the key articles and their general comments establish that there is an international responsibility to ensure that these key rights are realised, particularly though international assistance.[15] The main articles and their general comments establish that humanitarian aid is a core part of the strategy of implementation of these rights.

The obligations set out in the ICESCR are based on three principles, to respect, to protect and to fulfil. While the principle to respect is the classical non-interference in rights approach, a negative obligation, the principles to protect and fulfil imply responsibilities on the part of states to take measures to ensure that individuals are not deprived of their basic necessities for survival, including the right to food, shelter and health are all positive obligations.[16] The first level of these obligations is the domestic legal obligations resulting from any state ratifying the Convention. That the ICESCR imposes positive obligations through the 'minimum core obligation' concept is supported by the jurisprudence of the Constitutional Court of South Africa in *The Government of the Republic of South Africa and others v Grootboom and others.*[17] In this case relying on General Comment 3[18] to the ICESCR the Court stated:

> The concept of minimum core obligation was developed by the [Committee on Economic Social and Cultural Rights] to describe the minimum expected of a state in order to comply with its obligation under the Covenant. It is the floor beneath which the conduct of the state must not drop if there is to be compliance with the obligation. Each right has a 'minimum essential level' that must be satisfied by the states parties.[19]

Scott and Alston in their analysis of the Cape High Court decision in *Grootbroom* (before it was affirmed in the South African Constitutional Court) discussed the issue of progressive *versus* immediate realisation of the economic right of housing discussed in the judgment. They argued that there was a conceptual concordance between the presumption of immediacy contained in the International Covenant on Civil and Political Rights 1996[20] and the ICESCR jurisprudence and noted that the obligation to progressively realise economic, social and cultural rights includes the obligation to give special priority to ensuring a core minimum entitlement without delay.[21] This notion of minimum core obligations and the necessity to act without delay has also been confirmed in the jurisprudence of Argentina and Latvia.[22]

At the second level, emerging from notions of positive obligations and minimum core obligations is international responsiblity if compliance domestically drops beneath the floor described above. According to Mbazira the international community has a duty to ensure the realisation of these rights, and he bases his arguments on the evidence of aid and development activity in support of economic, social and cultural rights in various African states by the international community, including international organisations and civil society.[23] However, there is also support for international obligation, not just in the actions of the international community in delivering aid and development, but in the provisions and General Comments to the ICESCR itself since the main issue in humanitarian emergencies, such as the types described in part I of the article, is the provision of the necessities for survival.

This thesis of international responsibility is supported, first, by the general statement contained in Article 2(1) of the ICESCR which states:

> Each State Party to the present Covenant undertakes to take steps, individually and through international assistance and co-operation, especially economic and technical, to the maximum of its available resources, with a view to achieving progressively the full realization of the rights recognized in the present Covenant by all appropriate means, including particularly the adoption of legislative measures.

The duties under the the ICESCR have also been termed obligations of conduct and obligations of result in General Comment 3 drafted by the Committee on Economic Social and Cultural Rights (CESCR).[24] This positive obligation to fulfil all of the provisions of the ICESCR is not restricted to sovereign states but on all states that make up the international community. The General Comment to this Article emphasises that international cooperation for development and the realisation of economic, social and cultural rights is an obligation placed on all states. In the absence of an active programme of international assistance and cooperation on the part of all of those states that are in a position to undertake such a programme, the full realisation of economic, social and cultural rights will 'remain an unfulfilled aspiration in many countries'.[25] It would therefore be correct to say that the framework of economic, social and cultural rights includes within the positive obligations, the duty of all states in the international community, which are in a position to do so, to provide humanitarian assistance not just within the framework of a humanitarian emergency but within the framework of providing aid to realise these critical human rights.

Academic opinion also supports this interpretation of the ICESCR by the CESCR. Dennis and Stewart, for instance, argue that the CESCR has consistently documented that the realisation of these rights contains a dimension of international obligation including the General Comments as discussed above, though they caution that the degree of this international obligation is not specified in the ICESCR.[26]

Another pertinent provision in the ICESCR mandating humanitarian aid is Article 11 which states in part:

> The States Parties to the present Covenant recognize the right of everyone to an adequate standard of living for himself and his family, including adequate food, clothing and housing, and to the continuous improvement of living conditions. The States Parties will take appropriate steps to ensure the realization of this right, recognizing to this effect the essential importance of international co-operation based on free consent.

Even within this most basic provision for the necessities of life, food, clothing and housing, the importance of international cooperation is set out and is further amplified in the General Comment to this article.[27]

This approach is further developed in the analysis of the right to physical and mental health in Article 12 which states in part:

> The States Parties to the present Covenant recognize the right of everyone to the enjoyment of the highest attainable standard of physical and mental health. …

The international obligation to secure this highest attainable standard is set out in the very developed General Comment 14 adopted by the CESCR in 2004. It includes a framework for international cooperation in providing adequate health care including economic and technical international assistance and cooperation which will be accomplished by joint and separate action.[28] This General Comment argues that there is inequality in the health status of the people, particularly between developed and developing countries, as well as within countries, which is politically, socially and economically unacceptable and is, therefore, of common concern to all countries.[29] This General Comment includes a critical comment in paragraph 40 which is of direct relevance to the issues addressed in this chapter:

> States Parties have a joint and individual responsibility, in accordance with the Charter of the United Nations and relevant resolutions of the United Nations General Assembly and of the World Health Assembly, to cooperate in providing disaster relief and humanitarian assistance in times of emergency, including assistance to refugees and internally displaced persons. … [30]

Whilst General Comments admittedly are only interpretive instruments with respect to the ICESCR, it must be noted that they are highly influential and agreed upon by human rights experts in the area representing the international community of states.

In support of their thesis of international obligation, Dennis and Stewart analyse the analysis of states' reports by the CESCR. Although the ICESCR does not require any specific amount of international cooperation or assistance, consideration by the CESCR has involved the controversial issue of whether a given state has provided a sufficient level of financial assistance. In its Concluding Observations to States Reports, the CESCR urges developed countries to ensure that their official development assistance meets the UN target of 0.7% of GNP.[31]

Another highly influential international declaration that impacts on humanitarian aid is the Millennium Declaration adopted in 2000 on consensus by all states. Within this declaration adopting Millennium Development Goals is a pivotal statement on international responsibility under the heading 'shared responsibility', which states:

> Responsibility for managing worldwide economic and social development, as well as threats to international peace and security, must be shared among the nations of the world and should be exercised multilaterally. As the most universal and most representative organization in the world, the United Nations must play the central role.[32]

It is therefore clear that within the human rights discourse, international assistance is an important feature in the realisation of economic social and cultural rights as part of a development agenda, particularly in the positive obligation to fulfil these key rights.

8.3.2 Human security

The notion of international responsibility can be further supported within a human security framework. This is a much newer concept than the development of human rights norms. The first mention of the idea is contained in Chapter Two of the Human Development Report of 1994 published by the United Nations Development Programme (UNDP). Human security is based on a concern for human life and dignity and includes two components:

> [F]irst, safety from such chronic threats as hunger, disease and repression. And second, it means protection from sudden and hurtful disruptions in the patterns of daily life … [33]

The three essential characteristics of the concept are: (1) human security is a universal concern; (2) it is easier to ensure through early prevention rather than later intervention; and (3) it is people rather than state centered.[34] The UNDP Report predicts that the idea of human security is likely to revolutionise society in the twenty-first century.[35] The authors further indicate that freedom from fear and freedom from want have been recognised as interdependent rights from the beginning by the United Nations. In fact, these are two of the original four freedoms introduced by President Roosevelt in his speech to Congress prior to the US entry into the Second World War.[36] The concept of human security brings together these fundamental freedoms into a coherent notion that would change the focus from territorial security to people's security.[37]

The idea of human security developed further in the wake of the conflict in Kosovo. A succinct definition of the concept is provided by the Commission on Intervention and State Sovereignty in its seminal report, *The Responsibility to Protect*, commissioned by the Government of Canada to consider humanitarian intervention. The definition states that 'human security means the security of people – their physical safety, their economic and social well-being, respect for their dignity and worth as human beings, and the protection of their human rights and fundamental freedoms'.[38] It is evident from this definition that humanitarian emergencies are a direct threat to human security and by implication interference with humanitarian aid can be a direct threat to human security.

The United Nations Secretary-General Kofi Annan assumed a leadership role in the development of the notion of human security and in a statement to the 54th session of the General Assembly he stated that he intended to 'address the prospects for human security and intervention in the next century'.[39] For the Millennium Assembly, Annan released a report entitled *We the Peoples: The Role of the United Nations in the 21st Century*. In this Report he states:

> Two of the founding aims of the United Nations whose achievement eludes us still: freedom from want and freedom from fear.[40]

In discussing the internal armed conflicts of the 1990s, Annan introduced the new notion of human security:

> In the wake of these conflicts, a new understanding of the concept of security is evolving. Once synonymous with the defence of territory from external attack, the requirements of security today have come to embrace the protection of communities and individuals from internal violence. The need for a more human-centered approach to security is reinforced by the continuing dangers that weapons of mass destruction, most notably nuclear weapons, pose to humanity: their very name reveals their scope and their intended objective, if they were ever used.[41]

Annan argues that reducing poverty and achieving economic growth are essential steps in conflict prevention. His formula for conflict prevention also prescribes the protection of human rights, protection of minority rights, instituting political arrangements in which all groups are represented, assuring transparency in governance asserting the centrality of international humanitarian and human rights law, supporting the creation of an International Criminal Court.[42] Prevention, for Annan, is the 'core feature in our efforts to promote human security'.[43]

The Secretary-General's High Level Panel on Threats Challenges and Change, in its report to the Secretary-General entitled *A More Secure World*, is the first to bring together human security and humanitarian aid in the context of civil wars.[44] This report argues that humanitarian aid is a vital tool for helping governments to protect those civilians caught in wars and that the core purpose of the aid 'is to protect civilian victims, minimise their suffering and keep them alive during the conflict so that when war ends they have the opportunity to rebuild shattered lives'. It goes on to assert that donors *must* fully and equitably fund humanitarian protection and assistance operations.

Annan developed the notion of human security further in his report for the United Nations 60th Anniversary Summit entitled *In Larger Freedom* further,[45] and his analysis ties together development, security and human rights as reinforcing each other and argues that the human community is entitled to freedom from fear together with freedom from want. Human insecurity has come about as a result of technological advance, increasing economic interdependence, globalisation and dramatic geopolitical change. Although he argues that poverty and denial of human rights may not be said to 'cause civil wars', they greatly increase the risk of instability and violence. As a result, we will not enjoy development without security or security without development and we will not enjoy either without respect for human rights.

The notion of human security as developed by Annan embodies humanitarian aid not only in crisis situations but also humanitarian aid construed as aid for the purposes of development and in this it goes beyond the definitions of humanitarian aid as provided, for instance by the IDA, the EU Regulation and the definition put forward by the authors. Regardless, it must be noted that the notion of human security is sufficiently wide to include humanitarian aid that is provided in response to natural and man-made disasters.

Annan, in this report, also analyses the humanitarian response system. Part and parcel of the humanitarian response system as discussed in the definition part of this chapter is the provision of humanitarian aid. Whilst Annan does not address the issue of corruption, he does propose three courses of action which should include freedom from corruption at each level. The first is that the humanitarian system must have a more predictable response capacity ranging from the provision of water and sanitation to shelter and camp management. He argues that when crises are under way there is a need to operate quickly and flexibly particularly in complex emergencies.[46] The relevant United Nations country team, under the leadership of the humanitarian coordinator is in the best position to identify the opportunities and constraints.[47] Part of these constraints is the likelihood of corruption in the delivery of the aid.

He further supports the responsibility of the United Nations by arguing that there is a clear need to strengthen field coordination structures, by better preparing and equipping United Nations country teams, strengthening the leadership of the humanitarian coordinator and ensuring that there are sufficient resources immediately available.[48]

The second action proposed by Annan is the issue of predictable funding which engages the obligations of individual states. He argues that the generous outpouring of global support which was evident in the South-east Asia tsunami crisis becomes the rule. He proposes that 'more predictable and flexible funding be made available for humanitarian operations, particularly in the initial emergency phases'.[49]

A third step according to *In Larger Freedom* is a predictable right of access and guaranteed security for humanitarian workers and operations in the field. Annan argues that humanitarian personnel are too often blocked from providing assistance because government forces or armed groups prevent them from doing their jobs and elsewhere, terrorists attack unarmed aid workers and paralyse operations, in violation of basic international law.[50] Annan could have taken this opportunity to also include corruption as a feature blocking humanitarian workers from providing the assistance, since the government forces or armed groups in many instances require bribes or a portion of the aid in order for aid workers to carry on with the delivery.

As a result of both *A More Secure World* and *In Larger Freedom*, the 60th Anniversary Summit of the United Nations provided an opportunity to consider a wide variety of issues of concern to the international community including human security and humanitarian aid. The outcome document of the 60th anniversary summit is disappointing since, as evident from the following paragraph, there is only a modest endorsement of the concept of human security:

> We stress the right of people to live in freedom and dignity, free from poverty and despair. We recognize that all individuals, in particular vulnerable people, are entitled to freedom from fear and freedom from want, with an equal opportunity to enjoy all their rights and fully develop their human potential. To this end, we commit ourselves to discussing and defining the notion of human security in the General Assembly.[51]

If one examines the work already done in the United Nations system it is clear that there has to be a multifaceted approach to humanitarian aid within the analytical framework of human security. As seen from the Introduction, corruption in humanitarian aid is a denial of fundamental human rights. Yet in the following part of the chapter we see that although this might be an international responsibility, the scourge of corruption is still a large part of the difficulties in the delivery of humanitarian aid.

8.4 Humanitarian aid and acts of corruption[52]

The system of providing assistance,[53] be it short term to deal with immediate needs of food and shelter or reconstruction of the infrastructure such as roads, hospitals and schools, involves a multitude of actors and is normally tailored to the emergency, the needs of the people affected and the existing infrastructure for distribution of assistance within the targeted state, and the ability of the affected state to respond to the needs without international assistance.[54] It comprises donor organisations, UN agencies, government agencies, international non-governmental organisations (NGOs), Red Cross, local NGOs, international defence forces and a multitude of local actors such as local village chiefs and community representatives.[55]

The multitude of actors normally contract with each other in the implementation of the relief response. There is no set formula of how the relief operation is realised, since it is dependent on the circumstances such as the scale of the disaster and the availability of local organisations. In many instances, international organisations are likely to be directly involved to a large extent in the relief operations due to the 'fear that local actors may be more likely to abuse aid, although this is usually implicit and unsaid'.[56] However, it is common place for international NGOs to sub-contract or partner with local NGOs.

In order to provide assistance to the affected, the agencies have to engage in diverse activities ranging from procuring the items for distribution, transporting the items first to the country and then within the country, targeting specific areas, setting up camps, registration of the affected to assess the needs and actual distribution, to construction work. Alongside these activities, the relief organisations have also to employ staff and independent contractors to carry out the various operations from transport through to distribution. In each and every stage of the operation there is scope for corruption. These can range from an international organisation having to bribe the customs officials to cross the border, an individual beneficiary having to bribe the distribution official in order to receive food and shelter, diversion of funds paid to the local agency for relief operations, provision of sub-standard goods, over-estimation of numbers of people requiring assistance, to favouritism in the engagement of local staff for relief operations. There are numerous field studies on corruption in the aid context and a few of the studies are referred to below. For instance, investigations by aid agencies in Sierra Leone showed that the distribution of food did not reach all of the needy but was diverted to those close to the chiefs.[57] Sexual harassment and exploitation is another feature that emerged from the study conducted by Care International in Burundi, where food aid was dependent on giving of sexual favours by women to chiefs or other administrators in charge of food distribution.[58] False claims by contractors and favouritism in employment opportunities was revealed in the food for work programme in Andhra Pradesh, India, which was affected by severe drought over a long period.[59]

Unfortunately, many of the states[60] that have received humanitarian assistance from external sources are highly corrupt according to the Corruption Perceptions Index of Transparency International.[61] While it is realised that getting relief to those affected is the primary objective in providing humanitarian assistance, it cannot be denied that corruption affects the quality of the relief that is provided with the result that the relief does not reach many of those affected.[62] So in these circumstances it is fair to ask 'What is being done to combat corruption internationally?' and 'To what extent do international efforts to combat corruption impact upon combating corruption in the context of humanitarian assistance?'.

8.4.1 International law measures to combat corruption

Corruption is not a modern phenomenon. It is as old as humanity. It is, however, a politically sensitive subject and it is only since the mid-1990s that the international community has responded to the calls for an international effort to combat corruption. Before examining this response, the UN documents dealing with humanitarian assistance are briefly examined with a view to establishing whether they address corruption in the context of humanitarian assistance.

All of the major organs of the United Nations dealing with issues of humanitarian aid and the General Assembly and the Security Council have engaged in specific actions with respect to the provision of delivery of aid.

8.4.1.1 Security Council

An important development in international practice is the willingness of the international community to intervene and deliver aid with force in situations of internal or international armed conflict. This involves action by the Security

Council under its Chapter VII powers after finding a situation a threat to international peace and security. However, it must be noted that this has not thus far been the case in a situation of a natural disaster but rather only applicable to the delivery of humanitarian aid in the situation of internal armed conflict. However, there are now numerous incidents of international practice. Two of the first were Bosnia/Herzegovina and Somalia. In the 1992 Security Council Resolution 770 with respect to the situation in Bosnia/Herzegovina, the provision of humanitarian assistance was seen as an important step in the restoration of international peace and security.[63] The resolution called upon states to take all measures necessary to facilitate the delivery of humanitarian assistance to Sarajevo and wherever needed in other parts of Bosnia and Herzegovina, both nationally and through regional agencies or arrangements.[64]

The provision of aid was even more robustly confirmed in Somalia. In Resolution 794 the Security Council determined that the magnitude of the human tragedy caused by the conflict exacerbated by the obstacles being created to the distribution to humanitarian assistance constituted a threat to international peace and security. Significantly, the resolution authorised the use of military force to 'promote the process of relief distribution'.[65]

A more recent example is the mandate of the United Nations Organization Mission in the Democratic Republic of Congo established by Security Council Resolution 1279 (1999) of 30 November 1999. Resolution 1291 of 24 February 2000 was the first resolution that determined that the threat in the Congo constituted 'a threat to international peace and security in the region as a result of the failure to implement the Lusaka Accord'. The resolution expressed 'deep concern at all violations and abuses of human rights and abuses of international humanitarian law'. This resolution expanded the United Nations Mission in the Democratic Republic of Congo's (MONUC)[66] mandate including:

> (g) to facilitate humanitarian assistance and human rights monitoring, with particular attention to vulnerable groups including women, children and demobilized child soldiers, as MONUC deems within its capabilities and under acceptable security conditions, in close cooperation with other United Nations agencies, related organizations and non-governmental organizations ... [67]

This resolution gives a robust mandate to the troops that comprise MONUC to ensure the delivery of humanitarian assistance. There are other examples in Burundi, Cote D'Ivoire and Darfur, which provide mandates to armed forces to protect aid workers and to facilitate the delivery of humanitarian aid.[68]

However, in none of these situations has the Security Council dealt explicitly with the issue of corruption. Yet the fact that aid was not reaching the intended recipients in Somalia and Yugoslavia and the Congo was precisely the reason why the Security Council decided to enact robust peace enforcement mandates to allow aid to be delivered. Violence interfered with the delivery of aid but the aid was also being stolen and diverted to other persons. Furthermore, where the delivery of aid was under the United Nations supervision, it does not follow that no 'payments' were made to agents to ensure its effective delivery. It must, however, be said that the Security Council's mandate is to deal with threats to international peace and security and it is unlikely it will be seen as best placed to provide assurance that corruption does not interfere with the delivery of aid.

8.4.1.2 General Assembly

The General Assembly has also been involved in standard setting and statements concerning humanitarian assistance and in the 60th Anniversary Summit besides the general statement on human security there were specific statements concerning humanitarian assistance. First, with respect to children and armed conflict it states:

> 118. We therefore call upon all States concerned to take concrete measures to ensure accountability and compliance by those responsible for grave abuses against children. We also reaffirm our commitment to ensure that children in armed conflicts receive timely and effective humanitarian assistance, including education, for their rehabilitation and reintegration into society.

There is also the general statement on the responsibility to protect which includes the obligation to use humanitarian means to protect populations:

> 139. The international community, through the United Nations, also has the responsibility to use appropriate diplomatic, humanitarian and other peaceful means, in accordance with Chapters VI and VIII of the Charter, to help to protect populations from genocide, war crimes, ethnic cleansing and crimes against humanity ... [69]

A problem with these statements is that as with the Security Council action these are directly related to situations of armed conflict and not natural disasters. An excellent recent example was Myanmar when the despotic regime refused to allow humanitarian aid to reach the victims.[70] During that debate the concept of the responsibility to protect seemed to be widened to include victims of natural disasters. Although the concept was originally developed to deal with genocide, crimes against humanity and war crimes, it makes sense to widen it to include responsibility to ensure that humanitarian aid reaches those most in need. Recently, Lord Hannay, one of the drafters of the report of the High Level Panel on Threats, Challenges and Change, acknowledged that a situation such as Myanmar could trigger the responsibility to protect.[71] Allowing a population to starve or perish from disease means that a national government is not protecting its population and a crime against humanity could result which could trigger the international responsibility to protect. The current situations in Darfur and the

Democratic Republic of Congo are examples where far more people die from disease and starvation than violence, but the international community has embraced its responsibility to protect in a number of Security Council Resolutions. Certainly, there was also robust international pressure on Myanmar to allow the delivery of foreign aid.

Significantly, in the outcome document of the 60th Anniversary Summit of the General Assembly there was a specific section dealing with promoting system-wide coherence in providing humanitarian assistance. In the paragraph on improving system-wide coherence, there is a particular provision on humanitarian assistance which provides that the international community of states agree to:

- Upholding and respecting the humanitarian principles of humanity, neutrality, impartiality and independence and ensuring that humanitarian actors have safe and unhindered access to populations in need in conformity with the relevant provisions of international law and national laws;
- Supporting the efforts of countries, in particular developing countries, to strengthen their capacities at all levels in order to prepare for and respond rapidly to natural disasters and mitigate their impact;
- Strengthening the effectiveness of the United Nations humanitarian response, inter alia, by improving the timeliness and predictability of humanitarian funding, in part by improving the Central Emergency Revolving Fund;
- Further developing and improving, as required, mechanisms for the use of emergency standby capacities, under the auspices of the United Nations, for a timely response to humanitarian emergencies.[72]

It is unfortunate that the provision did not go further to include consideration of combating corruption in humanitarian aid.

Within the first section of the action plan is the statement that the United Nations must ensure that humanitarian actors have 'safe and unhindered access'. By implication, this could be taken to mean that humanitarian aid must be delivered without corruption. If there is systemic corruption such as in the regimes of Myanmar and Zimbabwe, the question can be posed as to whether the responsibility to protect is triggered and thus requiring the international community to ensure the principled delivery of the aid. However, at this juncture the only international practice is in situations of internal armed conflict, not in systematic failure to provide the necessities of life.

8.4.1.3 The United Nations Convention Against Corruption, 2003

Whilst the standard setting statements from the General Assembly may not make any specific references to combating corruption in humanitarian assistance, there is an international framework to combat corruption. Since the 1990s there has been intense activity on anti-corruption from international organisations and we have a plethora of legal instruments solely devoted to fighting corruption.[73] Of the many instruments the United Nations Convention against Corruption 2003 (UNCAC)[74] is the most comprehensive[75] and is widely ratified,[76] and therefore attention will focus on this Convention in this chapter.

It would be normal to expect a convention on corruption to provide a generic definition of corruption. The UNCAC, not unlike the other anti-corruption conventions, fails to provide a definition and this is perhaps due to the complexity of the notion. The word 'corruption' is interpreted variously in common parlance from moral turpitude to undue economic or material benefit obtained by an individual in a position of power by virtue of that individual's role within an organisation.

Due to the multi-dimensional character of corruption which makes defining the term difficult, the UNCAC lists offences that are to be criminalised by the States Parties. The language of UNCAC varies from the mandatory to the discretionary so that not all of the offences listed in the Convention have been criminalised by the States Parties in their implementing legislation. Of the list the States Parties are required to establish as criminal offences are the following:

- Bribery of public officials (Article 15);
- Bribery of foreign public officials or officials of an international organisation (Article 16); and
- Embezzlement, misappropriation or other diversion of property by a public official (Article 17).[77]

Before examining the above offence it is important to consider the definitions of 'public officials', 'foreign public officials' and 'officials of an international organisation' provided by UNCAC. The ambit of these definitions is clearly important in a humanitarian context since, as stated earlier, such activities involve a multitude of actors and if corruption is to be combated in this environment it is important that all actors, be they local chiefs, members of NGOs, armed forces or civil servants from international organisations are included. The term 'public official' is defined in Article 2(a) as:

> (i) any person holding a legislative, executive, administrative or judicial office of a State Party, whether appointed or elected, whether permanent or temporary, whether paid or unpaid, irrespective of the person's seniority; (ii) any person who performs a public function, including for a public agency or public enterprise, or provides a public service, as defined in the domestic law of that State Party; (iii) any other person defined as a 'public official' in the domestic law of the State Party. … .

The above definition would include without doubt public officials such as customs officials, mayors, officials in government departments and ministers. It is, however, not immediately apparent whether the local chief or the village elder who is authorised in the humanitarian context to oversee, for instance, the distribution of food aid or register beneficiaries in affected areas will be included. However, there seems to be sufficient scope for saying that they would be since they perform a public service, albeit temporary. Unfortunately, the above provision states that it is subject to the domestic law of the State Party, which means the answer to the question whether a village elder or chief is or is not a 'public official' will depend on the national law.

'Foreign public official' is defined in Article 2(b) as:

> any person holding a legislative, executive, administrative or judicial office of a foreign country, whether appointed or elected, any person exercising a public function for a foreign country, including for a public agency or a public enterprise.

The above definition is wide enough to include public officials in a third state and includes those who, for instance, work in state enterprises or parastatals responsible for procurement of vital supplies for affected areas as part of a humanitarian assistance programme.

'Official of public international organisation' is defined in Article 2(c) as:

> an international civil servant or any person who is authorised by such an organisation to act on behalf of that organisation.

The above definition clearly includes officials of international organisations such as the United Nations but it certainly does not include employees of international NGOs such as Oxfam and Christian Aid, which are major actors in humanitarian relief operations.

From the above definitions it is apparent there are some obvious gaps – the non-inclusion of employees of NGOs – which may be pertinent for the purposes of combating corruption in the humanitarian aid context. It is possible that the national anti-corruption laws of countries may have addressed this specific issue.

Returning to the issue of the substantive offences the UNCAC in Article 15(a) requires State Parties to criminalise active bribery or bribery from the supply side when committed intentionally. That is:

> the promise, offering or giving, to a public official, directly or indirectly of an undue advantage, for the official himself or herself or another person or entity, in order that the official act or refrain from acting in the exercise of his or her official duties.

To illustrate, where an employee of an international NGO which has sent food aid to state X suffering drought, promises a luxury holiday to be enjoyed by the parents, aunts and uncles of a customs official of state X so that the goods are cleared without delay he would have committed the offence of active bribery of a public official provided the requisite intention is present.

UNCAC in Article 15(b) also requires State Parties to make passive bribery, that is the demand side of bribery, an offence when committed intentionally. That is:

> the solicitation or appearance or acceptance by a public official, directly or indirectly, of an undue advantage, for the official himself or herself or another person or entity, in order that the official act or refrain from acting in the exercise of his or her official duties.

So using the illustration given in the context of Article 15(a), if the customs official were to ask for a luxury holiday for members of his family in return for clearing the customs formalities without delay, he would have committed an offence.

The active bribery of a foreign public official is another offence that State Parties are required to establish as a criminal offence. Article 16(1) states:

> Each State Party shall adopt such legislative and other measures as may be necessary to establish as a criminal offence, when committed intentionally, the promise, offering or giving to a foreign public official or an official of a public international organisation, directly or indirectly, of an undue advantage, for the official himself or herself or another person or entity, in order that the official act or refrain from acting in the exercise of his or her official duties, in order to obtain or retain business or other undue advantage in relation to the conduct of international business.[78]

The important limitation to Article 16 is that it is restricted to bribery of foreign public officials in the international business context. So does this provision have an impact on bribery of foreign public officials in the humanitarian assistance context? The answer is not in all contexts. It would be necessary to show there was an international business relationship. 'International business' is not defined in UNCAC but is likely to include sale and service contracts. So for instance, where a partner of a firm located in the UK offers a bribe to a minister in state Y, who has been given funds by a donor agency as part of a humanitarian assistance package to purchase seismic activity detectors, so that state Y buys that firm's equipment, an offence of bribery of a foreign public official would have been committed as long as the requisite intention is present.

As stated earlier, a constant issue in the context of humanitarian assistance is the diversion of funds and other resources by those engaged in the distribution of assistance. Article 17 addresses the issue of embezzlement and diversion as follows:

> Each State Party shall adopt such legislative and other measures as may be necessary to establish as criminal offences when committed intentionally, the embezzlement, misappropriation or other diversion by a public official for his or her benefit or for the benefit of another person or entity, of any property, public or private funds or securities or any other thing of value entrusted to the public official by virtue of his or her position.

In the humanitarian assistance context, a chief (provided he comes with the definition of 'public official') diverting food aid for feeding members of his tribe to the exclusion of other needy beneficiaries would have committed an offence as long as the requisite intention is present.

The UNCAC provides in its mandatory provisions a minimum threshold for combating corruption but there are some shortcomings, e.g. the definition of a public official. The biggest drawback with any international convention, even where it is ratified, is the issue of its implementation into national law and its effective enforcement. Enforcement at times can prove to be difficult since it may not always be possible to obtain evidence and witnesses to bring about successful prosecution. Given these difficulties, it may be possible to fight corruption through the adoption of best practices in the disbursement of humanitarian aid, as indicated in the following part of the chapter.

8.5. Recommendations and conclusion

As stated in the third part of the chapter, Annan raised the need for responding quickly to humanitarian emergencies and putting in place adequate structures which include the identification of constraints. Since one of the commonplace constraints faced in humanitarian assistance is corruption. NGOs such as Transparency International and the Overseas Development Institute have put forward various recommendations to minimise the risks of corruption faced in the delivery of humanitarian assistance at various levels. Among these strategies are:

- Assessment of the risks of corruption and fraud in the delivery of humanitarian assistance on the basis of which adequate systems – financial, monitoring and auditing – should be put in place;
- Management of procurement processes that reflect international best practice in tenders such as open invitation for quotes, decisions by procurement committees;
- Agencies sharing their experiences and strategies so there could be a common formulation of policies to prevent corruption;
- Have clear policies in respect of corruption that are widely publicised not only to the internal staff but also to external actors such as contractors and others the agency deals with;
- Work to remove taboos in discussing or bringing up the talk of corruption and provide adequate whistleblower protection;
- Making corruption training part of the induction programme for NGO personnel, local contractors and others;
- Sensitising the vulnerable to what aid they are entitled to through widespread dissemination of information and provide mechanisms for receiving feedback and complaints; and
- Auditing post emergency.[79]

But of course the downside is that all these suggested recommendations add yet another layer of processes and practices, to the already stretched processes and systems set up to meet the emergency needs. More research needs to be done on how the recommendations suggested can be effectively implemented without them being seen as tedious, and the fundamental tools for fighting corruption, transparency and accountability at all levels of the delivery process can be introduced.

The provision of humanitarian aid is a key part of the realisation of human rights. Regrettably, humanitarian aid due to corruption does not in all instances reach the people it is intended for. The international community has to view this aspect as a fundamental threat to the notion of human security. The recommendations listed above are just small beginnings.

Notes

1 Professor of International Law, School of Law, Flinders University.

2 Professor of Law, School of Law, University of Surrey. I would like to thank the Arts and Humanities Research Council (AHRC) for funding my project on 'Corruption in International Business: Limitations of Law', which enabled me to gain a holistic understanding of the wider impact of corruption on society. I also wish to thank Dr Brian Carr for in-depth discussions on concepts such as compassion, pity, sympathy and humanitarianism. The idea for this chapter emerged during the course of my seminar on the impact of corruption on the vulnerable at TRACC, American University, Washington DC in 2007. For further information on the corruption project visit <www.surrey.ac.uk/corruption> (accessed 21 March 2010).

3 Article 11(1) for instance states: 'The States Parties ... recognize the right of everyone to an adequate standard of living for himself and his family, including adequate food, clothing and housing, and to the continuous improvement of living conditions'.The text of the ICESR is available at <www2.ohchr.org/english/law/pdf/cescr.pdf> (accessed 21 March 2010). The list of ratifications or accessions is available at <http://treaties.un.org/Pages/ViewDetails.aspx?src=TREATY&mtdsg_no=IV-3&chapter=4&lang=en> (accessed 21 March 2010). As of 23 September 2009 there were 160 parties to the Covenant.

4 See, for instance, K Savage with M S Jackollie, D M Kumeh and E Dorbor, *Corruption Perceptions and Risks in Humanitarian Assistance: A Liberia Case Study* (London: ODI, 2007).

5 *Ibid*, pp 20–1.

6 The Liberian Case Study cites an example where non-governmental organisations (NGOs) from abroad were supporting several orphanages that did not exist or where the number of children claimed as residing in an orphanage was far greater than the actual numbers.

7 This chapter does not make any distinction between the phrase 'humanitarian aid' and 'humanitarian assistance' and the two phrases are used interchangeably.

8 For an exploration of some of the cognitive and emotional dimensions of such altruistic notion, see B Carr, 'Pity and Compassion as Social Virtues' (1999) 74(3) *Philosophy* 411.

9 By no means is this list of illustrations meant to be exhaustive.

10 The United Nations Security Council has acted to enforce the delivery of aid in man-made disasters, see for example UNSC Res 770 (13 August 1992) (Bosnia and Herzegovina), UNSC Res 794 (3 December 1992) (Somalia), UNSC Res 1291 (24 February 2000) (Democratic Republic of Congo).

11 The Committee on Economic Social and Cultural Rights General Comments provide greater specificity to these standards *see* General Comment 4, The Right to Adequate Housing, General Comment 12, The Right to Adequate Food, General Comment 14, The right to the highest standard of Health, all available at <www2.ohchr.org/english/bodies/cescr/comments.htm> (accessed 25 September 2009).

12 Council Regulation (EC) No 1257/1996 (20 June 1996) (OJ L 163, 02/07/1996, 1–6).

13 Emphasis added.

14 Articles 11 and 12 of the ICESCR.

15 See General Comment 3 to the ICESCR developed by the Committee on Economic, Social and Cultural Rights, 'The Nature of States Parties Obligations' (New York, NY: CESCR, 14 December 1990).

16 D Marcus, 'The Normative Development of Socioeconomic Rights through Supranational Adjudication' (2006) 42 *Stanford Journal of International Law* 53, 57 with reference to the right to food.

17 *Government of the Republic of South Africa and Others v Grootboom and Others* [2001] (1) SA 46 (CC) (right to shelter); see also *Minister of Health et al v Treatment Action Campaign et al* [2002] (5) SA 721 (CC) (right to health); for the first case establishing justiciability of economic, social and cultural rights in South Africa, see *Ex Parte Chairperson of the Constitutional Assembly: In re Certification of the Constitution of the Republic of South Africa* [1996] (4) SA 744 (CC), [1996] (10) BCLR 1253 (CC).

18 The General Comments are published periodically by the Committee on Economic Social and Cultural Rights (CESCR) and these provide clarification on the rights set out in the ICESCR, available at <www2.ohchr.org/english> (accessed 21 March 2010).

19 *Grootboom*, above, fn 17, paras 29–31.

20 Text available at <www2.ohchr.org/english/law/ccpr.htm> (accessed 21 March 2010). It came into force on 23 March 1976.

21 C Scott and P Alston, 'Adjudication Constitutional Priorities in a Transnational Context: A Comment on Soobramoney's Legacy and Grootbroom's Promise' (2000) 16 *South African Journal on Human Rights* 206, 227; and see the lower court decision in *Grootboom v Osstenberg Municipality* [2000] (3) BCLR 277 (C), judgment of David J.

22 *Cámara Nacional de Apelaciones en lo Federal y Constencíosco-adminstrativo de la capital Federal [CNFED] [Court of Appeals in Administrative Matters] 2/6/1998, Viceonte, Mariela Cecila v Estado National-M° de Salud y Acción,* Social/ampara ley 16.986, Causa No 31, 777/96 (2 June 1998), translated at <www.escr-net.org> (accessed 21 March 2010), and Constitutional Court, 2001, Case No 2000–2008-0109 (Latvia) (13 March 2001), translated at <www.satv.tiesa.gov.lv/Eng/Spriedumi/08–0109(00) htm> (accessed 21 March 2010). For a regional decision on social and economic rights, see *Social and Economic Rights Action Center for Social and Economic Rights v Nigeria*, African Commission on Human and Peoples' Rights, Case No ACHPR/Comm/A044/1. Decision regarding Comm No 155/96 (27 May 2002) available at <www1.umn.edu/humanrts/africa/comcases/155–96.html> (accessed 21 March 2010), known as the *Ogoni* case.

23 C Mbazira, 'A Path to Realizing Economic, Social and Cultural Rights in Africa? A Critique of the New Partnership for Africa's Development' (2004) 4 *African Human Rights Law Journal* 34, 39; see also D Rieff, 'Charity on the Rampage: The Business of Foreign Aid' (1997) 76 *Foreign Affairs* 132, in which he illustrates the pressure on states to provide aid in emergency situations such as Bosnia, Rwanda and eastern Zaire, but see his analysis that there are 'scoundrels' in the aid world.

24 General Comment 3, 'The Nature of States Parties Obligations' (New York, NY: CESCR, 14 December 1990).

25 *Ibid*, para 14.

26 M J Dennis and D P Stewart, 'Justiciability of Economic, Social and Cultural Rights: Should there be an international complaints mechanism to adjudicate the rights to food, water, housing and health?' (2004) 98 *American Journal of International Law* 462, 498–500.

27 General Comment 12 on the right to food discusses the international obligations set out in the article. Paragraph 36 states: 'In the spirit of article 56 of the Charter of the United Nations, the specific provisions contained in articles 11, 2(1), and 23 of the

Covenant and the Rome Declaration of the World Food Summit, States Parties should recognize the essential role of international cooperation and comply with their commitment to take joint and separate action to achieve the full realization of the right to adequate food. In implementing this commitment, States parties should take steps to respect the enjoyment of the right to food in other countries, to protect that right, to facilitate access to food and to provide the necessary aid when required. States parties should, in international agreements whenever relevant, ensure that the right to adequate food is given due attention and consider the development of further international legal instruments to that end'. General Comment 12, E/C.12/1999/5 (12 May 1999).

28 General Comment 14, 'The right to the highest attainable standard of health' (New York, NY: CESCR, 11 August 2004).

29 *Ibid*, para 38 and para 39 which states: 'To comply with their international obligations in relation to article 12, States parties have to respect the enjoyment of the right to health in other countries, and to prevent third parties from violating the right in other countries, if they are able to influence these third parties by way of legal or political means, in accordance with the Charter of the United Nations and applicable international law. Depending on the availability of resources, States should facilitate access to essential health facilities, goods and services in other countries, wherever possible and provide the necessary aid when required … States parties which are members of international financial institutions, notably the International Monetary Fund, the World Bank, and regional development banks, should pay greater attention to the protection of the right to health in influencing the lending policies, credit agreements and international measures of these institutions'.

30 *Ibid*, para 40, which goes on to state, 'Each State should contribute to this task to the maximum of its capacities. Priority in the provision of international medical aid, distribution and management of resources, such as safe and potable water, food and medical supplies, and financial aid should be given to the most vulnerable or marginalized groups of the population. Moreover, given that some diseases are easily transmissible beyond the frontiers of a State, the international community has a collective responsibility to address this problem. The economically developed States parties have a special responsibility and interest to assist the poorer developing States in this regard'.

31 Op. cit., Dennis and Stewart, fn 26, pp 500–1; and see *Concluding Observations of the ESCR Committee Ireland* (2002) UN Doc E./C./12.1/Add.77, para 38, *Concluding Observations of the ESCR Committee Germany* (2001) UN Doc E/C.12/1/Add.68, para 33.

32 United Nations Millennium Declaration, UNGA Res 55/2 (18 September 2000). The Declaration also contains a specific provision for international responsibility in humanitarian aid. It states:

> VI. Protecting the vulnerable
>
> 26. We will spare no effort to ensure that children and all civilian populations that suffer disproportionately the consequences of natural disasters, genocide, armed conflicts and other humanitarian emergencies are given every assistance and protection so that they can resume normal life as soon as possible.
>
> We resolve therefore:
>
> - To expand and strengthen the protection of civilians in complex emergencies, in conformity with international humanitarian law.
> - To strengthen international cooperation, including burden sharing in, and the coordination of humanitarian assistance to, countries hosting refugees and to help all refugees and displaced persons to return voluntarily to their homes, in safety and dignity and to be smoothly reintegrated into their societies.

33 United Nations Development Programme, *Human Development Report 1994* (New York, NY: Oxford University Press, 1994), p 23.

34 *Ibid*, pp 22–3.
35 *Ibid*, p 22.
36 FD Roosevelt, 'Address to Congress, January 6, 1941' (1941) 87 *Congressional Record* Pt I.
37 Op. cit., UNDP, fn 33, p 24.
38 International Commission on Intervention and State Sovereignty, *The Responsibility to Protect* (Ottawa: ICISS, 2001).
39 K Annan, 'Statement to United Nations General Assembly 54th session'.
40 K Annan, *We the Peoples; The Role of the United Nations in the 21st Century* (New York, NY: United Nations, 2000), p 17.
41 *Ibid*, p 43.
42 *Ibid*, pp 45 and 46.
43 *Ibid*, p 46.
44 High Level Panel Report, Report of the High Level Panel on Threats Challenges and Change, *A More Secure World: Our Shared Responsibility* (2004), UN Doc A/59/565, para 234.
45 K Annan, 'In Larger Freedom: Towards Development, Security and Human Rights for all' (21 March 2005), UN Doc A/59/2005.
46 Complex emergency is defined as 'a humanitarian crisis in a country, region or society where there is total or considerable breakdown of authority resulting from internal or external conflict and which requires an international response that goes beyond the mandate or capacity of any single agency and/or the ongoing United Nations country program' (Geneva: IASC, December 1994).
47 Op. cit., Annan, fn 45, para 204.
48 *Ibid*.
49 *Ibid*, para 205.
50 *Ibid*, para 206.
51 UN General Assembly, *2005 World Summit Outcome*, UNGA Res A/60/1 (24 October 2005), para 143.
52 We have not concentrated on the assessment process that takes place prior to the delivery of assistance in this chapter.
53 The funding for the humanitarian assistance comes from various sources: donor agencies, NGOs, UN agencies, monies raised through public appeals, and the national budget of the affected state.
54 For instance, India did not seek international assistance for the displacement of people during the tsunami in 2004.
55 For more on how these agencies work together, see J Macrae, *et al*, *Uncertain Power: The Changing Role of Official Donors in Humanitarian Action* (London: ODI, 2002) and J Macrae, *The New Humanitarianism: A Review of Global Trends in Humanitarian Action* (London: ODI, 2002).
56 P Ewins, P Harvey, K Savage, and A Jacobs, *Mapping the Risks of Corruption in Humanitarian Aid* (London: ODI, 2006).
57 R Farnthorpe, 'Humanitarian Aid in Post-War Sierra Leone: the Politics of Moral Economy', in S Collinson (ed), *Power, Livelihoods and Conflict: Case Studies in Political Analysis for Humanitarian Aid*, HPG Report 13 (London: ODI, 2003); see also TIRI, *Corruption in Post-Conflict Reconstruction: Breaking the Vicious Circle* (London: TIRI, 2005); ADB, OECD and TI, *Curbing Corruption in Tsunami Relief Operations* (Manila: Asian Development Bank, 2005).
58 Care International in Burundi, *Using Innovative Approaches to Better Understand Sexual Harassment and Exploitation within the Food Aid Program* (Bujumbara: Care International, 2005).
59 P Deshingkar, C Johnson and J Farrington, 'State Transfers to the Poor and Back: The Case of the Food-for-Work Program in India' (2005) 33(4) *World Development* 575. See also Transparency International, *Global Corruption Report 2005: Corruption in Construction and Post Conflict Reconstruction* (London: Pluto Press, 2005).

60 For example, Indonesia, Sri Lanka, Pakistan and Burundi.

61 The index is available at <www.transparency.org> (accessed 21 March 2010). The Index uses a scale of 1 to 10 with '1' being the least corrupt and '10' being the most corrupt. The methodology of the index has been criticised. See for instance I Carr, 'Fighting Corruption through Regional and International Conventions: A Satisfactory Solution?' (2007) 15(2) *European Journal of Crime, Criminal Law and Criminal Justice* 121.

62 See Op. cit., *Savage et al* , fn 4.

63 UNSC Res 770 (13 August 1992) (Bosnia and Herzegovina).

64 *Ibid*, para 2.

65 UNSC Res 794 (3 December 1992) (Somalia).

66 Mission de l'Organisation des Nations Unies en ED Congo, <http://monuc.unmission.org> (accessed 21 March 2010).

67 UNSC Res 1291 (24 February 2000) (Democratic Republic of Congo).

68 UNSC Res 1528 (27 February 2004) (Cote D'Ivoire), UNSC Res 1545 (21 May 2004) (Burundi), UNSC Res 1706 (31 August 2006).

69 The rest of the provision states, 'In this context, we are prepared to take collective action, in a timely and decisive manner, through the Security Council, in accordance with the Charter, including Chapter VII, on a case-by-case basis and in cooperation with relevant regional organizations as appropriate, should peaceful means be inadequate and national authorities are manifestly failing to protect their populations from genocide, war crimes, ethnic cleansing and crimes against humanity. We stress the need for the General Assembly to continue consideration of the responsibility to protect populations from genocide, war crimes, ethnic cleansing and crimes against humanity and its implications, bearing in mind the principles of the Charter and international law. We also intend to commit ourselves, as necessary and appropriate, to helping States build capacity to protect their populations from genocide, war crimes, ethnic cleansing and crimes against humanity and to assisting those which are under stress before crises and conflicts break out'.

70 For a complete discussion of the disaster in Myanmar, see J Wong, 'Reconstructing the Responsibility to Protect in the Wake of Cyclones and Separatism' (2009) *Tulane Law Review* 84, <http://ssrn.com/abstract=1446364> (accessed 21 March 2010), and R Barber, 'The Responsibility to Protect the Survivors of Natural Disaster: Cyclone Nargis. A Case Study' (2009) 14 *Journal of Conflict and Security Law* 3.

71 In response to a question at a seminar at the University of Surrey on 14 May 2008.

72 Op. cit., UNGA, fn 51.

73 The other conventions are:

(1) Organisation of American States Inter-American Convention Against Corruption 1996. Came into force on 6 March 1997.

(2) OECD Convention on Bribery of Foreign Public Officials in International Business Transactions 1997. Came into force on 15 February 1999. See I Carr and O Outhwaite, 'The OECD Convention Ten Years on' (2008) 5(1) *Manchester Journal of International Economic Law* 3.

(3) Convention drawn up on the basis of Article K.3(2)(c) of the Treaty of European Union on the Fight Against Corruption involving Officials of the European Union Communities or Officials of Member States of the European Union 1999 (EU Convention), which is still in the process of receiving ratifications. See also Council Framework Decision 2003.568/JHA of 22 July 2003 on combating corruption in the private sector (OJ L 192 of 31.07.2003). According to Article 249 of the EC Treaty as amended by the Treaty of Amsterdam, a decision is binding in its entirety upon those to whom it is addressed.

(4) Council of Europe Criminal Law Convention on Corruption 1999. Came into force on 1 July 2002.

(5) Council of Europe Civil Law Convention on Corruption 1999. Came into force on 1 November 2003.
(6) Southern African Development Community Protocol on Corruption 2000. Not yet in force. For further on this Convention, see I Carr, 'Corruption, the Southern African Development Community Anti-corruption Protocol and the Principal–Agent–Client Model' (2009) 5(2) *International Journal of Law in Context* 147.
(7) Economic Community of West African States Protocol on the Fight Against Corruption 2001. Not yet in force.
(8) African Union Convention of Preventing and Combating Corruption 2003. Came into force on 5 August 2006; for further on this convention, see I Carr, 'Corruption in Africa: Is the African Union Convention on Combating Corruption the Answer?' (2007) *Journal of Business Law* 111.

74 This Convention was drafted by the Ad Hoc Committee for the negotiation of a Convention against Corruption which carried out its work at the headquarters of the United Nations Office on Drugs and Crime (UNODC) in Vienna. The UNODC serves at the secretariat.
75 It is said to be comprehensive, in comparison to other anti-corruption conventions, since it covers a range of issues related to corruption, e.g. laundering of the proceeds of crime and asset recovery. For more on UNCAC, see I Carr, 'The United Nations Convention on Corruption: Improving the Quality of Life of Millions in the World?' (2006) 3(3) *Manchester Journal of International Economic Law* 3.
76 So far, 140 states have ratified or acceded to this Convention. Many of them are in the process of adopting implementing legislation. Full list of ratifications available at <www.unodc.org> (accessed 21 March 2010).
77 Among the list of offences where the state has the discretion to adopt them as criminal offences or not in its legislation are bribery in the private sector (Article 21), trading in influence (Article 18), embezzlement of property in the private sector (Article 22), abuse of functions (Article 19) and illicit enrichment (Article 20).
78 Emphasis added.
79 These recommendations are derived from the following documents: op. cit., ADB, OECD and TI, fn 57; Feinstein International Center, HPG and Transparency International, *Preventing Corruption in Humanitarian Assistance Final Research Report* (Berlin: Transparency International, 2008).

Bibliography

ADB, OECD and TI, *Curbing Corruption in Tsunami Relief Operations* (Manila: Asian Development Bank, Manila, 2005).

Annan, K, *We the Peoples; The Role of the United Nations in the 21st Century* (New York, NY: United Nations, 2000).

Barber, R, 'The Responsibility to Protect the Survivors of Natural Disaster: Cyclone Nargis. A Case Study' (2009) 14 *Journal of Conflict and Security Law* 3.

Care International in Burundi, *Using Innovative Approaches to Better Understand Sexual Harassment and Exploitation within the Food Aid Program* (Bujumbara: Care International, 2005).

Carr, B, 'Pity and Compassion as Social Virtues' (1999) 74(3) *Philosophy* 411.

Carr, I, 'Fighting Corruption through Regional and International Conventions: A Satisfactory Solution?' (2007) 15(2) *European Journal of Crime, Criminal Law and Criminal Justice* 121.

——, 'Corruption in Africa: Is the African Union Convention on Combating Corruption the Answer?' (2007) *Journal of Business Law* 111.

——, 'Corruption, the Southern African Development Community Anti-corruption Protocol and the Principal–Agent–Client Model' (2009) 5(2) *International Journal of Law in Context* 147.

——, 'The United Nations Convention on Corruption: Improving the Quality of Life of Millions in the World?' (2006) 3(3) *Manchester Journal of International Economic Law* 3.

Dennis, M J and Stewart, D P, 'Justiciability of Economic, Social and Cultural Rights: Should there be an international complaints mechanism to adjudicate the rights to food, water, housing and health?' (2004) 98 *American Journal of International Law* 462, 498–500.

Deshingkar, P, Johnson, C and Farrington, J, 'State Transfers to the Poor and Back: The Case of the Food-for-Work Program in India' (2005) 33(4) *World Development* 575.

Ewins, P Harvey, P, Savage, K and Jacobs, A, *Mapping the Risks of Corruption in Humanitarian Aid* (London: ODI, 2006).

Farnthorpe, R, 'Humanitarian Aid in Post-War Sierra Leone: the Politics of Moral Economy', in Collinson, S (ed), *Power, Livelihoods and Conflict: Case Studies in Political Analysis for Humanitarian Aid*, HPG Report 13 (London: ODI, 2003).

Feinstein International Center, HPG and Transparency International, *Preventing Corruption in Humanitarian Assistance Final Research Report* (Berlin: Transparency International, 2008).

International Commission on Intervention and State Sovereignty, *The Responsibility to Protect* (Ottawa: ICISS, 2001).

Macrae, J, *The New Humanitarianism: A Review of Global Trends in Humanitarian Action* (London: ODI, 2002).

Macrae, J, *et al Uncertain Power: The Changing Role of Official Donors in Humanitarian Action* (London: ODI, 2002).

Marcus, D, 'The Normative Development of Socioeconomic Rights through Supranational Adjudication' (2006) 42 *Stanford Journal of International Law* 53, 57.

Mbazira, C, 'A Path to Realizing Economic, Social and Cultural Rights in Africa? A Critique of the New Partnership for Africa's Development' (2004) 4 *African Human Rights Law Journal* 34, 39.

Rieff, D, 'Charity on the Rampage: The Business of Foreign Aid' (1997) 76 *Foreign Affairs* 132.

Roosevelt, F D, 'Address to Congress January 6, 1941' (1941) 87 *Congressional Record* Pt I.

Savage, K, with Jackollie, M S, Kumeh, D M and Dorbor, E, *Corruption Perception and Risks in Humanitarian Assistance: a Liberia Case Study* (London: ODI, 2007).

Scott, C and Alston, P, 'Adjudication Constitutional Priorities in a Transnational Context: A Comment on Soobramoney's Legacy and Grootbroom's Promise' (2000) 16 *South African Journal on Human Rights* 206, 227.

TIRI, *Corruption in Post-Conflict Reconstruction: Breaking the Vicious Circle* (London: TIRI, 2005).

Transparency International, *Global Corruption Report 2005: Corruption in Construction and Post Conflict Reconstruction* (London: Pluto Press, 2005).

United Nations Development Programme, *Human Development Report 1994* (New York, NY: Oxford University Press, 1994).

Wong, J, 'Reconstructing the Responsibility to Protect in the Wake of Cyclones and Separatism' (2009) *Tulane Law Review* 84.

Index

Printed in the USA/Agawam, MA
June 2, 2014
590428.166